IMPORT/EXPORT

How to Take Your Business Across Borders

Fourth Edition

Author
Dr. Carl A. Nelson

Translators
Chongwen Ding

Fan Xu

Yulin Yin

进出口业务

——带领企业走出国门

第4版，双语教学版

〔美〕卡尔·纳尔逊 著

丁崇文 徐 凡 尹珏林 译

人民邮电出版社

北京

图书在版编目（CIP）数据

进出口业务——带领企业走出国门（第 4 版）：双语教学版 /（美）纳尔逊（Nelson，C. A.）著；
丁崇文，徐凡，尹珏林译 .
– 北京：人民邮电出版社，2011.6
高等学校教材
ISBN 978-7-115-25532-7

Ⅰ . ①进… Ⅱ . ①纳… ②丁… ③徐… ④尹… Ⅲ . ①进出口贸易—双语教学—高等学校—教材
Ⅳ . ① F740.4
中国版本图书馆 CIP 数据核字（2011）第 096705 号

Dr. Carl A. Nelson

Import / Export, 4th Edition
ISBN 978-0-07-148255-4

Copyright © 2009 by McGraw-Hill Education, Inc.

进出口业务——带领企业走出国门（第 4 版）：双语教学版

◆ 著 [美]卡尔·纳尔逊
  译 丁崇文 徐 凡 尹珏林
  策 划 刘 力 陆 瑜
  责任编辑 刘晓庆
  装帧设计 陶建胜

◆ 人民邮电出版社出版发行 北京市崇文区夕照寺街 14 号 A 座
  邮编 100061 电子邮件 315@ptpress.com.cn
  网址 http://www.ptpress.com.cn
  电话 （编辑部）010-84937150 （市场部）010-84937152
  （教师服务中心）010-84931276
  三河市李旗庄少明装订厂印刷
  新华书店经销

◆ 开本：787×1092 1/16
  印张：19.75
  字数：310 千字 2011 年 6 月第 1 版 2011 年 6 月第 1 次印刷
  著作权合同登记号 图字：01-2009-6951
  ISBN 978-7-115-25532-7/F

定价：48.00 元
本书如有印装质量问题，请与本社联系 电话：（010）84937153

内 容 提 要

本书英文版是国外有关国际贸易业务最畅销的教科书之一，本书基于新近出版的第 4 版英文版，在保留原版英文的同时，对重点和难点的段落、句子、生词、术语等进行了中文翻译及注释。

本书分为 2 编，共 9 章。书中主要从进口和出口共性与差异的独特角度，展示了国际贸易基本原理和基础知识，并讲述了国际贸易发展的新趋势。全书体例编排独特，内容均衡，案例鲜活，指导务实。最大特点是在操作层面上凸显其实用性，使读者在语言研习和业务提升方面均有所收获。

本书作为一本实践指导性的专业书籍，不仅适用于商务专业的学生，特别是商务英语专业的学生，同时也适用于从事进出口贸易的在职人士，以及有意加入国际竞争、分享贸易成果的有识之士。

译注者序

  经济贸易全球化的浪潮和中国经济持续的腾飞，不仅为企业带来了无限商机，也为人才带来了良好的发展机遇。日益频繁的中外商贸交往，呼唤精通英语、掌握国际贸易知识，又熟悉进出口业务的专业人士。培养和造就语言、知识和技能兼备的复合型专业人才，并使其在这一广阔天地大显身手，成为时代前进和个人发展的共同需求。人民邮电出版社推出的译注版《进出口业务——带领企业走出国门》正是对上述诉求的积极响应。

  本书的英语原版作者卡尔·纳尔逊博士是加州国际管理大学的国际商务教授，从事国际事务，特别是国际贸易，已有近半个世纪的丰富经验。由著名的 McGraw-Hill 出版公司出版的这部书，从 1987 年问世以来畅销不衰，不断再版，深受读者追捧。本译注版基于 2009 年的第 4 版，即纳尔逊博士根据世界经济的新发展和进出口业务的新趋势增补修订的最新力著。

  作为国际贸易业务书籍，《进出口业务——带领企业走出国门》颇有特色：

1. **体例编排独特**。不同于常见版本，作者将进出口业务的共同点和差异之处分为两编详细介绍。本书结构新颖、逻辑缜密，从概念到操作脉络都非常清晰，有助于读者更加准确地理解。

2. **内容均衡**。作者概括了国际贸易基本原理和基础知识，不仅涵盖了进出口业务中最为精华实用的部分，而且还与时俱进地体现了国际贸易发展的新趋势。书中理论与实践均衡得当且紧密结合。

3. **案例鲜活**。从开篇首章，作者就以 9 个真实案例，展示了国际贸易能为我们提供的营利良机，以及那些从平凡起步但富有眼光、充满激情的创业者成功捕捉商机获得丰厚回报的精彩历程。全书选取的鲜活实例为读者生动地再现了进出口业务的真实过程。

4. **操作指导务实**。本书得益于作者的丰富阅历，众多的案例不仅使读者将无形思维转化为有形资源，更使读者能够跟随作者周游世界，甚至进入作者亲历亲为的公司或机构，从而获得国际贸易过程的真实体验。本书在操作层面凸显了实用性，在许多关键贸易环节上，不仅展示了详细的操作技巧，而且提供了业内实务专家独到的思路点拨。

　　此外，阅读本书的又一好处是，读者能够一箭双雕地在语言研习和业务提升两方面均有收获。由美国资深国际贸易从业者、国际商务教授撰写的这本《进出口业务——带领企业走出国门》，具有语言流畅、文字鲜活、表述专业的明显优势。当然，由于原著作者的国别身份难免带有美国视角，读者在阅读原著时，应当注意这一文化因素。译注版则以译注者双向把握英汉语言的功力和熟悉进出口业务的基础，加倍助力读者了解西方业者国际贸易的思维方式和沟通方法，从而使之能够更有效地在全球化环境中开展商务交流，促成贸易合作，拓展并尽享进出口业务的成果。

　　译注版涵盖了原著的主体部分，省略了国际贸易规范中部分关于国别和区域组织的那些比较容易变化的章节。此项安排使译注版凸显了原著的核心，也减少了书价可能带给读者的压力。

　　译注版适于商务专业的学生，特别是商务英语专业学生用以快速提升进出口业务知识和语言运用能力。本书也适用于希望在熟悉国际贸易的同时，能够扫除英语沟通障碍的企业在职人士。对于希望加入国际竞争、分享贸易成果的有识之士而言，《进出口业务——带领企业走出国门》真正是——开卷有益。

对外经济贸易大学

丁崇文

2011 年春于惠园

This fourth edition is dedicated to my daughter Monica who helped me bring this book to birth way back in 1987 and watched as it took a life of its own and remained a bestseller for more than two decades.

作者简介

卡尔·纳尔逊博士在政府部门和私人企业中从事管理国际事务长达 45 年之久，编撰出版了 7 本国际商务及贸易领域的著作。

作为美国前海军军官、企业主管、国际贸易专家，纳尔逊博士国际阅历丰富。他在日本生活了两年，在越南一年，对欧洲、夏威夷、韩国、澳大利亚、新西兰、菲律宾、印度以及印度洋区域的国家和地区颇为熟悉。供职于美国国际发展署，参与运营加利福尼亚州 / 墨西哥北美自由贸易协定以及保税加工区等工作，这些背景使他对第三世界经济发展也有丰富的经验。

纳尔逊博士是职业作家，其作品涵盖小说、短篇小说、非小说作品、报刊文章及技术论文。他的非小说著作包括《全球的成功》、《全球管理》、《出口》、《营利协议》、《国际商务》和《赢得贸易游戏》。1999 年出版的小说《顾问》曾在 1989 年第一届南加利福尼亚州作家会议上获得最佳小说奖。他的第 2 本小说《秘密推手》，获得了由圣地亚哥图书奖协会颁发的最佳政治惊悚小说奖。第 3 本《经理人》进入过国家最佳图书奖最终入围名单，并获普利策奖提名。

他在圣地亚哥加州国际商务大学担任国际商务教授，并执教研究生课程。

纳尔逊博士早年毕业于马里兰州首府安纳波利斯美国海军军官学院，后获得了加利福尼亚州圣地亚哥美国联盟国际大学的金融学方向工商管理博士学位。他曾在美国海军战争学院学习过指挥，并在加利福尼亚州蒙特雷海军研究生学院取得了管理学硕士学位（主攻经济学 / 系统研究）。1989 年，他荣获了美国国际大学颁发的优秀校友称号，2003 年获得了由加利福尼亚州国际商务大学授予的杰出国际教育家奖。

纳尔逊博士的名字被载入《2006 年美国名人录》、《2006 年美国教育名人录》、《2007 年世界名人录》以及《1984 年加利福尼亚州名人录》。

目　　录

CHAPTER 4 SELLING WITH E-COMMERCE 73　第 4 章　使用电子商务进行销售

FOREWORD

Welcome to the world of international commerce. It began in a big way with the Phoenicians over 3,000 years ago and has been a prime mover in the development of civilization ever since.

It is a long, continuous story of people trading products unique to their regions for the products unique to other regions. For the early traders, this was often arduous work involving long and treacherous sea voyages and overland passages. As trade volumes and competition grew, strong pressures developed to produce the best product at the best price, to market these products more effectively, and to deliver them more efficiently and expeditiously. There was also pressure to improve accounting and communication systems to facilitate trade. For example, it was the Phoenicians who were responsible for the alphabet we use today. To simplify their business transactions, they replaced the cuneiform alphabet's 550 characters with a 22-letter system, which was further altered by the Greeks and Romans.

Over the centuries, commercial goals have spurred advances in a wide range of human pursuits, including transportation, communication, information technology, manufacturing, research, medical care, insurance, and entertainment, among others. The same commercial goals have created a need to travel to distant lands, learn other languages, and deal with other cultures. While the business ambitions of individual nations or regions led to conflicts at times, the overall effect of global trade has been to promote business growth and prosperity. In fact, I believe strongly that the continuous expansion of world trade to include the impoverished regions of the world is the surest path to world peace. This is because constructive trade leads to economic development, understanding, and trust, which are essential ingredients for peace.

To be sure, the international trade landscape has changed dramatically since the early days, and this is especially true of the last decade. Pulitzer Prize-winner Thomas Friedman has famously said, "The world is flat." He, of course, refers to the ability of nations previously isolated by vast distances to now compete successfully with developed countries through improved and low-cost communications and other technologies.

But one thing has not changed—and it will never change. Success in world trade will go to those individuals who are best prepared for it, including having an understanding of products, services, markets, suppliers, distribution, documentation, regulations, financial tools, and other aspects of world trade too numerous to mention.

In reading this book, you have made a good start to acquire the knowledge you will need to be successful. I hope it will lead to a rewarding career for you, and I wish you every success in this and all your future endeavors.

Guy F. Tozzoli
President
World Trade Centers Association

ACKNOWLEDGMENTS

I will always be deeply indebted to my daughter Monica Askari who helped me in the earliest stages to develop this successful book. Then there are those who have given of their precious time to update the four editions. These include Julie Osman of the Export Assistance Center, U.S. Department of Commerce, San Diego, California, for her expert advice on the chapter about exporting from the United States.

I am grateful for the research Helen Guvichy provided to update this fourth edition as well as that of my wife Dr. Dolores Hansen Nelson, who kept me on track. Last but not least, I'm thankful to McGraw-Hill associate editor Melissa Bonventre's guidance in preparing this new edition.

引　言

　　科技的进步使世界的变化日新月异。谈及这些,许多人不禁会想到"全球化"。在 19 世纪中叶,航海绕地球一周大概耗时一年,而现在乘飞机环绕地球只需一天;即时收发的电子邮件可快捷地往来于天涯海角;数十亿球迷还可以同时共享世界杯决赛盛宴。然而,全球化也不是新奇之物。它源于 20 世纪革命性的变化,特别是在信息通信领域的变化。上述变化加快了世界各国经济相互依赖的步伐,也增加了商品与服务跨境交易的数量和种类。这不仅加快了科技传播的速度,扩大了科技传播的范围,也加速了国际金融服务的自由流动。与此同时,人力资本也在自由流动,这意味着不是工作岗位向劳动力聚集地靠拢,就是劳动力追逐工作岗位而居。许多新词,像"一体化"、"外包"、"内包",已经成为了我们的常用语。

　　德国汽车、哥伦比亚咖啡、中国服装、埃及棉花以及印度软件都在贸易范围内。结果是,家家户户都能在众多的商品和服务中,以最优惠的价格获得满意的选择。

　　全球化给我们带来了"世界贸易组织(WTO)"、"欧元"和"北美自由贸易区(NAFTA)"。每天都有百十亿美元的资金,以几乎零成本的电子方式在全球进行流通。

　　全球化拓展了一切。它把市场理论推至全盛期,并且使新古典主义经济模式成为历史,这些经济模式是建立在阻碍商品与服务在经济区域间流动的基础上的。一些专业概念像"比较优势"、"一般均衡"似乎也不再适用。

　　在转型过程中,我们发现,融于全球化之中的国家的经济发展欣欣向荣:商品、资本和劳动力在各国之间自由地流动。这些国家间的不平等现象也在减少。

　　自第二次世界大战以来,全球化需要贸易谈判达到新的高度。在当初的"关税及贸易总协定(GATT)"以及现在的"世界贸易组织(WTO)"和"世界海关组织(WCO)"的主办下,一轮又一轮的贸易纠纷和关税争端得到解决,这为商品和服务的流动做出了巨大贡献。

　　世界商品和服务出口总量,由第二次世界大战结束时的不足 1 亿美元飙升到现在的 11 万亿美元。预计，全球生产总值（GGP）也将由 20 世纪 70 年代的不足 5 万亿美元，增加到 21 世纪中叶的 100 万亿美元。届时，国际贸易总量可能高达 40 万亿美元，而这两项数据在以前都是无法想象的。图 I.1 展示了世界贸易急剧发展的真实数据。

这种发展的结果将使得本世纪的经济比以往更加繁荣。因为，自由开放的国际贸易是经济发展的坚实推动力，而且所有人都将置身其中。

这本第 4 版的《进出口业务——带领企业走出国门》，致力于揭开国际贸易的神秘面纱，使每个人都能体验全球化的浪潮，感受弄潮的乐趣。

本书的成功之处在于延续了其一贯鲜活、贴切的特点，从而持续稳坐"畅销书、最受欢迎书籍"的宝座[1]。付梓 20 多年来，多次不断重印再版，已有成千上万的读者学习此书，并把学到的知识付诸实践。

我们（McGraw-Hill 出版公司和作者）坚持为读者奉上一本实用作品。本书以简洁明了的方式，介绍了国际贸易交易中的基础知识，而每一新版的内容都力求与时俱进、体现前沿。

第 4 版对基本内容进行了扩展和更新，并且增添了新信息，如网络零售指南，内包和外包等内容。本版还说明了怎样利用网络新利器进行进出口贸易，等等。

本书介绍进口和出口的方方面面，讲解详细、实用，成功案例丰富。它传递的核心信息是：跨国贸易并不难，走出国门受益多。

本书采用的方法

本书的初衷在于通过紧凑和富有逻辑的结构，以精炼的理论结合众多实用内容，展现进出口交易的各个方面，为读者提供一本实践指导性的专业书籍。

与以往出版的国际贸易图书不同的是，本书从进口和出口共性与差异的角度，展示了进出口的基本知识。而其他相关书籍往往把进口和出口分开处理，以示两者的截然不同。实际上，进口和出口的基本原理是大体相同的，进口就像出口的镜像（共性部分）。例如，进口和出口贸易的专业

---

1 基于在 Amazon.com 和 Barnes and Noble.com 的销售统计数据。

Figure I.1 World Exports of Merchandise, Goods, and Services

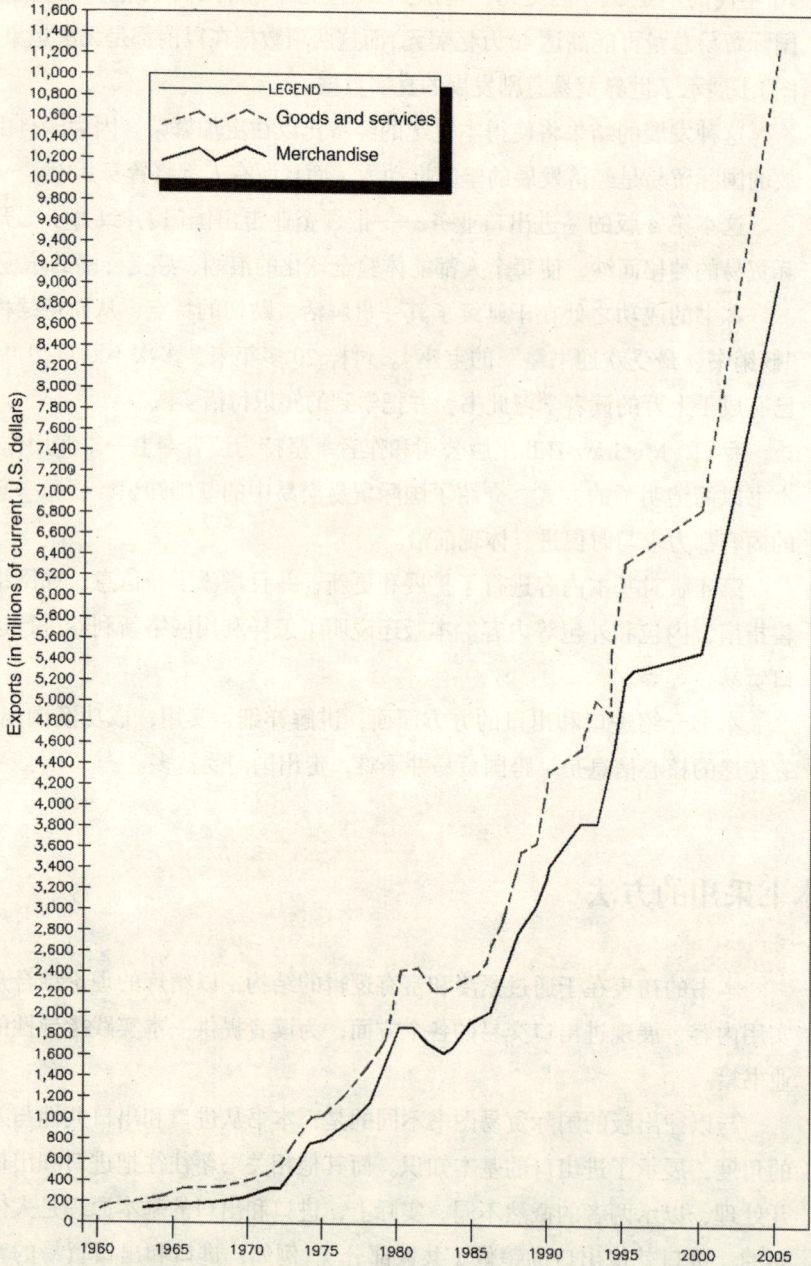

Source: World Bank

术语和交流方式都一样。

进口和出口的共性并不局限于某一国家，也就是说，它适用于世界上的任何国家，因此本书具有国际性。本书仅有两章内容（第 7 章和第 8 章）具体到美国，然而，即使是这两章的内容也具有普遍性，因为其贸易过程同样适用于其他国家。

关于国际贸易的原理没有改变，在第 1 版写作时，国际贸易所采用的基本方法依然适用于今天。国际贸易的焦点不仅仅在于了解进出口贸易，更在于怎样在交易中获益。若要成功，从事贸易者必须把握对方的问题所在，也就是要做到知己知彼。

本书的目标读者

《进出口业务——带领企业走出国门》适合小型制造业主或服务性企业主、第二职业开拓者，或者期望学习怎样涉入身价高达 11 万亿美元国际市场的企业家。本书对于女性和少数族群拥有的企业意义尤为重大，这些企业的增长高于全国平均水平。那些想在国际发展中提升自己的公司管理人员，想在不断拓展的全球市场里寻找机会的在校学生和企业家，都将继续从此书中受益。而对于那些缺乏实务知识、实践经验，想要学习进出口贸易技巧的中小型制造业和服务业公司，本书具有独到的指导价值。在世界范围内，越来越多的制造业和服务性企业卷入了国际贸易的浪潮，然而在全球化的席卷下，只有参与贸易游戏才能获得生存和发展。

本书由美国作者撰写，但是这并非意味着此书仅限于美国人使用。世界各国都有企业在生产商品并且远销海外。即使国家的制度和语言有所不同，人们跨境做生意的过程也是相同的。此书描述的就是这种跨境贸易过程，并且由此为任何想在全球贸易中获利的人士提供宝贵帮助。

国际贸易让许多人兴趣盎然：启动大把赚钱的业务，向海外推销自产和他人的产品，这其中的挑战令人着迷。他们看到了尚未开发的市场和营利前景，渴望了解怎样跻身于不断增长的国际贸易活动之中。进出口业务为他们提供了周游世界的良机，并且还能使其尽享与世界各国的客户开展业务合作的美誉。

众多在校学生（甚至包括高级商科学位拥有者）希望进入国际贸易发展，并且能在该领域拥有自己的一席之地。通过学习此书，他们可以将所学理论与实践相结合。很多讲师和教授发现本书适合用于课堂教学，因为它以独特的视角帮助学生了解进出口的全过程，有助于学生把自己的前程与进出口业务发展的宏大背景融为一体。

从古至今，女性从来没有像今天这样在世界经济活动中拥有如此之多的机会和自由。在 2002 年，美国女性拥有的公司超过 1 200 万家，占小型企业的 30%，总收入达到 9 500 多亿美元，比 1997 年提高了 22%。女性拥有公司的增长率为 20%，而少数族群拥有的公司也增长了 67%。由于这些公司的总量在增加，参与国际贸易的这些企业数量也在相应地增加。

对于移居他国的人来说，许多原本意料中的障碍反倒成为了优势。譬如说，在非洲许多地方，你的黑色肌肤将为你的生意带来很多便利。许多新移民已经具有能说另一种语言或者了解另一种文化的优势。因为已经身居他国，又有海外联系，所以这时起步从事国际贸易往往会更加容易。

本书涵盖内容

本书基于通俗易懂、生动有趣的原则组织内容，适合从企业家到决策者的各类人员使用。

《进出口业务——带领企业走出国门》包含下述内容：

- 采用生动有趣的方式阐释进出口贸易；
- 通过比较异同揭示进出口贸易的基本原理；
- 通过列举具体的案例和轶事，展现怎样将进出口贸易基本原理付诸实践，获得高额利润；
- 教授读者如何利用互联网来促进销售；
- 解释怎样在全球市场买到制造成本最低的商品；
- 向读者展示怎样在经济全球化的市场中做生意；
- 介绍美国国土安全部在贸易中的地位。

进出口的共性知识

本书列举了 16 个在进出口业务中意思相同的基本概念：其中第 3 章有 6 个，第 4 章 6 个，第 5 章 4 个。

为方便读者的理解和掌握，每个基本概念都按照现实买卖交易的通常流程来呈现。但是，一定不要错误地认为概念呈现的先后顺序代表着它们的重要性，或者每个概念都能独立存在。实际上，国际贸易中的每一步骤都环环相扣、密切联系，各个基本概念都同等重要。在进出口贸易中获得成功的人都深谙这些概念的关键所在，他们就像第 6 章介绍的那样创建公司，然后把这些概念原理应用到业务中去。

进出口的差异特性

进口和出口的某些方面存在差异，或者说进出口的某些方面仅限于某些国家。譬如说，除了进口配额以外，"控制手段"仅在出口中使用；但是关税仅在进口中使用。这些进出口中的显著差别在本书第 6 章和第 7 章分别加以阐述。这种处理方式明确突出了差异特性，有助于读者迅速地理解和掌握。

本版新增内容

新版采用了许多新的方式阐述进出口贸易的交易过程，并且紧跟时代发展增添了新内容。例如：

- 提供了大量的网络资源和网址；
- 修订了如何使用电子商务的章节；
- 改进了在全球化影响下怎样开展业务的部分；
- 更新了世界贸易中心的有关章节；
- 增补了关于产品标准的信息；
- 增补了像北美自由贸易区和欧盟等一体化经济区的信息；

- 介绍了使用信用证的技巧；
- 介绍了美国国土安全部在国际贸易中的地位；
- 新增了怎样开设和利用网店的指南。

如何使用本书

不管是从事国际贸易的进口还是出口，你都要知道进出口的基本知识。因此，用好本书的上策，即首先学习第 2 至 5 章中的基本概念。当然，组建自己的公司是从事外贸交易活动的前提。所以，接下来的第 6 章将告诉你怎样创建和管理公司，然后将书中的基础知识付诸实践，在进出口贸易的实际活动中使自己的公司获利。这就是本书的妙处所在。

本书的最后一章给读者提供了进出口贸易的 20 条基本原则。

本书回答了数百条诸如下面的问题。按照作者的建议去做，必将获益匪浅。

- 怎样开始我的进出口业务；
- 如何选择产品来开展进出口贸易；
- 国土安全对我的业务有何影响；
- 怎样签订海外订货合同；
- 怎样签订营销合同；
- 怎样使用网络从事贸易；
- 怎样创建企业网站；
- 怎样制作网站首页；
- 怎样给产品制定有利可图的价格；
- 怎样准备市场策划；
- 怎样从事贸易谈判；
- 怎样保护产品专利和商标；
- 海外旅行的秘诀有哪些；
- 怎样筹集进出口交易资金；
- 什么是"外包"；
- 什么是"信用证"；
- 到哪里去申请出口许可证；

- 怎样迅速通关；
- 如何使用协调关税表；
- 怎样计算进口关税；
- 怎样为进出口企业撰写计划书；
- 北美自由贸易区有哪些好处；
- 怎样在欧洲单一市场从事贸易；
- 从哪里能够获取与中国和印度从事贸易的相关信息。

小　结

本书为读者提供了无限良机。它带来的不仅是阅读的乐趣，还有独特的视野和巨大的营利潜力。我们希望此书能激发你去环游世界，体验异国风情，接触各国奇人，朋友遍天下。最主要的是，祝愿你能收获国际贸易中那笔尚未开发的巨大财富。

《进出口业务——带领企业走出国门》将会改变你的生活。别犹豫啦，赶紧加入进出口贸易大市场，时不我待！

PART I

THE COMMONALITIES

共性知识

CHAPTER 1

WINNING THE TRADE GAME
制胜商场

International trade is the exchange of goods and services across national boundaries. *Exports* are the merchandise individuals or nations sell; *imports* are the goods individuals or nations purchase. By these methods, products valued at more than US$11 trillion worldwide are exchanged every year. When we as consumers enjoy fresh flowers from Latin America, tropical fruits in the middle of winter, or a foreign car, we are participants in, and beneficiaries of, international trade. International trade is not a zero-sum game of winners and losers; it is a game in which everyone wins.

国际贸易就是在不同国家之间交换商品和服务。所谓出口货品，就是个人或者国家卖出的商品。而进口货品，则是个人或者国家买入的商品。

国际贸易并不是一个有成功者就必定会有失败者的零和游戏，相反，它是一场所有参与者可以共赢的盛宴。

全球的机遇
Global Opportunities

Major changes that took place in the twentieth century have had a significant effect on international trade in the new century and have provided unprecedented opportunities.

The age of globalism has brought about worldwide distribution, the Internet, satellite communications, and speedy transportation systems. People all over the world seek the same luxuries and standards. They see things and, naturally, they want them.

全球化时代造就了世界分销体系、互联网络、卫星通信以及快捷的运输系统。

---

participant 参与者。beneficiary 受益者。a zero-sum game 零和游戏（一方得益招致另一方相应受损的博弈）。unprecedented 前所未有的。

全球化不再只是个时髦的口号，而是现实。

因此，国际贸易不是静态的过程，如果生产厂商试图把产品销往海外，就必须时常进行调整。

Globalization is no longer a buzzword; it is a reality. National governments have a large stake in its outcome because this change affects their societies. As the process goes forward, the need for harmonizing interstate laws becomes more serious. Therefore international trade cannot be a static process, and businesses that make products and attempt to sell them across borders must constantly adjust.

美国的赤字和盈余
U.S. Deficits and Surpluses

图 1.1 展示了始于最早时期的美国贸易史。

这表明，美国是世界上盈余和赤字最多的国家。这意味着，世界各地有很多能够赚钱的商品在转手交易，而你也能置身其中。

Figure 1.1 shows the history of American trade since the earliest days. You will note that it was not until about 1975 that trade began its chronic fall into significant deficits. Nevertheless, as Figures 1.2 and 1.3 show, the United States is at or near the top of the list in merchandise trade and commercial services. That is, America has the largest surpluses and deficits of any nation in the world, which means there is a lot of profitable merchandise moving around the world and you can have a part of that.

什么是进出口企业
What Is an Import/Export Business?

The questions most frequently asked by interested parties are: "What is an import/export business?" and "What organizational methods do traders use?" The answers depend on whether you work for a manufacturer or are independent (for more detail see Chapter 6).

If you own or work for a manufacturer of an exportable product, your company can create and organize its own export department. Today, however, many manufacturers outsource their export function to import/export companies.

现在很多公司把他们的出口业务外包给专门的进出口公司打理。

一家独立的进出口商业实体，实际上就是充当国际中间代理人的个人或公司。也就是说，它出售外国制造的产品（进口），或把本国的产品销售到别的国家（出口），或者两者兼做。

An independent import/export business is an individual or company that acts as an international middleman (a unisex term); that is, it sells foreign-made products (imports), sells domestic (home country) products in other countries (exports), or does both. See the Glossary at the back of book for an extensive list of the most commonly used trade terms.

Every manufacturer that is not already exporting can be a potential client for you; there are still many businesses all over the world that do

---

buzzword 时髦词汇。interstate〔美国〕各州间的，州际的。stake 利益，利害关系。chronic 长期的。significant deficits 巨额赤字。merchandise trade 货物贸易。commercial services 商贸服务。outsource 外包。middleman 中间代理人。unisex 不分男女的。home country 东道国。

图 1.1 1960 至 2004 年间美国贸易差额
Figure 1.1 U.S. Balance of Trade: 1960–2004

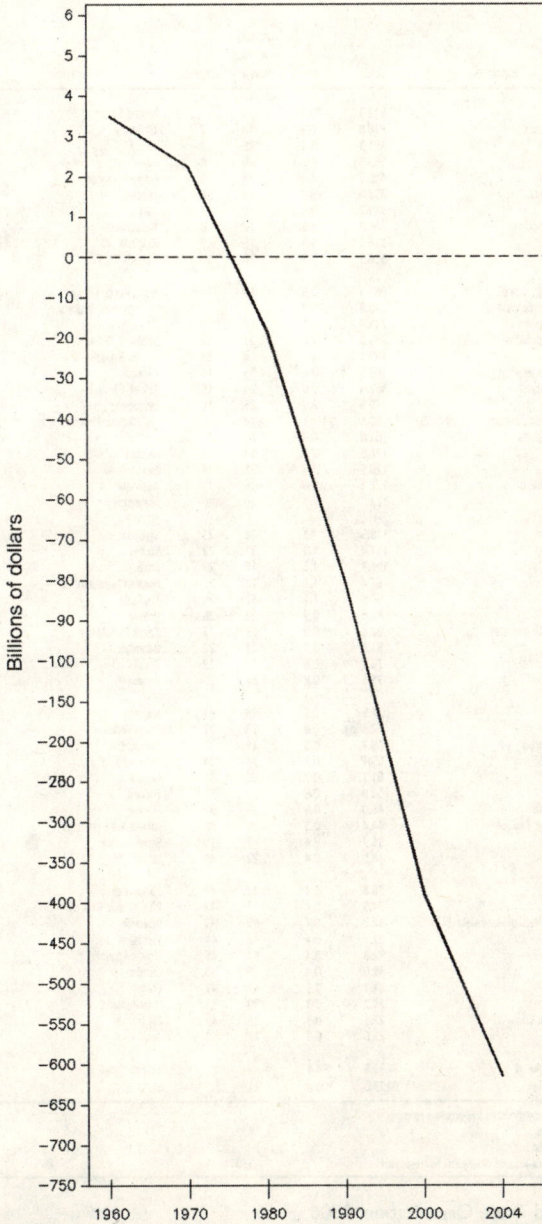

Y axis: Billions of dollars

Source: U.S. Department of Commerce

U.S. Department of Commerce 美国商务部。

图 1.2   2004 年世界货物贸易主要进口商和出口商排行榜

Figure 1.2 Leading Exporters and Importers in World Merchandise Trade: 2004 (in billions of dollars and percents)

Rank	Exporters	Value	Share	Annual percentage change	Rank	Importers	Value	Share	Annual percentage change
1	Germany	912.3	10.0	21	1	United States	1525.5	16.1	17
2	United States	818.8	8.9	13	2	Germany	716.9	7.6	19
3	China	593.3	6.5	35	3	China	561.2	5.9	36
4	Japan	565.8	6.2	20	4	France	465.5	4.9	17
5	France	448.7	4.9	14	5	United Kingdom	463.5	4.9	18
6	Netherlands	358.2	3.9	21	6	Japan	454.5	4.8	19
7	Italy	349.2	3.8	17	7	Italy	351.0	3.7	18
8	United Kingdom	346.9	3.8	13	8	Netherlands	319.3	3.4	21
9	Canada	316.5	3.5	16	9	Belgium	285.5	3.0	22
10	Belgium	306.5	3.3	20	10	Canada	279.8	2.9	14
11	Hong Kong, China	265.5	2.9	16	11	Hong Kong, China	272.9	2.9	17
	domestic exports	20.0	0.2	2		retained imports a	27.3	0.3	13
	re-exports	245.6	2.7	17					
12	Korea, Republic of	253.8	2.8	31	12	Spain	249.3	2.6	20
13	Mexico	189.1	2.1	14	13	Korea, Republic of	224.5	2.4	26
14	Russian Federation	183.5	2.0	35	14	Mexico	206.4	2.2	16
15	Taipei, Chinese	182.4	2.0	21	15	Taipei, Chinese	168.4	1.8	25
16	Singapore	179.6	2.0	25	16	Singapore	163.9	1.7	28
	domestic exports	98.6	1.1	24		retained imports a	82.8	0.9	30
	re-exports	81.0	0.9	26					
17	Spain	178.6	2.0	14	17	Austria	117.8	1.2	18
18	Malaysia	126.5	1.4	21	18	Switzerland	111.6	1.2	16
19	Saudi Arabia b	126.2	1.4	35	19	Australia	109.4	1.2	23
20	Sweden	122.5	1.3	20	20	Malaysia	105.3	1.1	26
21	Switzerland	118.5	1.3	18	21	Sweden	99.3	1.0	19
22	Austria	117.4	1.3	21	22	Turkey	97.5	1.0	41
23	Ireland	104.3	1.1	12	23	India	97.3	1.0	37
24	Thailand	97.4	1.1	21	24	Russian Federation c	96.3	1.0	27
25	Brazil	96.5	1.1	32	25	Thailand	95.4	1.0	26
26	Australia	86.4	0.9	21	26	Poland	89.2	0.9	31
27	United Arab Emirates	82.8	0.9	23	27	Czech Republic c	69.5	0.7	34
28	Norway	81.8	0.9	21	28	Denmark	68.2	0.7	19
29	Denmark	76.8	0.8	15	29	Brazil	65.9	0.7	30
30	India	75.6	0.8	32	30	Ireland	60.7	0.6	13
31	Poland	74.9	0.8	39	31	Hungary	59.3	0.6	24
32	Indonesia	72.3	0.8	13	32	South Africa b	57.1	0.6	39
33	Czech Republic	68.7	0.8	41	33	Portugal	54.9	0.6	16
34	Turkey	63.1	0.7	34	34	Indonesia	54.9	0.6	30
35	Finland	61.3	0.7	15	35	Greece	52.6	0.6	17
36	Hungary	54.9	0.6	27	36	Finland	50.8	0.5	20
37	South Africa	46.0	0.5	26	37	Norway	48.1	0.5	19
38	Iran, Islamic Rep. of	44.4	0.5	31	38	United Arab Emirates	47.6	0.5	21
39	Philippines	39.7	0.4	7	39	Saudi Arabia	44.6	0.5	21
40	Israel	38.5	0.4	22	40	Israel	42.9	0.5	18
41	Portugal	35.8	0.4	13	41	Philippines	42.3	0.4	7
42	Argentina	34.5	0.4	17	42	Iran, Islamic Rep. of	34.7	0.4	33
43	Bolivarian Rep. of Venezuela b	34.2	0.4	43	43	Romania	32.7	0.3	36
44	Ukraine	32.7	0.4	42	44	Viet Nam	31.1	0.3	23
45	Algeria	32.3	0.4	31	45	Slovak Republic c	29.5	0.3	31
46	Chile	32.0	0.4	49	46	Ukraine	29.0	0.3	26
47	Nigeria	31.1	0.3	57	47	Chile	24.9	0.3	28
48	Kuwait	28.7	0.3	39	48	New Zealand	23.2	0.2	25
49	Slovak Republic	27.5	0.3	26	49	Argentina	22.3	0.2	61
50	Viet Nam	25.6	0.3	27	50	Iraq	21.3	0.2	114
	Total of above d	8639.8	94.4	-		Total of above d	8795.2	92.6	
	World d	9153.0	100.0	21		World d	9495.0	100.0	21

a Retained imports are defined as imports less re-exports.
b Secretariat estimates.
c Imports are valued f.o.b.
d Includes significant re-exports or imports for re-export.

Source: World Trade Organization, 2006

---

rank 排名。value 金额。share 份额。annual percentage change 年变化率。World Trade Organization 世界贸易组织。

图 1.3   2004 年世界服务贸易主要进口商和出口商排行榜

Figure 1.3 Leading Exporters and Importers in World Trade in Commercial Services: 2004 (in billions of dollars and percents)

Rank	Exporters	Value	Share	Annual percentage change	Rank	Importers	Value	Share	Annual percentage change
1	United States	318.3	15.0	11	1	United States	260.0	12.4	14
2	United Kingdom	171.8	8.1	18	2	Germany	193.0	9.2	13
3	Germany	133.9	6.3	15	3	United Kingdom	136.1	6.5	14
4	France	109.5	5.1	12	4	Japan	134.0	6.4	22
5	Japan	94.9	4.5	25	5	France	96.4	4.6	18
6	Spain	84.5	4.0	11	6	Italy	80.6	3.8	10
7	Italy	82.0	3.9	17	7	Netherlands	72.4	3.5	11
8	Netherlands	73.0	3.4	16	8	China	71.6	3.4	31
9	China	62.1	2.9	34	9	Ireland	58.4	2.8	12
10	Hong Kong, China	53.6	2.5	18	10	Canada	55.9	2.7	12
11	Belgium	49.3	2.3	14	11	Spain	53.7	2.6	18
12	Austria	48.3	2.3	14	12	Korea, Republic of	49.6	2.4	25
13	Ireland	46.9	2.2	24	13	Belgium	48.3	2.3	14
14	Canada	46.8	2.2	11	14	Austria	47.1	2.2	14
15	Korea, Republic of	40.0	1.9	27	15	India	40.9	2.0	...
16	India	39.6	1.9	...	16	Singapore	36.2	1.7	23
17	Sweden	37.8	1.8	25	17	Denmark	33.4	1.6	18
18	Switzerland	36.8	1.7	11	18	Sweden	33.0	1.6	15
19	Singapore	36.5	1.7	19	19	Russian Federation	32.8	1.6	24
20	Denmark	36.3	1.7	15	20	Taipei, Chinese	29.9	1.4	20
21	Greece	33.2	1.6	37	21	Hong Kong, China	29.8	1.4	16
22	Luxembourg	33.1	1.6	34	22	Australia	25.6	1.2	22
23	Norway	25.9	1.2	21	23	Norway	24.0	1.1	21
24	Taipei, Chinese	25.5	1.2	11	24	Thailand	23.0	1.1	28
25	Australia	24.8	1.2	20	25	Luxembourg	22.3	1.1	35
26	Turkey	23.8	1.1	25	26	Indonesia a	21.3	1.0	...
27	Russian Federation	20.2	0.9	25	27	Switzerland	21.1	1.0	10
28	Thailand	18.9	0.9	21	28	Mexico	19.3	0.9	10
29	Malaysia	16.7	0.8	24	29	Malaysia	18.8	0.9	8
30	Israel	14.2	0.7	16	30	Brazil	16.1	0.8	12
31	Egypt	14.0	0.7	30	31	United Arab Emirates a	13.4	0.6	...
32	Mexico	13.9	0.7	12	32	Greece	13.4	0.6	25
33	Portugal	13.8	0.6	21	33	Israel	13.3	0.6	13
34	Poland	13.3	0.6	19	34	Poland	12.3	0.6	17
35	Brazil	11.5	0.5	20	35	Finland	11.8	0.6	18
36	Hungary	10.1	0.5	17	36	Saudi Arabia	11.0	0.5	39
37	Czech Republic	9.7	0.5	25	37	Turkey	10.3	0.5	33
38	Croatia	9.6	0.5	11	38	Hungary	10.0	0.5	11
39	Finland	8.9	0.4	14	39	Czech Republic	9.1	0.4	26
40	South Africa	8.1	0.4	10	40	South Africa	9.1	0.4	16
	Total of above	1950.0	91.7	-		Total of above	1900.0	90.6	-
	World	2125.0	100.0	18		World	2095.0	100.0	17

a Secretariat estimate.
Note: Figures for a number of countries and territories have been estimated by the Secretariat. Annual percentage changes and rankings are affected by continuity breaks in the series for a large number of economies, and by limitations in cross-country comparability.

Source: World Trade Organization, 2006

not export. According to the U.S. Department of Commerce, less than 10 percent of all American manufacturers currently sell their products overseas.

不论你经营的业务是源自家庭产业还是基于国内现有生产厂家的增设业务，进出口企业的启动往往都不需要太多的资本投资。

Whether you run your business from your home or as an expansion of an existing domestic manufacturing firm, an import/export business often requires little capital investment for start-up. Of course it can grow into a giant business with billions of dollars in annual sales. An import/export business also offers great opportunities to travel and to enjoy the prestige of working with clients from all over the world.

进出口商在哪里进行交易
Where Do Importers and Exporters Trade?

一旦开始国外贸易，新的商机就会接踵而至。

Everyone is trading internationally. And once trade begins with one country, new opportunities spring out of nowhere. A business person who successfully starts importing very soon learns of exporting opportunities and vice versa. In any case, a whole lot of money can be made. More than $11 trillion wouldn't be traded worldwide if it weren't profitable to do so.

世界贸易组织（世贸组织）
The World Trade Organization (WTO)

世界贸易组织创建于1995年1月1日，和世界银行以及国际货币基金组织拥有旗鼓相当的地位。它的创立对全球贸易起到了促进作用。

其核心是由众多贸易国协商签订并由各自国会认可的世贸组织协定。

世贸组织的目标就是帮助商品和服务的生产商，进口商和出口商，开展他们的业务。

Created on January 1, 1995, the World Trade Organization (WTO), with equal status alongside the World Bank and the International Monetary Fund, has strengthened global trade. It is the only international organization that deals with the rules of trade between nations. At its heart are the WTO agreements, negotiated and signed by the bulk of the world's trading nations and ratified by their parliaments. As of 2005, it has over 149 national members making it easier to do business across borders by reducing tariffs and harmonizing laws and practices that are barriers to trade. The WTO's goal is to help producers of goods and services, exporters and importers, conduct their business.

---

prestige 声誉。client 客户。out of nowhere 突然地。vice versa 反过来／反之亦然。the World Bank 世界银行。the International Monetary Fund 国际货币基金组织。the rules of trade 贸易规则。tariff 关税。barriers to trade 贸易壁垒。

网上交易
Cyber Trading

There is no president or congress of the Internet, and it has no boundaries; therefore, cyber communication is the international trader's connection without barriers (see Chapter 4).

世界贸易中心协会
World Trade Centers Association (WTCA)

Founded in 1970, the World Trade Centers Association (WTCA) is a not-for-profit, nonpolitical association dedicated to the establishment and effective operation of world trade centers as instruments for trade expansion. To date, the WTCA membership about 300 centers in 75 countries. These world trade centers service more than 750,000 international affiliated businesses.

World trade centers, dedicated to providing services to facilitate international trade, are located in over 170 cities with about 100 more in the planning stages. In other words, they are in virtually every major trading city in the world. To learn more about world trade centers, see Chapter 9.

建于 1970 年的世界贸易中心协会（WTCA）是一个非营利性、非政治性的组织，它致力于建立有效合理运行的世界贸易中心，以促进全球贸易的发展。

贸易一体化
Trade Integrations

Trade integrations are preferential arrangements between two or more nations to facilitate commerce across borders.

贸易一体化是两个或多个国家促进双边或多边贸易的优惠协定。

北　美
North America

The North American Free Trade Agreement (NAFTA)—the world's largest trading bloc—is expanding to include many of the nations of the Caribbean basin and South America.

北美自由贸易协定（NAFTA），作为世界最大的贸易区域集团，正在扩张，力图将加勒比海沿岸和南美的许多国家收入麾下。

欧　洲
Europe

The European Union (EU) formed a single internal market that has resulted in the removal of essentially all physical, technical, and fiscal

欧盟（EU）建立了一个单一内部市场，这个市场几乎消除了欧洲共同市场上所有关于物质、技术和财政等方

---

to date 到目前为止。affiliated business 会员企业。planning stages 筹划阶段。preferential arrangement 特惠（贸易）协定，特惠协议。trading bloc（国家间建立的）贸易集团。Caribbean basin 加勒比沿岸。

面阻碍商品和服务贸易的壁垒。

一些公认的变化包括：

- 相同的增值税；
- 运输管制的宽松；
- 行业和安全基本标准的建立；
- 欧盟范围内政府采购招投标机制的开放。

barriers to the exchange of goods and services within the European common market. The EU is now becoming larger to include some of the newly independent states of Central and Eastern Europe. Some of the changes agreed to are:

- A common value-added tax
- Deregulation of transportation
- Establishment of minimum industrial and safety standards
- Broadening of the EU-wide bidding process for government procurement

亚　洲
Asia

亚洲及太平洋沿岸国家和地区，包括澳大利亚、新西兰、日本和亚洲"五小虎"（韩国、新加坡、泰国以及中国台湾和中国香港特别行政区），正展现出极大的贸易机会。

The Asian/Pacific Basin nations of Australia, New Zealand, Japan, and the "Tigers" (Repubic of Korea, Singapore, Thailand as well as China Taiwan, China Hong Kong SAR) are the countries that today present the greatest trade opportunities. Trade in this region has expanded faster than any other part of the world.

中国和印度
China and India

中国和印度，世界上人口最多的两个国家，在国际贸易中取得了巨大进步。它们值得密切关注——其贸易势头不容小觑！

China and India are the two most populated countries and are making special progress in international trade. They are worthy of focused research—they are doing business!

非　洲
Africa

The latest world trade emphasis is focused on the countries of the African continent, particularly those south of the Sahara where there are vast untapped resources and a need for modernization and economic development.

为何做贸易
Why Get into Trade?

There are three big reasons to get into the trade game:

1. Imports bring big profits.
2. Exports make big profits.

---

value-added tax 增值税。deregulation 解禁，放松管制。bidding process 招投标程序。government procurement 政府采购。the Sahara 撒哈拉沙漠。untapped resources 未开发的资源。

3. The world is interdependent. People have awakened to two realities—that people of each nation rely on people of other nations to exchange goods, services, and ideas—and that free trade creates jobs.

人们已经意识到了两大事实：每个国家都要依赖其他国家以互换商品、服务和创意；自由贸易能够创造就业机会。

Those who are winning the trade game know that, regardless of national deficits or surpluses, the time is always right for an import/export business to make profits. The winners simply swing with political and economic changes over which they have little or no control.

贸易赢家只是在个人无法掌控的政治经济变化中顺势而为。

成功案例
Success Stories

This book does not guarantee financial success—there are too many variables such as management, financial capitalization, and determination; however, the following are a few stories you might find interesting and stimulating. The intention is to motivate and offer a few ideas that might work for you.

本书并不保证获取财富上的成功，因为有太多的不确定因素在起作用，例如管理方法、金融投资以及个人的决心等。但是，下面这些故事也许能够引发你的兴趣，给你带来激励。

美国好莱坞
Hollywood USA

The president and CEO of a small New Jersey company with a Beverly Hills connection swears that it's true that customers in the Middle East are wild for products bearing American brand names and splashes of red, white, and blue on their packaging. His line of Hollywood USA high-quality body sprays, creams, baby products, deodorants, and shampoos has found buyers around the world—in Africa, Latin America, and, of course, the Middle East.

在美国新泽西洲贝弗利山附近有一家小型公司，其总裁兼首席执行官坚称，中东的消费者狂热追捧美国货，即那些包装上印有美国商标和涂有红、白、蓝色块的商品。

从空气到水
From Air to H_2O

Even in the driest part of the world, Hisham Fawzi's worldwide government customers don't wait for rain to quench their thirsts. As president and chairman of Excel Holdings, a small firm in Leesburg, Virginia, Fawzi develops and markets a patented line of machines that convert moisture from the air into drinkable water. Excel Holdings

美国弗吉尼亚州利兹堡（Leesburg）市的一家小公司 Excel Holdings 的总经理 Fawzi，开发并向市场推出了一组专利设备。该设备能将空气中的湿气转化成饮用水。

---

variable 变量。CEO 首席执行官。Beverly hills 贝弗利山。line 商品系列。body spray 香体喷雾。deodorant 除臭剂。government customer 政府客户。

currently markets its products in 14 countries with more potential customers in the waiting. Most of his customers are foreign governments or international organizations that often finance water purification efforts.

南瓜孕妇装
Pumpkin Maternity

一位摇滚乐手在荷兰旅行时想起了姐姐和最要好的朋友，当时那两人都已怀孕并抱怨过没有合适的衣服可穿。

While touring the Netherlands, a rock musician thought about her sister and her best friend, both pregnant and complaining that they had nothing to wear. She knew exactly what was needed—hip, quality maternity clothes that reflect today's fashions.

两年后，她的邮购业务和网店交易都很兴隆。

Two months later the Pumpkin Maternity catalog was printed, and she was in business. Two years later, she has thriving mail-order and Web site sales. You can check out Pumpkin Maternity at www.pumpkinmaternity.com and www.babystyle.com.

澳新地区
Down Under

1991 年以来，Amy Frey 的小公司 ATC 国际已经帮助很多澳大利亚制造商在利润丰厚的北美市场找到了获利机会。

Since 1991, Amy Frey has helped Australian manufacturers gain a niche in the lucrative North American market through her small business, ATC International. Frey nurtured her company from its humble origins in a spare bedroom to a 6,000-square-foot warehouse outside Washington, DC. From there, her four-person team provides market research, business management, distribution, and logistic services to clients in Australia and New Zealand.

帕洛玛技术公司
Palomar Technologies

帕洛玛技术公司是总部位于加利福尼亚州圣地亚哥市的一家高科技产业公司，是世界高精度微电子集成设备的主要供应商。

Palomar Technologies is a high-tech company headquartered in San Diego, California. It is the premier supplier of high-precision microelectronic assembly equipment in the world. Palomar provides best-in-class solutions for microelectronic component manufacturers worldwide. The unique concentration of telecom and bio-med companies in the San Diego region is renowned worldwide and provides instant credibility for a high-tech company such as Palomar to compete

---

water purification 水的净化。hip 时尚新潮的。maternity clothes 孕妇装。in business 做买卖。mail-order 邮购。niche 有利可图的机会，利基市场。distribution 分销。logistic services 物流服务。premier supplier 主要供应商。

against foreign suppliers for design, process development, custom manufacturing, and service business.

国际咨询集团公司
International Consulting Group

The International Consulting Group serves the Mexico–United States border area. Since its start-up in the mid-1980s, it has offered services to expand into Mexico or Latin America. The group assists clients with informed ideas and services that best suit their specialized needs in researching and penetrating markets.

集团公司为客户提供咨询服务，献计献策，充分满足客户在研发和拓展市场方面的特定需求。

自动喂狗器和阿里巴巴网站
Dog Feeders and Alibaba.com

This company started production of high-end dog feeders and learned that it's almost impossible to compete with the big guys if you don't produce offshore. Start-ups don't usually have the capital for actually going to China and visiting potential business partners before closing the deal. So instead, this company went to Alibaba.com and found the system very easy to use and helpful. It posted its need to find suppliers in Asia on Alibaba's Web site and started making contacts immediately.

这家公司开始生产高端自动喂狗器时就知道，除非去海外生产，否则几乎没有可能与大公司抗衡竞争。

于是，该公司访问了阿里巴巴网站，并发现了此系统便捷、有效。

DriveCam 国际公司
DriveCam International

Headquartered in San Diego, California, DriveCam reduces claims costs and saves lives by improving the way people drive. The company's product mitigates risk by improving driver behavior and assessing liability in collisions. Combining sights and sounds, expert analysis, and driver coaching, its approach has reduced vehicle damages, worker's compensation, and personal injury costs by 30 to 90 percent for more than 40,000 commercial, government, and consumer vehicles.

Launched in February 1998, DriveCam has received three patents for its innovative design with additional patents pending. By 2005, the company was ranked number 67 in the Inc. 500. Focusing on improving risky driving behavior by predicting and preventing crashes, DriveCam's exception-based video event recorder is mounted on the

总部位于加利福尼亚州圣地亚哥市的 DriveCam 国际公司，通过改善人们的驾驶方式，减少索赔成本，挽救生命。

通过音像结合、专家分析和司机培训，已经有 40 000 多辆车，包括商务、政府和家庭用车，在这家公司这些方法的帮助下，把车辆损失、员工赔偿和人身伤害费用等损失降低了 30% 到 90%。

---

process development 工艺开发。penetrating market 进入市场。start-ups 新公司。close the deal 达成交易。claim 索赔。assess liability 评估可能性。personal injury 人身伤害。patent 专利。

windshield behind the rearview mirror and captures sights and sounds inside and outside the vehicle. The company operates in 10 countries in North America, Europe, Africa, Australia, and Asia.

Candleworks 公司

Candleworks

位于爱荷华州爱荷华市的 Candleworks 公司，生产和销售家用自然芬香和香熏蜡烛，产品远销国外。

Located in Iowa City, Iowa, Candleworks is a company that makes and markets natural home fragrances and aromatherapy candles internationally. It was born out of struggle, has survived, and earned $800,000 in sales in their first year.

第 2 章讲述如何开始赚钱的交易（规划进出口的第一步），并且帮你更快找到能够成功和营利的国际贸易良机。

The next chapter explains how to launch a profitable transaction—the first steps of your import/export project—and speed you on your way toward international trade opportunities with profits and success.

---

windshield 挡风玻璃。rearview mirror 后视镜 。

CHAPTER 2

LAUNCHING A PROFITABLE TRANSACTION

开始赚钱的买卖

Some perceive the import/export transaction process as an obstacle, but don't let that deter you. The truth is that anyone can grasp the nuts and bolts of international trade. The bridge from producers to buyers has existed for many years, and it has been tested and retested. By investing some time and money in yourself, you can easily learn this process.

This chapter addresses the first six commonalities of the importing and exporting transaction. If you understand the steps outlined below, your import/export business will get off to an excellent start on the road to early profitability.

有人把进出口交易程序视为障碍，但是，千万不要因此而改弦易辙，影响你做进出口贸易的初衷。

本章首先介绍进出口交易的六大共同要点。如果理解掌握了下述步骤，你的进出口业务就会出师顺利，早日赚钱便指日可待。

1. Terminology
2. Homework
3. Choosing the product
4. Making contacts
5. Market research
6. What's the bottom line?

---

nuts and bolts 基本要点。 terminology 专业术语。 homework 前期调研。

不要误认为本书所列步骤是依照重要性来排序的，或者认为在进出口业务中都必须严格地按照此顺序行事。

Don't mistakenly assume that the order presented in this book represents a hierarchy of importance, or that these steps are in the precise order of every import/export project. In reality, sometimes things happen simultaneously.

贸易术语
Terminology

由于国际间的相互依赖日益增强，在当代商业中，贸易读写能力与互联网和电脑读写能力一样重要。

Because of increasing international interdependency, trade literacy has become as important in modern business as Internet and computer literacy. As you progress in your reading, refer frequently to the extensive glossary of commonly used terms found at the end of this book. Many of these terms are also defined when they first appear in the text. Don't be frightened by the new terminology—you can learn it!

前期调研
Homework

即使拥有一些国际贸易经验，不经过调研就急于开展一项业务也非明智之举。

Research is one of the keys to winning the trade game! Even if you have some experience in international trade, it's unwise to jump into an unresearched project. In fact, it's not unusual to spend several weeks learning about the product and its profit potential before getting serious. Think of it as an investment to reduce the number of inevitable mistakes.

选择产品或服务
Choosing the Product or Service

The question asked most often is, "What product should I select to import or export? Should it be rugs or machinery?" Of course, if your firm already manufactures merchandise or provides a service, that product or service is what you sell. But for your own import/export business, your job will be to sell someone else's product or service. In other words you will be the middleman.

---

literacy 读写能力。jump into 急切投入。inevitable mistake 常见错误。middleman 中间商。

The Personal Decision 个人决策

Most people begin with a single product or service that they know and understand or have experience. Others begin with a line of products or define their products in terms of an industry with which they are familiar. Above all, product selection is a personal decision, but the decision should make common sense. For example, if you aren't an engineer, don't begin by exporting gas turbine engines. Or, if you are an electronics engineer, don't start with fashionable textiles. A good example is the American house painter who began making excellent profits exporting a line of automated painting equipment to Europe. He knew the equipment before he began exporting.

最重要的是，虽然产品选择是一种个人决策，但是应当符合常理。

Start your business with a product or service with which you have an advantage. You can gain that advantage because of prior knowledge, by doing library research about a product, by making or using contacts, or by understanding a language or culture.

从你有优势的产品或服务开始做起。前期知识储备可以为你取得优势，这些知识可通过去图书馆做产品调研、建立或运用关系网或者了解某种语言或文化来获取。

HOT TIP

In the beginning, keep it simple.

起步阶段，简单为重。

营销技术决策
The Technical Marketing Decisions

Keep in mind that the product you select may need to be adapted to the cultures of other countries.

- *Product standards.*   ISO is an organization that harmonizes world product standards such as flammability, labeling, pollution, food and drug laws, and safety standards. ISO 9000 (product registration) and ISO 14000 (environmental management registration) are the international quality assurance series. At the time of publication of this edition they have been in effect for more than 13 years and are unlikely to go away.

国际标准化组织是一个国际组织，协调全世界产品标准，对易燃物品、标签、污染、食品和药品的法律以及安全标准等有统一的规定。ISO9000（产品注册）和ISO14000(环境管理注册)是国际质量保证系列的认证。

---

define 确定。common sense 常理。prior knowledge 前期知识。ISO 国际标准化组织。

世界上大多数国家都使用
220 伏、50 赫兹的电源，然
而美国的产品则要使用 120
伏、60 赫兹的电源。

在产品创新的生命周期中，
新产品往往首先在发达国家
推出，为早期型号在最欠发
达国家的销售留出余地。

例如，在美国，摩托车和自
行车大多为消遣之用，而在
其他许多国家，它们却是基
本的交通工具。

Therefore, it is important to check your products for compliance. Be sure to check www.iso.org

- *Technical specifications and codes.*   Most of the world uses 220 V, 50 Hz but products used in the United States are 120 V, 60 Hz. Similarly, most of the world uses the metric system of weights and measures. Determine how you can convert your product to meet the appropriate specifications and codes.
- *Quality and product life cycle.*   In the life cycle of product innovation, new products are typically introduced first to developed countries leaving an opportunity for sales of earlier models to least-developed countries. Assess the stage in the life cycle in which you find your export/import product.
- *Other uses.*   Different countries use some products for purposes different from those that we apply here. For example, motorcycles and bicycles are largely recreation vehicles in the United States, but in many countries they are the primary means of transportation.

何谓世界水平

What Is World Class?

"世界水平" 意味着，尽管
也许存在品质同样优良的产
品，但世界上绝没有任何产
品能够略胜一筹。但是有些
市场无法受用世界级高端产
品，因此需要确保所选产品
和服务适合你的市场。

较发达的工业化国家，包括
世界经济合作发展组织的所
有成员国，有别于 "发展中"
或 "欠发达" 国家。

What does it mean to have *world-class products*? Don't deceive yourself. Some things are better than others; you know it, we all know it. *World class* means there may be something as good, but there is nothing better in the world. But some markets can't absorb world class, so make sure that the products and services you select are right for your market.

> *Developed countries.* Distinguishes the more industrialized nations, including all member countries of the Organization for Economic Cooperation and Development (OECD) from "developing"—or "less developed"—countries.
>
> *Least-developed countries.* Forty-nine of the world's poorest countries are considered by the United Nations to be the least developed of

---

technical specification 技术规格。metric system 公制。product life cycle 产品生命周期。
Organization For Economic Cooperation and Development (OECD) 世界经济合作发展组织（世界经合组织）。

the least-developed countries. Most of them are small in terms of both area and population, and some are land-locked or small island countries. They are generally characterized by:

➤ Low per capita incomes, literacy levels, and medical standards
➤ Subsistence agriculture
➤ Lack of exploitable minerals and competitive industries

Many least-developed countries are in Africa, but a few, such as Bangladesh, Afghanistan, Laos, and Nepal, are in Asia. Haiti is the only country in the Western Hemisphere classified by the United Nations as "least developed."

最不发达的国家一般具有如下特点：

➤ 人均收入低、文化水平低、医疗标准低；
➤ 生存农业水平；
➤ 可开发的矿藏和有竞争力的产业匮乏。

建立联系
Making Contacts

Importers and exporters need contacts to get started. The exporter must convince a domestic manufacturer of his or her ability to sell the manufacturer's product or service internationally. The importer, on the other hand, must find an overseas manufacturer or middleman from whom to buy the product or service.

进口商和出口商需要先建立联系，然后再开展业务。

Contacts are classified in two categories. The two ways to make contacts overlap, and they can be used to expand your import/export network:

有两种方法可将建立的联系网结合起来，它们可以拓宽进出口网络：

1. *Sourcing* (finding) a manufacturer or provider of the product or service you wish import or export
2. *Marketing* (selling) that product or service

1. 找到生产者或供应商，他们为你提供你打算做的进出口产品或服务。
2. 营销（售卖）这种产品或服务。

货源联系
Sourcing Contacts

If you are an exporter, any product or service you select falls into an industry classification, and that industry very likely has an association. Almost every industry has a publication—if not a magazine, at least

如果你是出口商，你选的产品或服务总能归为某种行业分类，而这一行业很可能有行业协会。

---

per capita 每人。subsistence agriculture 生存农业，温饱型农业。contact 联系。industry classification 行业分类。association 协会。publication 出版物。

可以开始在合适的行业出版物上寻找所需产品或服务的生产商。

a newsletter. Begin looking for manufacturers of your product or service in the appropriate industry publication. Under "Information Sources" in Chapter 7, you will find other information that may help you make contacts for products to export.

对于进口商来说，获得这类的信息略为复杂。

Contacts for importers are only slightly more difficult to obtain. Assuming you know in which country your product is manufactured, you need a contact in that industry in that country. Start with the nearest consulate office and then contact that country's international chamber of commerce. You can also make contacts through your embassy or through a corresponding industry association. Furthermore, you can make direct contact with the government of the country in which you have an interest.

你也可以通过本国的大使馆或通过相应的行业协会进行联系。

Next, establish communications with the overseas contact to seek further information or to ask for product samples and prices. You can make contact by letter or by electronic means such as fax or e-mail. (See "Communications" in Chapter 3.)

最后，你需要去一趟你想与之贸易的国家，这很重要。

Eventually, you will need to take a trip to the country with which you intend to trade. It will make a big difference. (Travel is also discussed in Chapter 3.)

营销联系
Marketing Contacts

Marketing methods and channels of distribution are similar in most countries. Agents, distributors, wholesalers, and retailers exist everywhere, and you make marketing contacts through these channels.

国内营销联系的建立，除了可以利用旧货交换会、跳蚤市场、家庭聚会或者批发商，还可以借助贸易展销会、直销、直接寄售和厂家代表等。

For domestic marketing contacts, use trade shows, direct sales, direct mail, and manufacturer's representatives, as well as swap meets, flea markets, home parties, or wholesalers. Most governments will also help you find contacts.

Foreign sales representative. A representative or agent residing in a foreign country who acts as a salesperson for a U.S. manufacturer,

---

newsletter 简讯。information sources 信息来源。consulate office 领事馆。international chamber of commerce 国际商会。product sample 产品样品。agent 代理商。distributor 经销商。wholesaler 批发商。retailer 零售商。foreign sales representative 海外销售代表。

usually for a commission. Sometimes referred to as a *sales agent* or *commission agent*.

Distributor. A firm that: (1) sells directly for a manufacturer, usually on an exclusive basis for a specified territory, and (2) maintains an inventory of the manufacturer's goods.

经销公司应当：（1）通常基于特定区域的独家销售代理，直接销售生产商的产品。（2）持有生产商产品，维持一定的库存水平。

The international marketeer (trader) also can make contacts through world trade centers (WTCs) (see Chapter 9), trade shows, direct sales, a distributor, or an agent who is the equivalent of a manufacturer's representative. Trade fairs or shows are often the single most-effective means to make contacts and to learn about products, markets, competition, potential customers, and distributors. The term *trade show* or *fair* includes everything from catalog shows through local exhibits to major specialized international industry shows. At these shows, exhibitors offer literature and samples of their products.

贸易"展览会"或"交易会"包罗万象，从目录展示到国内展会到重大的专业国际行业展会。在这些展会上，参展商提供自己产品的文字资料和样品。

Lists of worldwide trade shows and international conferences are available from most large airlines as well as from the U.S. Department of Commerce and Chamber of Commerce (COC). Your industry association will know when and where the appropriate trade shows take place. Table 2.1 offers a range of ideas that should assist you, the importer or exporter, in making either sourcing or market contacts.

市场调研
Market Research

Market research is vital to the success of your import/export business. Is your product salable? Does anyone care? You must be able to sell enough of the product or service to justify undertaking the import/export project. If you are presenting a new product, you may have to create a market. But a good rule of thumb for the new import/export business is, "If the market isn't there, get out of the project and find another product."

但是开拓一项新的进出口业务时有条宝贵的经验法则：如果尚无市场，最好放弃手头项目，另寻他路。

---

commission 佣金。sales agent 销售代理。commission agent 佣金代理。marketeer 商人。world trade centers 世界贸易中心。literature 文字资料，印刷品。department of commerce 商务部。chamber of commerce 商会。care 关注，感兴趣。rule of thumb 经验法则。

表2.1　建立联系

Table 2.1　Making Contact

	Source	Market
Import	Consulate offices	Swap meets
	International COC	Direct mailers
	Industrial organizations	Mail orders
	Foreign governments	Home parties
	WTCA	Trade shows
	The Web (Internet)	Wholesalers
		Associations
		Representatives
		Retailers
		U.S. government
		WTCA
		The Web (Internet)
Export	*Thomas Register*	Distributors
	Contacts Influential	Trade shows
	Yellow Pages	Retailers
	U.S. Department of Commerce	Foreign governments
	Trade journals	U.S. Department of Commerce
	Trade associations	Direct mailers
	WTCA	United Nations
	The Web (Internet)	USAID
		Sell Overseas America
		Business America
		State trade promotion offices
		Journal of Commerce
		WTCA
		The Web (Internet)

出口商调研一览表
Exporter Checklist

糟糕的是，有太多新手还没有搞清产品销售能否赚钱就投入进出口业务。

International market research will save money and time. Unfortunately, too many newcomers plunge into import/export without determining whether they can sell the product at a profit.

Following are checklists of research items for importers and exporters:

该产品的交易量有多大?谁占有市场份额，占有多少?

- Is there already a market for the product?
- What is the market price?
- What is the sales volume for that product?
- Who has market share, and what are the shares?

International COC 国际商会。WTCA 世界贸易中心协会。Thomas Register 托马斯登记。USAID 美国国际开发署。

- What is the location of the market; what's its size and population? (Note that people in major urban areas generally have more money than people do elsewhere.)

  市场的位置在哪里，何等规模以及人口多少？

- What are the climate, geography, and terrain of the market country?
- What are the economics of the country, its gross national product (GNP), major industries, and sources of income?
- What is its currency? How stable is it? Is barter commonplace?

  易货贸易是否频繁？

- Who are the employees of the country? How much do they earn? Where do they live?
- Is the government stable? Is it friendly to Americans? Does the country have a good credit record?
- What are the tariffs, restrictions, and quotas?
- What are the other barriers to market entry, such as taxation and repatriation of income?
- What language is spoken there? Are there dialects? Does the business community speak English?
- How modern is the country?
- Do people there use the Internet?
- Do they have electric power?
- How do they move their goods?
- How good is the hard infrastructure (roads, trains, etc.)?

  硬件设施（公路、铁路等等）如何？

- What about the soft infrastructure (schools, etc.)?

  软件设施（如学校）如何？

- Does the country manufacture your product? How much does it produce? How much is sold there?
- What kind and how much advertising is generally used? Are there local advertising firms? Are there trade fairs and exhibitions?
- What distribution channels are being used? What levels of inventory are carried? Are adequate storage facilities available?
- Who are the customers? Where do they live? What influences the customers' buying decisions? Is it price, convenience, or habit?
- What kinds of services are expected? Is the custom to throw away or repair? Can repair services be set up?

  人们期待何种服务？其习俗是丢弃还是修补？能开设维修服务吗？

- What about competition? Does the competition have sales organizations? How does it price?

---

geography 地理环境。terrain 地域范围。gross national product 国内生产总值。barter 易货贸易。credit record 信用记录。tariffs 关税。quota 配额。market entry 市场准入。taxation 税收。distribution channel 经销渠道。storage facilities 存储设施。

进口商调研一览表
Importer Checklist

产权的含义是什么?

- What are the property rights implications?
- Is there already a market for the product?
- What is the market price?
- What is the sales volume for that product?
- Who has market share, and what are the shares?
- What is the location of the market; what's its size and population? (Major urban areas are generally where the people have more money than elsewhere.)
- Who are the wholesalers?
- What sort and how much advertising is generally used? Are there local advertising firms? Are there trade fairs and exhibitions?
- What distribution channels are being used? What levels of inventory are carried? Are there adequate storage facilities available?
- Who are the customers? Where do they live? What influences the customers' buying decisions? Is it price, convenience, or habit?
- What kinds of services are expected? Is it the custom to throw away or repair? Can repair services be set up?
- What about competition? Does the competition have sales organizations? How does it price?

解决上述问题可以去众多好一点的图书馆、你所在国的商务部和商会或者私营市场调查公司（请见第7章和第8章关于进出口信息资源的列表）

The answers to these questions are available through most good libraries, your equivalent of the U.S. Department of Commerce, your Chamber of Commerce, or private market research companies. (See Chapters 7 and 8 for a list of export and import information sources.)

何为底线
What's the Bottom Line?

利润是内部的、个人化的决定。随产品、行业、市场渠道的差异而不同。

Profit is an internal, individualized decision that varies from product to product, industry to industry, and within the market channel. Desirable profit relates to the goals you plan for your import/export business. For instance, one person's goal might be to cover expenses, take a small salary, and be pleased if the business supports travel to exotic places. Another might have the goal to expand the business to eventually become

---

equivalent 对应部门。cover expenses 支付全部费用。

a major trading company. Yet another might set a goal to work for only five or six years, sell the business at a profit, and retire on the capital gain.

This segment of the chapter discusses the profit aspects of international trade, beginning with initial quotations, terms of sale, the market channel, and pricing.

本章接下来讨论国际贸易利润的方方面面，首先是初始报价、销售术语、市场渠道和定价。

初始报价

Initial Quotations

Initial quotes begin either with a request for quotation (RFQ) sent by the importer to the exporter or with an unsolicited offer from the exporter. A simple letter or e-mail can be a request for a quotation. Figure 2.1 shows a sample letter of inquiry.

初始报价可通过进口商向出口商询价或者出口商自报价开始。

图2.1　询盘信样信

Figure 2.1 Typical Letter of Inquiry

Our Company, Inc.
Hometown, U.S.A.

Ref:
Date:

XYZ Foreign Co.
2A1 Moon River
Yokohama, Japan

Our company is a medium-sized manufacturing company. We are interested in your products.

Please send us a pro forma invoice for five of your machines, CIF Los Angeles. Please indicate your payment terms and estimated time of delivery after receipt of our firm order.

Sincerely,

W.T. Door
President

---

capital gain 资本收益。request for quotation 询价。unsolicited offer 卖方自报价。pro forma invoice 形式发票。CIF 成本、保险费和运费。payment terms 支付条件。firm order 实盘。

形式发票即票面上印有"形式"字样的普通发票，它是发起贸易谈判的常用方式。形式发票是临时单证，在货物计划装运之前，由卖方给买方，以提示产品的种类、数量、总额和其他有关货物的重要规格数据（重量、大小等）。

The pro forma invoice, a normal invoice document visibly marked "pro forma," is the method most often used to initiate negotiations. This provisional invoice is forwarded by the seller of goods prior to a contemplated shipment; it advises the buyer of the kinds and quantities of goods to be sent, their value, and important specifications (weight, size, etc.). Its purpose is to describe in advance certain items and details, and it contains the major elements of a contract, which will be used later in shipping and collection documents such as letters of credit (discussed in Chapter 5).

Keep in mind that everything in a pro forma invoice is negotiable, so carefully think through any terms entered on this document. Once accepted by the purchaser, it becomes a binding sales agreement or legal contract, and the seller is bound to the terms stated. Figure 2.2 is an example of a pro forma invoice which shows the key elements of the contract which are:

图 2.2 是形式发票的样例，它体现了合同的几个关键要素：

• 产品描述及规格；
• 材料费；
• 单价；
• 数量；
• 运费；
• 交货条款；
• 程序。

• Product description and specifications
• Material costs
• Price
• Quantity
• Shipping costs
• Delivery terms
• Procedures

销售术语

Terms of Sale

在国际贸易中，卖方使用的定价术语叫做销售术语。

In international business, suppliers use pricing terms, called *terms of sale*. These pricing terms quite simply define the geographical point where the *risks* and *costs* of the exporter and importer *begin* and *end*.

长期以来，国际商会开发建立了一套用来解释最常用的一些贸易术语的国际准则，这些准则被称为"国际贸易术语解释通则"。

The International Chamber of Commerce (ICC) has, over time, developed a set of international rules for the interpretation of the most commonly used trade terms called INCOTERMS. If, when drawing up the contract, both buyer and seller specifically refer to INCOTERMS, they can be sure of clearly defining their respective responsibilities. In

---

shipping documents 运输单证。 collection documents 托收单证。 a binding sales agreement 约束性销售协议。
INCOTERMS 国际贸易术语解释通则。

图2.2 形式发票示例

Figure 2.2 Typical Pro Forma Invoice

XYZ Foreign Co.
2A1 Moon River
Yokohama, Japan

Our Company, Inc.
Hometown, U.S.A.

Purchase Order Date:
Invoice Date:
Invoice Ref.No.:
  PRO FORMA 00012

Terms of Payment:
 Confirmed
 Irrevocable Letter of Credit
 Payable in U.S. dollars

Invoice To:
Ship To:
Forwarding Agent:

Via: Country of Origin:

QUANTITY	PART NO.	DESCRIPTION	PRICE EACH	TOTAL PRICE
10	A2Z	Machines	$100.00	$1,000.00

Inland freight, export packing & forwarding fees	$ 100.00
Free alongside (FAS) Yokohama	$1,100.00
Estimated ocean freight	$ 100.00
Estimated marine insurance	$ 50.00
CIF Long Beach	$1,250.00

Packed in 10 crates, 100 cubic feet
Gross weight 1000 lbs.
Net weight   900 lbs.
Payment terms: Irrevocable letter of credit by a U.S. bank.
Shipment to be made two (2) weeks after receipt of firm order.
Country of Origin: Japan
We certify this pro forma invoice is true and correct.

Issu A. Towa
President

---

irrevocable letter of credit 不可撤销信用证。country of origin 原产国。gross weight 毛重。

so doing, buyer and seller eliminate any possibility of misunderstanding and subsequent dispute. A copy of INCOTERMS 2000 (effective January 1, 2000) can be ordered in 31 languages for about 40 Euros or US$50 via the Internet (Web site: www.iccbooks. com); it is available as a paper or as an e-book. You can also write to: The ICC Publishing Corporation, Inc., 156 Fifth Ave., Suite 417, New York, NY 10010; telephone 1-212-206-1150; fax (212) 633-6025; e-mail: pub@iccwbo.org

There are many variant terms of sale. INCOTERMS organizes them into four groups: "E group" for Ex words; "F group" for FCA, FAS, and FOB; "C group" for terms where the seller has to contract for carriage (CFR, CIF, CPT, CIP); and "D group" for terms in which the seller has to bear all costs and risks to bring the goods to the place of destination (DAF, DES, DEQ, DDU, and DDP).

Among all these terms there are four—EXW, FAS, CIF, and DAF—that are most commonly used. Figure 2.3 graphically shows how these terms function.

国际贸易术语解释通则，将所有术语整理归纳为四组：E组，包括 EX 字头术语；F组，包括 FCA、FAS 和 FOB；C 组术语是指由卖方拟订运输合同（包括 CFR、CIF、CPT 和 CIP）；D 组术语中卖方承担到达进口国交货地点之前的所有费用和风险（包括 DAF、DES、DEQ、DDU 和 DDP）。

最为常用的四个术语是 EXW、FAS、CIF 和 DAF。

图 2.3 风险与费用（责任）的起点与终点

Figure 2.3 Where the Risks and Costs (Obligations) Begin and End

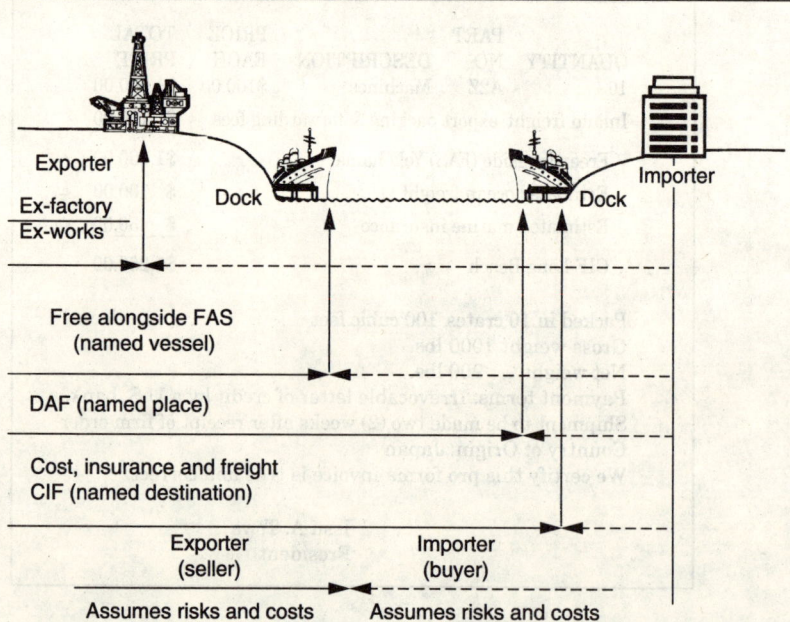

Exporter
Ex-factory
Ex-works
Dock
Dock
Importer

Free alongside FAS
(named vessel)

DAF (named place)

Cost, insurance and freight
CIF (named destination)

Exporter
(seller)

Importer
(buyer)

Assumes risks and costs

Assumes risks and costs

---

effective 生效。variant terms 术语变体。graphically show 以图示说明。

EXW is used with a named place or point of origin. Examples are Ex-Factory (named place) and Ex-Works (named place). These terms mean that the seller agrees to cover all charges to place the goods at a "specified delivery point." From that point on all other costs are the buyer's responsibility.

工厂交货（EXW）使用时带有指定交货地点或原产地。

FAS (free alongside a ship) is usually followed by a named port of export. A seller quotes this term for the price of goods that includes charges for delivery alongside a vessel at the port. The buyer is responsible thereafter.

船边交货（FAS）一般有约定的出口装运港紧接其后。

CIF (cost, marine insurance, freight) is used with a named overseas port of import. The seller is responsible for charges up to the port of final destination.

成本、海上保险及运费（CIF）与指定海外的进口目的港一起使用。

DAF (delivered at frontier) is used with a named place of import. The seller delivers when the goods are placed at the disposal of the buyer on the arriving means of transport. The goods are not unloaded; they are cleared for export but are not cleared for import at the frontier—that is, they must still pass the customs border of the named adjoining country.

边境交货（DAF）使用时要有指定的进口地点。

Marine insurance. An insurance that will compensate the owner of goods transported on the seas in the event of loss if such loss would not be legally recovered from the carrier. Also covers overseas air shipments.

Specific delivery point. A point in sales quotations that designates specifically where and within what geographical locale the goods will be delivered at the expense and responsibility of the seller (e.g., FAS named vessel at named port of export).

海上保险，当海上货物运输受到损失，并且依照法律该损失不属于承运人的责任时，海上保险要补偿货物所有者的该项损失。

指定交货地点，在销售条款／报价中特别约定的地点，要在该地点以及明确的地理位置内交货，此前的费用和责任由卖方承担。

市场渠道
The Market Channel

In general the international market channel includes:

- The manufacturer
- The foreign import/export agent

Ex-Factory/Ex-Works 工厂交货。 at the disposal of 随意支配。 clear for export 出口报关。 air shipments 航空货物。

图 2.4   市场渠道
Figure 2.4 Market Channel

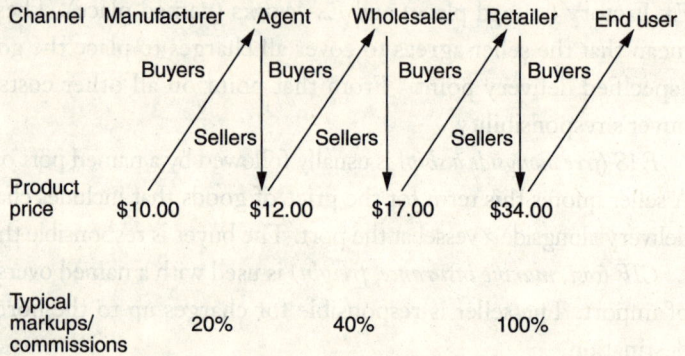

Channel	Manufacturer	Agent	Wholesaler	Retailer	End user
	Buyers	Buyers	Buyers	Buyers	
	Sellers	Sellers	Sellers		
Product price	$10.00	$12.00	$17.00	$34.00	
Typical markups/ commissions		20%	40%	100%	

- Any distributors (wholesalers)
- Any retailers
- The buyers or customers

Figure 2.4 shows how this might look.

定　价
Pricing for Profit

产品定价既要足够高，以生成合理的利润，同时也要足够低，使产品具有价格竞争力。

The price of your product should be high enough to generate a suitable profit but low enough to be competitive. Ideally, the importer or exporter should strive to buy at or below factory prices. This can be done by eliminating the manufacturer's cost of domestic sales and advertising expenses from the overseas price.

Each step along the market channel has a cost. If a product is entirely new to the market or has unique features, you may be able to command higher prices. On the other hand, to gain a foothold in a very competitive market, you can use marginal cost pricing. *Marginal cost pricing* is the technique of setting the market entry price at or just above the threshold at which the firm would incur a loss. [Under GATT (General Agreement on Tariffs and Trade) rules, now an integral part of the WTO, it is illegal to dump—that is, gain market share—by incurring a loss.]

边际成本定价法是一项制订市场进入价格的技术，它使价格等于或略高于企业盈亏点。

---

markups 加成率。factory prices 出厂价。foothold 立足点。threshold 盈亏点。dump 倾销。

Most new importers/exporters simply use the domestic factory price plus freight, packing, insurance, and so on. Depending on the volume and value of the transaction, the buyer and seller may mutually agree on which currency they will use. However, there are a number of countries where the seller or buyer will prefer to use U.S. dollars or Euros for their transaction or, depending on the volume and value of the transaction, they may agree to a currency basket.

It is important that you understand not only the elements that make up your price, but also those of your overseas trading associate. Remember there are no free lunches; everything has a cost.

Figure 2.5 illustrates how a product might move from one country to another by an importer or exporter. In particular, it shows how the

从事进出口贸易的新手大都会简单地在国内出厂价格基础上，加上运费、包装费、保险以及其他费用。

图 2.5 展示了出口商或进口商如何把产品从一个国家转送至另一个国家，特别说明了一国的卖价如何转变为另一国的买价。

图 2.5　定价模型

Figure 2.5　Pricing Model

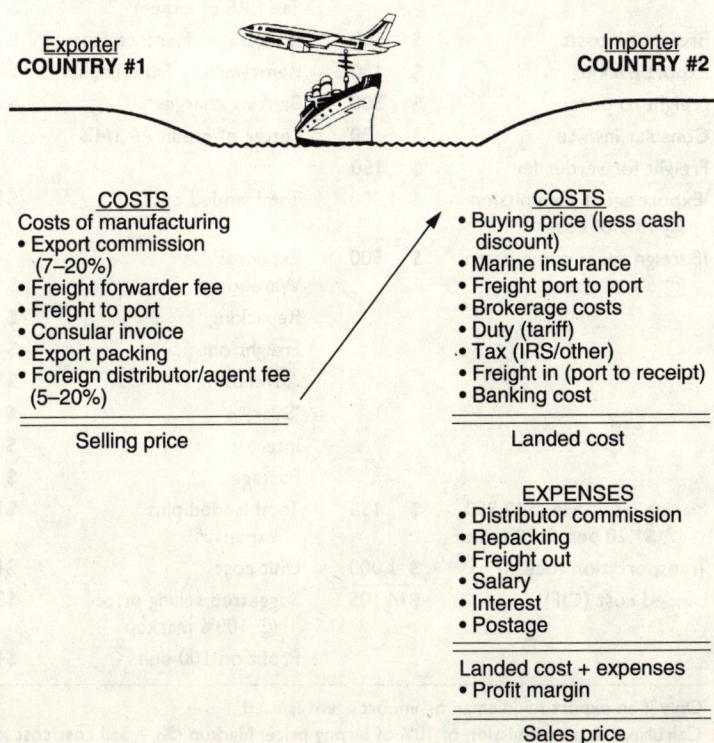

transaction volume 交易量。currency basket 一揽子货币。freight forwarder fee 运输费用。less cash discount 扣除现金折扣。brokerage costs 经纪费。banking cost 银行业务费。landed cost 到岸成本。

尽管佣金率可能低至1%或者高达40%，一般出口中间商的佣金在7%~20%之间，而进口中间商（即国外分销商或海外销售代理）在5%到20%之间。

selling price in one country becomes the buying price in the other. Typical commission percentages are between 7 and 20 percent for an export middleman and between 5 and 20 percent for an import middleman (in other words, a foreign distributor or agent), although commissions may be as low as 1 percent and as high as 40 percent. The key issues are the price of the product and the number of units (sales

表 2.2　成本构成要素示例

Table 2.2 Examples of Cost Elements

Terms of Sale: CIF

Export		Import	
Cost Elements	**Cost**	**Cost Elements**	**Cost**
Factory cost of 100 units @ $100/unit	$10,000	Landed cost (CIF)	$14,105
Expenses:			
		Duty @ 5.5%	$ 776
		Tax (IRS or other)	$ 150
Brokerage costs	$ 100	Brokerage clearance fees	$ 50
Export packing	$ 150	Reforwarding from broker	$ 100
Freight to port	$ 500	Banking charges	$ 50
Consular invoice	$ 50	Letter of credit @ 1/4%	$ 75
Freight forwarder fee	$ 150		
*Export agent commission @ 15% of cost	$ 1,500	Total landed cost	$15,306
†Foreign agent commission @ 5% of cost	$ 500	Expenses	
		Warehouse	$ —
		Repacking	$ 100
		Freight out	$ 100
		Advertising	$ 500
		*Salary	$ 1,410
		Interest	$ —
		Postage	$ 100
Marine insurance ($12,950 @ $1.20 per $100 value	$ 155	Total landed plus expenses	$17,516
Transportation (ocean)	$ 1,000	Unit cost	$175.16
Landed cost (CIF)	$14,105	Suggested selling price @ 100% markup	$350.32
		Profit on 100 units	$17,516

*Only if an export middleman or import agent is used.
†Calculated at a commission of 10% of buying price: Markup (%) = Sell cost/cost × 100.

---

unit price 单位成本。

图 2.6   出口成本计算表
Figure 2.6 Export Costing Worksheet

Reference Information
Our reference_____   Customer reference_____

Customer Information
Name _____   E-mail_____
Address _____
             _____   Fax_____

Product Information
Product _____   Dimensions _____ × _____ × _____
No. of units _____   Cubic measure _____ (sq. in.)
Net weight _____   Total measure _____
Gross weight _____

Product Charges
Price (or cost) per unit _____ × units _____ Total _____
Profit (or markup)   _____
Sales commissions   _____
FOB, factory   _____

Fees–packing, marking, inland freight   _____
Freight forwarder   _____
Financing costs   _____
Other charges   _____
Export packing   _____
Labeling/marking   _____
Inland freight to   _____
FOB, port city (export packed)   _____

Port Charges
Unloading (heavy lift)   _____
Loading (aboard ship)   _____
Terminal
   Consular document (check if required) _____
   Certificate of origin (check if required) _____
   Export license (check if required) _____
FAS vessel (or airplane)   _____

Freight
Based on_____ Weight_____ Measure
Ocean _____ Air _____
Rate _____ Minimum_____ Amount _____

Insurance
Coverage required _____
Basis _____ Rate _____ Amount _____
CIF, port of destination

_____
dimension 外形尺寸。cubic measure 体积。coverage required（承保）范围。

图 2.7 进口成本计算表
Figure 2.7 Import Costing Worksheet

Reference Information
Our reference _____   Customer reference _____

Customer Information
Name_____   E-mail_____
Address _____
        _____   Fax_____

Product Information
Product _____   Dimension _____ × _____ × _____

No. of units _____   Cubic measure _____ (sq. in.)
Net weight _____   Total measure _____
Gross weight _____

Note: If quote is FOB factory, use export
Costing sheet to determine price at
CIF, Port of destination

Landed cost (CIF, port of destination)   _____
Customs duty   _____
Customs house broker fees   _____
Banking charges   _____
Taxes: federal   _____
      state   _____
      other   _____
Total landed   _____

Expenses   _____
Inland freight (from port city)   _____
Warehouse costs   _____
Repacking   _____
Inland freight (from warehouse)   _____
Advertising/promotion   _____
Overhead (% of annual)   _____
Salary (% of annual)   _____
Loans (principal/interest)   _____
Total landed plus expenses   _____

Unit cost   _____

Selling price   _____
Margin _____%

Profit   _____

---

overhead 日常开支。margin 利润率。

volume) that you can sell. If, for instance, the product is a big-ticket item (i.e., having a high sales price), the commission percentage may be quite low, but a small percentage of a million-dollar sale can be very good business.

Table 2.2 shows a set of fictitious cost elements associated with a CIF quotation which corresponds to the steps shown in Figure 2.5. Figures 2.6 and 2.7 are offered as work lists to aid you in accurate costing of your product.

表 2.2 展示了在 CIF 报价下一套假设的成本构成，它和图 2.5 中的步骤相对应。

Is there sufficient profit at the *volumes* (number of units) you can sell to make it worth your while and meet your personal profit goals? Recall that the same amount of work goes into importing or exporting a product that makes no profit as one that makes a good profit.

HOT TIP

A word of caution for manufacturers: If at first exporting doesn't appear profitable, check your manufacturing costs. It may be necessary to import less costly components in order to compete internationally.

对生产者提醒一句：假若最初的出口贸易不营利，那就审核一下生产成本。为了更具国际竞争力，也许需要进口价位更低的组件。

Be satisfied that you have a viable project. Then take the next step to lay out a long-range market plan. The next chapter explains how to develop that plan and then how to put it into action to make a transaction.

---

big-ticket item 高价货物。work list 工作清单。viable project 可行性项目。put into action 付诸实施。

CHAPTER 3

PLANNING AND NEGOTIATING TO WIN
制 胜 之 道 —— 计 划 与 洽 谈

If you have a marketable and profitable product or service that will sell in sufficient volume, you now are ready to commit resources (time and money) to the project. But before you do, make sure you complete the following homework steps:

1. Develop a market plan
2. Prepare for negotiations
3. Understand the tips and traps of culture
4. Consider intellectual property rights
5. Learn about communications
6. Get ready to travel

Face up to the fact that international marketing is a step up from domestic marketing because it involves more complexity. The more countries, languages, and cultures with which you become involved, the more your planning will require special attention. Don't hesitate to call in consultants and other experts to read over your plan and offer criticism. This can pay off and save you money in the long run.

如果你的产品或服务有销路且可营利，你现在应准备对项目投入资源（时间和金钱）

在行动之前，要保证完成下列准备步骤：

1. 展开营销策划；
2. 洽谈准备；
3. 了解文化细节和文化陷阱；
4. 仔细考虑知识产权问题；
5. 学习沟通技巧；
6. 做好旅行准备。

---

marketable 有销路的。profitable 盈利的。sufficient volume 充足的数量（文中指有良好销路）。commit 投入。
tip 小建议。intellectual property right 知识产权。

营销策划
The Market Plan

你已经确定你的项目切实可行；现在写一份长期的营销策划，然后执行。

营销策划只是一个记录在纸上的过程，它能为你联系采购商并说服他们购买商品提供许多合理的方法。

按照以下步骤，逐步写出营销策划：

1. 目标——例如，第二年年底的销售额，第三年年底营销区域扩展至 A 和 B 国。

2. 具体策略——例如，在两个城市广播广告，向特定名单上所列的公司和个人发送 3 封直接邮件，建立网站并为地址做广告。

3. 活动或行动计划时间表——例如，你将出席的商业展览清单，要包括访问海外采购商的日期和持续时间，要分别列出采购商的姓名、地址以及联系方式；明确的责任分配（行动计划的重要特征）。

4. 完成行动计划的预算——包括有关产品营销每项可以想到的成本，很多新兴公司会低估这部分成本，初始营销成本将会很高。

You have determined that your project is viable; now write a long-range market plan, and then execute it.

A *market plan* is simply a process, recorded on paper, that allows you to think through the many logical ways to reach buyers and convince them to agree to a sale. It is important to integrate the international market plan with the firm's overall strategic business plan. See Chapter 6 ("How to Set Up Your Own Import/Export Business") for details about how to write a business plan.

Follow the following logical, step-by-step process to write your market plan:

1. *Objectives:*
   Examples:

   * Sales of $XXX,XXX by the end of the second year
   * Expansion into countries A and B by the end of the third year

2. *Specific tactics:*
   Examples:

   * Radio advertising in two cities
   * Three direct mailings to each company or person on a specific list
   * Develop an Internet Web site and advertise the address

3. *Schedule of activities or action plan:*
   Examples:

   * A list of trade shows indicating those that you will attend, including dates and duration of trips to visit overseas distributors, with their names, addresses, and phone numbers
   * Specific assignments of responsibility (an essential feature of an action plan)

4. *Budget for accomplishing the action plan:*

   * Include every conceivable cost associated with marketing the product. This is where most start-up firms underestimate. Initial marketing costs will be high.

---

viable 切实可行的。long-range 长期的。direct mail 直接邮件（未经索取就直接邮寄给预期客户的有关商业内容的印刷品）。assignment of responsibility 责任分工。conceivable 可想到的。underestimate 低估。

市场细分
Segmenting the Market

Marketing segmentation enables an import/export organization to choose its customers and fashion its marketing strategy based both on identified customer wants and requirements, and on response to the startup's specific desires and needs. You should visualize segmentation on both a macro and a micro level.

市场细分使进出口组织能够根据确定的客户要求和新兴公司的特殊需求来选择客户并制订市场营销策略。

> *Macro.* From the Greek word *makros* meaning long. It is a combining form meaning large.
> *Micro.* From the Greek word *mikros* meaning small. A combining term meaning little, small, microscopic.

宏观市场细分
Macro Segmentation

Macro segmentation divides a market by such broad characteristics as industry shipments, location, firm size, and the like. An import macro segment might be dividing a city into marketing segments. On a larger scale, it might involve dividing the United States into regions, prioritizing those regions, and then developing a micro plan for each region.

宏观细分根据较宽泛的特征分割市场，如工业运输、地理位置、公司规模及类似的特征等。进口宏观细分可能是对一个城市进行市场细分。

Export macro segments might include prioritizing of continents or of countries within a continent; better yet, export macro segments might sort by language, purchasing power, or cultural preference.

出口宏观细分可能根据语言、购买力或文化倾向进行分类。

微观市场细分
Micro Segmentation

Micro segmentation finds the homogeneous customer groups within macro segments and, therefore, attempts to find out who makes the decisions for each homogeneous group. Micro segmentation pinpoints where (by address) and who (by name) can say yes to a buying decision. From this analysis, a promotional strategy can be designed to target the decision-making units (DMUs).

微观市场细分是在宏观分区内寻找同质客户群，然后试图寻找同质客户群中的决策者。微观市场细分要准确定位购买决策者的地址和姓名。

---

fashion 制订。startup 新兴公司。purchasing power 购买力。cultural preference 文化倾向。homogeneous 同质的。

进口微观细分从市场调查结果中抽取数据并识别批发商的地理位置。

An import micro segmentation might take the data from your market research effort and identify where the wholesalers are located. If you list and prioritize these decision makers by name and address, you would have a logical and specific plan of attack for your marketing effort.

你要根据你所营销的产品类别、竞争对手以及目标市场，制订为期 3 至 5 年的营销策划和时间表。

Your market plan and schedule should cover a three- to five-year period, depending on the kind of product(s) you market, your competitor(s), and your target market(s). Be sure to write this plan no matter how small the import/export project. Only when it is in writing will it receive proper attention and adequate allocation of funds.

执行营销策划
Executing the Market Plan

接下来是营销策划的关键——将策划付诸实践，通过贸易展会、广告、电视推广、直接邮件等所有与预算策划相一致的方式，积极地营销产品。

Next comes the fun—putting the plan into action and actively marketing the product through trade shows, advertisements, television promotions, and direct mail, all in accordance with your budgeted plan. Remember that nothing happens in a business until something is sold.

人员销售
Personal Sales

进出口商进行国际销售的两种基本方式是直接销售和间接销售。直接销售方式指国内制造企业拥有自己的营销部门，专门负责向国外分销商、零售企业销售货物，并负责将货物运往海外。间接销售方式指通过中间人将货物向海外销售，并由中间人负责货物运输。

不管目标决策者处于市场渠道的哪个环节，记住国际销售与国内销售是相同的：与决策者（潜在客户）建立人际关系并向其展示产品组合、宣传册、价格表以及样品。

The two basic approaches to selling internationally for both imports and exports are direct and indirect sales. Using the *direct sales method*, a domestic manufacturing firm has its own marketing department that sells to a foreign distributor or retailing firm and is responsible for shipping the goods overseas. The *indirect sales method* uses a middleman, who usually assumes the responsibility for moving the goods. This is where your import/export business fits into the picture. You may sell directly to retailers or to distributors/wholesalers. Regardless of where your targeted DMU is in the market channel, keep in mind that international sales are just like domestic sales: someone makes personal contact and presents a portfolio, brochure, price list, and/or sample to decision makers (potential buyers) who can say yes.

---

market research 市场调查。put…into action 付诸实践。in accordance with 与……一致。distributor 分销商。middleman 中间人。regardless of 不管。portfolio 产品组合。

HOT TIP

Making sales requires persistence and determination. Follow up, and then follow up again.

贸易展会（展销会）
Trade Shows (Fairs)

If you're attending a trade fair or show for the first time, consider using it as the keystone of your sales trip. Allow time afterward to visit companies you meet at the fair.

The international trader attends trade shows for five basic reasons:

1. To make contacts
2. To identify products for import or export
3. To evaluate the competition (often done without exhibiting)
4. To find customers and distributors for import or export
5. To build sales for existing distributors

国际贸易商参加贸易展会的 5 个基本理由 :

1. 与客户取得联系 ;

2. 识别用于进出口的产品 ;

3. 评估竞争程度 ;

4. 寻找进出口客户和分销商;

5. 与已有分销商建立销售关系。

HOT TIPS: TRADE FAIRS

- If you are exhibiting to sell, don't over commit. You may get more business than you can handle reasonably.
- If you are searching for products to import, don't buy until you have done your homework!
- Take more business cards to the trade show than you think you will need. Have your fax number, Web site, and e-mail address on your card.
- Obtain language translation/interpreter help from a local university or college.
- If you are exhibiting to sell, consider prior advertising to let potential customers know that you will be there.

---

fairs 展销会。build sales 建立销售关系。

贸易代表团
Trade Missions

贸易代表团出访是为了促进和参与国际贸易。

Trade missions are trips made for the express purpose of promoting and participating in international trade. State, province, and local governments organize several kinds of trade missions for exporters.

特殊代表团
Special Missions

由政府组织并发起的出访，按照设计的预定行程进行访问，使你能与潜在客户和代理商建立联系

These are organized and led by government officials with itineraries designed to bring you into contact with potential buyers and agents. You pay your own expenses and a share of the costs of the mission.

研讨代表团
Seminar Missions

类似专业化贸易访问团，研讨代表团在出访期间可能会增加几个为期一至两天的由产业代表进行的专业展示。

Similar to the specialized trade mission, seminar missions add several one- or two-day technical presentations to the trip by a team of industry representatives.

产业组织，政府许可的贸易代表团
Industry-Organized, Government-Approved Trade Missions

尽管这些代表团由商务部、贸易组织或其他产业团体组织组成，政府仍会在出访前和出访过程中为其提供官方协助。

Though these missions are organized by chambers of commerce, trade associations, or other industry groups, government officials often provide assistance prior to and during the trip.

商品目录展会和视频／商品目录展览
Catalog Shows and Video/Catalog Exhibitions

视频／商品目录展览是促进大型机械销售的理想方式，因为大型机械的运输成本很高。

These are the least expensive way to develop leads, to test markets, and to locate agents because you don't have to be there. You simply send along product catalogs, brochures, and other sales aids to be displayed at exhibitions organized by governments and consultants.

Video/catalog exhibitions are ideal for promoting large equipment and machinery which are costly to ship.

---

mission 代表团。itinerary 预定行程。trip 出访。

贸易展览中心
Trade Show Central

This is a free Internet service that provides information on more than 50,000 trade shows, conferences, and seminars. It has 5,000 service providers and 8,000 venues and facilities around the world (www.tscentral.com).

这是一项提供 50 000 多条关于贸易展会、会议以及研讨会信息的免费网络服务。

广 告
Advertising

All companies advertise to communicate with customers. Exporters and importers must ask themselves whether advertising is both important to sales and affordable. The assistance of an agency familiar with the market environment you wish to target could be critical to the success of your advertising campaign. Some countries do not carry television and radio advertising. Additionally, cultural differences often require more than a simple translation of promotional messages.

所有的企业通过广告与客户进行交流。

In countries where illiteracy is high, you may prefer to avoid written forms of advertising such as magazines and concentrate instead on outdoor advertising such as billboards, posters, electric signs, and street car or bus signs. These reach wide audiences in most countries.

在文化水平比较低的国家，应尽量避免如杂志等书面形式的广告，要将重点放在户外广告上，使用如广告牌、海报、电子指示牌、街车以及公交车牌等广告方式。

分销商
Distributors

A *distributor* is a merchant who purchases merchandise from a manufacturer at the greatest possible discount and then resells it to retailers for profit. The distributor carries a supply of parts and maintains an adequate facility for servicing. The distributor buys the product in its own name, and payment terms are often arranged on a credit basis. A written contract usually defines the territory to be covered by the distributor, the terms of sale, and the method of compensation (see "Avoiding Risk" in Chapter 5). The work is usually performed on a commission basis, without assumption of risk, and the representative may operate on either an exclusive or a nonexclusive basis. The contract is established for a specific time frame such that it may be renewable based on satisfactory performance.

分销商以最低折扣价从制造商处购买产品，然后转卖给零售商以获取利润。

---

illiteracy 文盲，缺乏教育。billboard 广告牌。poster 海报。street car 街车。resell 转售。

进出口商很少将产品卖给终端用户，原因如下：(1) 耗费时间；(2) 当买家不了解他们自己的贸易制度时，会导致货物被扣押或被拍卖。

As with domestic sales, foreign retailers usually buy from the distributor's traveling sales force, but many buy through catalogs, brochures, or other literature.

Importers and exporters seldom sell directly to the end user. It is not recommended because: (1) it is time consuming, and (2) it leads to goods being impounded or sold at auction when the buyer doesn't know his or her own trade regulations.

海外贸易商清单
Overseas Trader's Checklist

你希望外商代表所具备的条件如下：

- 具有良好的信誉；
- 具有雄厚的财力；
- 有交易此货物或类似货物的经验；
- 拥有销售团队；
- 使用现代通信设备；
- 不断增长的销售记录；
- 客户；
- 仓储能力；
- 售后服务能力；
- 了解地区文化和商业实务；
- 熟练掌握英语和当地语言；
- 具备营销技能的相关知识。

What you want from a foreign representative is:

- A solid reputation with suppliers and banks
- Financial strength
- Experience with the product or a similar product
- A sales organization
- Modern communications such as Internet, fax, and so on
- A sales record of growth
- Customers
- Warehouse capacity
- After-sales service capability
- Understanding of regional culture and business practices
- Knowledge of both English and the language of the country
- Knowledge of marketing techniques (promotion, advertisement, etc.)

贸易伙伴清单
Trading Partner's Checklist

外商代表希望你所具备的条件如下：

- 出色的产品；
- 专属领域；
- 培训；
- 零件可获得性；
- 良好的担保；
- 广告和促销支持；

What the foreign representative wants from you is:

- Excellent products
- Exclusive territories
- Training
- Parts availability
- Good warranties
- Advertising and merchandising support

---

end user 终端用户。impound 依法扣押。after-sales service 售后服务。exclusive territory 专属区域。parts availability 零件可获得性。

- Credit terms, discounts, and deals
- Commissions on direct sales by the manufacturer in the distributor's territory
- Minimum control and/or visits
- Freedom to price
- Dealing with one person
- Security that the product will not be taken away once it is established in the territory
- The right to terminate the agreement when he or she pleases

- 信用证条款，折扣和协议；

- 最小控制；
- 价格自由；

- 保证货物安全；

- 给予他／她终止协议的权利。

洽　谈
Negotiations

Bargaining is a custom to people of many nations. But culturally nothing comes less naturally to Americans. The United States is a nation that operates on a fixed-price system, and most buyers have grown up with the notion of purchasing off the shelf at the price offered or not buying at all. Of course, comparative shopping is native to everyone's buying psyche, so when the international stakes and the competition increase, often companies from nations that are born cultural negotiators begin to force your hand. Your instincts should provide some basis for taking the right action and you can make the right moves if you prepare. An agent/distributor contract should be considered and should include issues of industrial property rights, territory covered (exclusive and nonexclusive contracts), the problems of terminating the contract, and the possibility of the host country switching from contract laws to labor laws according to the comparative size of the principal's company and distributor's company.

讨价还价在许多国家成为了一种惯例。

美国实行固定价格体系，多数买家形成了要么按价格买要么不买的观念。

你应该按照自己的意愿采取正确的行动，如果有备而来，你就能够采取正确的行动。

准　备
Preparations

Unfortunately, all too many people wander into international bargaining situations with no plan and no idea of how to proceed. For some, lack of preparation is the result of a sense of superiority, but for most it's pure ignorance about the number and competence of the ferocious competitors out there scouring the world for scraps of business.

不幸的是，太多人在国际谈判过程中没有计划，也对谈判过程没有概念。对于一些人来说，优越感导致了缺乏准备，但是对于大多数人来讲，纯粹是由于他们忽视了正在蚕食市场的激烈的竞争者的数量和能力。

---

custom 习惯。grow up with the notion 形成观念。instinct 本能。superiority 优越，优势。ferocious 激烈的。scour for 搜索。scrap 碎片。

准备国际谈判的第一步是对
公司能力进行完整的评估。
分析公司的优势和劣势，特
别是在管理技能、产品运输、
技能以及全球资源等方面。

下一步，分析你们的目标
——销售产品的目标公司和
国家。

The first step in preparing for international negotiations is to develop a complete assessment of your firm's capabilities. Analyze your strengths and weaknesses, particularly in terms of managerial skills, product delivery, technical abilities, and global resources.

Next, analyze your target—the company or country you intend to sell your product to. Keep in mind that the human and behavioral aspects of your negotiations will be vital. For example:

- Understand the place in the world where you will be traveling.
- Know its culture, history, and political processes.
- Play particular attention to the importance of face-saving to the people of the country where you will be negotiating.
- What is the host government's role in negotiations?
- How important are personal relations?
- How much time should you allow for negotiations?
- Be sure that the final agreement specifies terms for the cost, quality, and delivery of the product. Quality can be assured only by inspection of the actual product, but cost and delivery terms are the result of a quote agreed to by the seller.

在日本，年轻的执行官会在
他们做出最初报价之前进行
模拟洽谈。他们组队，围坐
在有黑板的模拟会议厅中，
进行模拟洽谈。

In Japan, young executives role-play negotiations before they make an initial quote. They form teams, sit around a table with a chalkboard nearby, and pretend to negotiate the deal. Each team has a set of negotiating alternatives related to the country they are pretending to represent. Sometimes they cut their offer price by 10 percent; if that doesn't work, they cut it by another 5 or 10 percent. Other ploys are: (1) offering loans with lower interest rates than their competitors; (2) offering better after-sales service warrantees; or (3) providing warehouses for parts. Sometimes even the cost of advertising can make the difference in the sale.

商定合同
Agreeing to a Contract

根据在第2章解释的步骤，
在获得最初报价后，任何国
际贸易计划的下一步都是与
海外合作伙伴签订协议或销
售合同。

After obtaining the initial quotations as explained in Chapter 2, the next step in any international business arrangement is to reach an agreement or a sales contract with your overseas partner.

---

strength and weakness 优势和劣势。managerial skill 管理技能。technical ability 技能。role-play 角色扮演。initial quote 最初报价

Negotiating is integral to international trade, and an importer/exporter should be ready to offer or ask for alternatives using simple letters, faxes, or e-mails. In the highly competitive international business world, a trader's ability to offer reasonable terms to customers may mean the difference between winning and losing a sale.

治谈是国际贸易的必要组成部分，进出口商应准备使用简单的信件、传真或邮件来提供或请求其他选择。

Exporters are finding it increasingly necessary to offer terms ranging from cash against shipping documents to time drafts, open accounts, and even installment payments spread over several years. More sophisticated business arrangements such as countertrade, which includes barter, product buyback, counterpurchase, and after-sales service, are also negotiables. Figure 3.1 illustrates the concept.

在更复杂的贸易计划中，如对销贸易中所包含的物物交换、产品回购、互购以及售后服务等，都可以经过治谈进行协商。

图 3.1　对销贸易

Figure 3.1 Countertrade

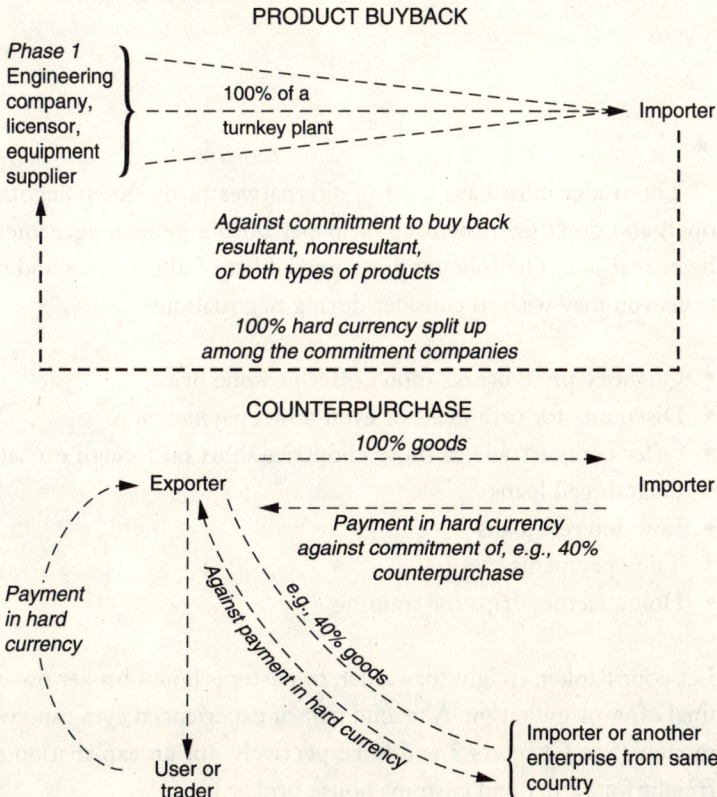

PRODUCT BUYBACK

Phase 1
Engineering company, licensor, equipment supplier

100% of a turnkey plant

Importer

Against commitment to buy back resultant, nonresultant, or both types of products

100% hard currency split up among the commitment companies

COUNTERPURCHASE

100% goods

Exporter

Importer

Payment in hard currency against commitment of, e.g., 40% counterpurchase

Payment in hard currency

Against payment in hard currency

e.g., 40% goods

User or trader

Importer or another enterprise from same country

---

integral 必要组成部分的。countertrade 对销贸易。barter 物物交换。product buyback 产品回购。counterpurchase 互购。

对销贸易，一系列进行对等贸易方法的国际贸易术语总称，意为出口方承诺从进口方购买等值或一定金额的商品或劳务，贸易双方的进出口货款全部或部分抵消。

物物交换，用一种商品换取另一种商品的贸易，贸易过程不涉及钱。

> *Countertrade.* A general international trade term for a variety of methods to conduct reciprocal trade in which the seller is required to accept goods or other instruments of trade, in partial or whole payment for its products.
> *Barter.* Trade in which merchandise is exchanged directly for other merchandise without the use of money.
> *Product buyback.* Principally applicable for the construction and supply of plant and equipment. Major characteristic is its long-term aspect.
> *Counterpurchase.* One of the most common forms of countertrade in which the seller receives cash but contractually agrees to buy local products or services as a percentage of cash received and over an agreed period of time.

公开谈判，在达成协议之前不要将谈判内容以书面形式确定下来。

The trader must have a list of alternatives ready. Keep negotiations open and don't firm them up on paper until a general agreement has been reached. The following is a partial list of alternatives and conditions you may wish to consider during negotiations:

- Quantity price breaks (don't offer just one price)
- Discounts for cash deals or even down payments
- Offer countertrade to those countries short on foreign exchange
- Guaranteed loans
- Low-interest loans
- Time payments
- Home factory trips for training

让你的银行经理、货运代理、报关行复审最终报价。有经验的人的再次审阅能够节省成本。

Let your banker, freight forwarder, or customs house broker review the final offer or quotation. A second pair of experienced eyes can save you money. (See Chapters 7 and 8, respectively, for an explanation of the freight forwarder and customs house broker.)

---

term 术语。reciprocal 对等的。firm up 确定，敲定（合同）。banker 银行经理。

海外行贿法案（FCPA）
Foreign Corrupt Practices Act (FCPA)

During your negotiations, make sure you stay on the right side of the Foreign Corrupt Practices Act (FCPA) of 1977, amended by the International Anti-Bribery and Fair Competition Act of 1998. In essence, this act makes it illegal for companies to bribe foreign officials, candidates, or political parties. Make certain that everything in the contract has a price. Don't get caught making illegal payments or gifts to win a contract or sale. Two kinds of penalties can be imposed for violation of the FCPA, criminal and civil.

在进行洽谈时，要遵守《1977年海外行贿法案》，该法案已被修订为《1998年国际反行贿与公平竞争法》。

违反了《海外行贿法案》会受到两种形式的处罚：刑事处罚和民事处罚

刑事处罚
Criminal Penalties

The following criminal penalties may be imposed for violations of the FCPA's antibribery provisions. Corporations and other business entities are subject to a fine of up to $2 million. Officers, directors, stockholders, employees, and agents are subject to fines of up to $100,000 and imprisonment for up to five years. Moreover, fines under the Alternative Fines Act may be quite a bit higher; the actual fine may be up to twice the benefit that the defendant sought to obtain by making the corrupt payment. You should also be aware that fines imposed on individuals may *not* be paid by their employer or principal.

对公司或其他企业实体处以200万美元的罚款。对官员、董事、股东、雇主和代理人处以10万美元的罚款，5年以下有期徒刑。

民事处罚
Civil Penalties

The U.S. Attorney General or the SEC, as appropriate, may bring a civil action for a fine of up to $10,000 against any firm *as well as* any officer, director, employee, or agent of a firm, or stockholder acting on behalf of the firm, who violates the antibribery provisions. The specified dollar limitations are based on the egregiousness of the violation, ranging from $5,000 to $100,000 for a natural person, and $50,000 to $500,000 for any other person.

美国司法部长或美国证券交易委员会，在适当的情况下，可以对违反行贿法规的任何公司以及代表公司做出违规行为的官员、董事、雇主、公司代理人或股东处以10 000美元以下的罚款。

The law does not address itself to "facilitating payments," those small amounts used to expedite business activities euphemistically called in various countries: "mordida," "grease," "bakshish" (small amount of

---

Foreign Corrupt Practices Act 海外行贿法案。Anti-bribery 反行贿。criminal penalty 刑事处罚。imprisonment 关押，监禁。civil penalty 民事处罚。attorney general 司法部长。SEC 美国证券交易委员会。

money), "rashoa" (big amount of money), "cumsha," or "squeeze." Nevertheless, great care should be exercised in this regard as well.

文化细节与文化陷阱
Tips and Traps of Culture

在外国文化中进行贸易，文化差异会成为洽谈的一大障碍，但是我们不应该让这种障碍存在。

The very thought of doing business in a foreign culture can be a major barrier to negotiations, but it shouldn't be. After all, traders are known for their spirit of curiosity, inquisitiveness, and risk taking.

Developing overseas alliances does present new elements of risk and due diligence, along with the inherent challenges brought by distance, differing cultural motivations and priorities, and the effective integration of differing approaches and objectives. But that's also what brings the rewards.

一种文化能够比另一种更优越吗？政治体制、陆军、海军、甚至是经济体制都可能更加优越，而文化不会。

了解另一种文化的最好方式是"身临其境"。即到另一个国家访问或居住，感受文化的异同。

Can one culture be superior to another? Political systems, armies, navies, and even economic systems may be superior, but cultures cannot.

The best way to appreciate another culture is to "walk in the other person's shoes"; that is, visit or live in the country and get a feel for the similarities and differences. Short of that, this section of this chapter is the next best thing, because its purpose is to help you break through culture barriers. You are cautioned that, to be effective in your business dealings, it is essential to be prepared. Do your homework before you interact in a new country, and then get on with doing business.

了解外国文化的价值观真的那么重要吗？当然！一个经常往返于国内外，广交异国朋友的人曾说："他们跟我们的相同点多于不同点。"

Does understanding foreign cultural values really make a difference? You bet it does! One person who had traveled overseas regularly and had made friends in many countries said, "They're more like us than they're different." What he meant was that they like kids, they want them to be educated, they understand business, and they work hard. What he didn't say was that it's the differences that affect attitudes, so much so at times that some managers won't even consider entering the market to do business with "them."

* 文化是一个群体（可以是国家、也可以是民族、企业、家庭）在一定时期内形成的思想、理念、行为、风俗、习惯、代表人物，以及由这个群体整体意识所辐射出来的一切活动。——译者注

什么是文化 *
What Is Culture?

Culture is a set of meanings or orientations for a given society or social setting. It's a complex concept because there are often many cultures

---

traps of culture 文化陷阱。superior 优越性。appreciate 体会，理解。social setting 社会环境。

within a given nation. For an international business person, the definition is more difficult because a country's business culture is often different from its general culture. Thus the environment of international business is composed of language, religion, values and attitudes, laws, education, politics, technology, and social organizations that are different.

对于国际贸易商来说，文化更难定义，因为一个国家的贸易文化往往与一般的文化不尽相同。

Whatever a nation's culture, it works for the people who live there. In order to function within it, you must get on the bandwagon.

无论一国的文化如何，它都为那里的居民服务。为了能使企业在外国文化中正常运转，你必须紧跟潮流。

The Japanese do it very well. They learn how to penetrate foreign markets by sending their managers to live and study in "the other person's shoes." Their mission is to develop relationships with contemporaries that will last for years. The Japanese don't try to change the way of life in the other country; they learn about it. When they go home, they are specialists in marketing and production in the country they researched.

日本在这一点上做得很好。他们通过外派经理到国外居住学习来了解国外市场。

It's a country's culture that regulates such things as sexuality, child rearing, acquisition of food and clothing, and the incentives that motivate people to work and buy products. All these things are of course major factors in marketing products.

文化影响着一个国家的方方面面，如性别、儿童抚养、食物和衣服的获取，人们工作和购买产品的激励等。

贸易文化中的九大因素
The Nine Elements of Business Culture

Business culture is secondary to a country's general culture, but it provides the rules of the business game and explains the differences and the priorities.

关 系
Relationships

Relationships developed over a long period of time are the thing that reduces mistrust. To meet this challenge, you need to understand the countries, their people, and the cultures where you intend to do business.

经过很长时间所建立的关系能够减少不信任。

语 言
Language

Ask international business people what language they speak, and they will say that they speak the language of the customer.

当你询问国际贸易人员使用什么语言时，他们会告诉你他们使用的是他们的客户所使用的语言。

---

work for 为……效力。 bandwagon 时尚，潮流。 penetrate 了解。 regulate 控制。 mistrust 不信任。

语言是将人类与其他生命体区分开的特征。

语言是文化中交流的工具。对于在特定文化中的人来说，语言标志着他们的交际范围。

Language is one of the things that sets humans off from other forms of life. It is the way you tell others about your history and your intentions for the future. Language is the means of communicating within a culture. For people in a given culture, their language defines their socialization.

肢体语言
Body Language

肢体语言在非语言交流中具有微妙的力量。

这种语言包括你的姿势、手势、面部表情、服装、走路姿态，甚至你对时间、物质和空间的看法。

Body language is the subtle power of nonverbal communication. It's the first form of communication you learn, and you use it every day to tell other people how you feel about yourself and them. This language includes your posture, gestures, facial expressions, costumes, the way you walk, and even how you view time, material things, and space.

宗　教
Religion

宗教对国与国之间的文化异同产生重要作用。

了解什么是禁忌以及什么是多种宗教而导致的社会推崇，影响营销策略。

Religion plays a major part in the cultural similarities and differences of nations. In itself religion can be a basis of mistrust and a barrier to trade. Religion is often the dominant influence for the consumer of products. Such things as religious holidays determine buying and consumption patterns. Knowing what is forbidden and what a society expects as a result of its various religions influences market strategy.

价值观和态度
Values and Attitudes

在国际贸易中，价值观和态度很难度量，但却至关重要。

一个社会的价值观决定了它对待财富、消费、成就、科技以及变化的态度，你必须从东道国文化的角度来评估社会价值。

The role of values and attitudes in international business is difficult to measure, but vital to success. Work ethic and motivation are the intangibles that affect economic performance.

Values of a society determine its attitudes toward wealth, consumption, achievement, technology, and change, and you must evaluate in terms of the host culture. Researching attitudes about openness and the receptivity to new technology is essential to marketing.

法律和法制环境
Laws and Legal Environment

社会的法律是其文化的另一个领域。它们是由权力机构和社会所制订的规则。

The laws of a society are another dimension of its culture. They are the rules established by authority and society. On the one hand, laws provide an opportunity to handle the mistrust of doing business across international boundaries; on the other hand, they can become barriers

---

socialization 交际。nonverbal communication 非口头信息交流。posture 姿势。gesture 手势。dimension 领域。

and constraints to operations. The laws of nations are often greatly different. In actuality, none of the world's legal systems are pure—each nation has its own unique laws, but one can find many similarities and mixtures among each classification.

国与国之间的法律往往大相径庭。

For most dealings you will be primarily interested in the law as it relates to contracts, but always view litigation as a last resort. Settle disputes in other ways if possible. Litigation is only for the stupid and the rich, because it usually involves long delays during which inventories are tied up and trade is halted. Lawsuits are costly, not just because of the money but also because of the broken relationship that results. Most international commercial disputes can be solved by conciliation, mediation, and arbitration. The International Chamber of Commerce provides an arbitration service that can often be written into a sales contract for use should the unspeakable happen.

对大多数贸易来讲，你会密切关注与合同相关的法律条文，而将诉讼视为最后的补救办法。

大多数国际贸易争端都可以通过调解、斡旋和仲裁来解决。

教　育
Education

Culture shapes our thoughts and emotions. Motivation is influenced by our education as well as other things such as values and religion which we have already discussed. The biggest international difference is the educational attainment of the populous. The next biggest difference is the educational mix. In some countries such as the United States there is little difference in the mix. Practically all Americans are educated from kindergarten through twelfth grade. In the United States education is no longer a function of wealth, but this is not so in many other countries. It is not unusual to find only the elite of some nations educated to the levels Americans assume for all people. The impact of education is therefore profound for marketing products as well as for establishing relationships, because good communications are often based on relative education capacities and standards.

文化塑造了我们的思想和情感。

国际间最大的差距在于大众的受教育程度。国际间第二大的差距在于教育结构。

对于营销产品和建立关系而言，教育的影响至关重要，因为良好的交流往往基于相对较高的教育能力和标准之上。

技　术
Technology

The most recent change in technology is our growing control over transportation, energy, and information communications including the

---

litigation 诉讼。conciliation 调解。mediation 斡旋。educational attainment 教育程度。educational mix 教育结构。

由技术这个词汇衍生出许多概念，如科学、发展、发明和创新等。

在最发达的国家和那些被我们称之为"传统社会"的国家之间存在很大差距。

你应该站在进口国的角度来看待技术。

Internet. The word *technology* begets concepts such as science, development, invention, and innovation. Some older languages don't even have words to express these concepts. Understanding the technological gaps among nations is an essential element to exporting products across borders. Wide gaps still exist between the most advanced nations and those that are still what we call "traditional societies." The implications are that you might need to consider such things as training needs for technology transfer and the impact of that transfer on social environments. You should always look at technology from the importing country's point of view.

社会组织
Social Organization

社会阶层的形成是在一个社会中形成等级制度的过程——包括相对权力、社会优先权、特权以及各个阶级的收入。一个系统内的每个阶层都有不同的品味、政治观点以及消费方式。

当你身处社会宗教等级制度中时，至关重要的是，你要学会如何应对，而非试图改变。

Social stratification is the hierarchy of classes within a society—the relative power, social priorities, privilege, and income of those classes. Each class within a system has somewhat different and distinct tastes, political views, and consumption patterns. Many countries have a socio-religious ideology that allows rank to be intrinsic and inherited biologically. This implies that different categories of humans are culturally defined as if consisting of different worth and potential for performance. Regardless of how you react to such noncompetitive socialization, such ideas are predictable in some countries. Faced with such a system of socio-religious rank, it is essential that you learn how to deal with it—not attempt to change it.

实际应用
Practical Applications

大多数商务旅行都是短期的。尽管如此，即使你只参观一个国家，也要尽可能了解这个国家的文化，这是十分重要的。

Now that you have an appreciation of culture, let's take a look at the practical side.

Most business trips are usually short term. Nevertheless, it's important to understand as much about the culture of a country as possible, even when you're just visiting. To begin, let's look at some generalities—some ideas that will help you make a good impression no matter where you're doing business.

---

beget 产生。gap 差距。stratification 阶层的形成。hierarchy 等级制度。business trip 商务旅行。

Saving face is not just an Asian concept, although it is particularly sensitive in Asian countries. Avoiding embarrassment to others, particularly ranking persons, is essential wherever you are in the world.

People of any country like to talk about their own land and people. If you ask questions that demonstrate genuine interest, it will cultivate their respect toward you. But no one likes critical questions such as, "Why don't you do it this way?" Or, "How come you do it that way?" Above all they don't want to hear how much better it is where you come from.

First impressions do count, and the wrong first impression can stop your business deal in its tracks. Bad first impressions are all but impossible to overcome. Following are some tips that will help you make that good first impression:

1. Smile! It's the universal business language and helps to avoid many problems.

2. But smile right. The smile in which the lips are parted in a sort of an ellipse around the teeth comes across as phony and dishonest. Smile easily—where your full teeth are exposed and the corners of your mouth are pulled up. This kind of smile says, "Hi, I'm pleased to meet you!"

3. Grooming is important all over the world. Studies indicate that most people are more attracted to others who are neat, well groomed, and crisply dressed.

4. Flash your eyebrows. That is, in most cultures raising the eyebrows almost instinctively in a rapid movement and keeping them raised for about a half-second is an unspoken signal of friendliness and approval.

5. Lean forward. Liking is produced by leaning forward.

6. Look for similarities. People tend to like others who are like them, so common experiences and interests are often a starting point for producing liking.

7. Nod your head. People like other people who agree with them and are attentive to what they are saying.

好面子不仅仅是亚洲的观念，尽管亚洲国家对此更加敏感。无论你在什么地方，避免尴尬都至关重要，特别是在与高层人员的交往中。

任何国家的人都喜欢谈论他们自己的风土人情。如果你的问题能够表明这是你发自内心的关注，这将帮助你赢得他们的尊重。

第一印象很重要，不好的第一印象会使交易突然中断。下列建议将帮助你赢得良好的第一印象：

1. 微笑。

2. 恰到好处的微笑。

3. 仪表整洁。

4. 抬眉。

5. 身体前倾。

6. 寻找共同点。

7. 点头示意。

---

saving face 好面子。embarrassment 尴尬。genuine 真正的。in one's tracks 突然。groom 使……整洁。raise one's eyebrows 抬眉。lean 倾斜。

8. 保持开放的姿态。

8. Open up. A position in which your arms are crossed in front of your chest may project the impression that you're resisting the other person's ideas. Open, frequently outstretched arms and open palms project the opposite.

给女性的建议
Tips for Women

下列建议对女性非常有用：

Following are some tips that might be especially useful for women travelers:

1. 不管商务关系多么密切，都不要送给男人礼物。

2. 应以公司的名义送礼，永远不要以自己的名义送礼。

3. 如果你结婚了，在海外要使用夫人的称谓。

4. 避免独自在公共场合饮食。

5. 进行晚宴邀请时，应毫不犹豫地邀请搭档的家庭，这对巩固交易相当有用。

6. 在与异性搭档交谈时，请提及你的配偶并问候对方的家人。

7. 拒绝调情。

8. 根据对方的文化进行合理着装，保守的着装一般是可行的。

1. Never give a man a gift, no matter how close the business relationship. A small gift for his family might do.
2. Give gifts from the company, never from you.
3. If you are married, use Mrs. when overseas, even if you don't at home.
4. Avoid eating or drinking alone in public. Use room service, or invite a woman from the office where you are doing business to join you at a restaurant.
5. If the question of dinner arises and is useful to cement the deal, avoid any doubts by inviting your counterpart's family.
6. Make a point to mention your husband and ask about your male counterpart's family. Some business women who are not married invent a fiancé or "steady" back home.
7. Turn off flirtations immediately with a straightforward no.
8. Be aware of the culture, and dress to fit it as closely as your wardrobe will permit. Conservatism works.

每个国家的人都喜欢幽默，他们都有自己的幽默故事，但向没有共同文化的商务伙伴讲复杂的笑话是很困难的，以下是几点建议：

1. 要记得不同文化对笑话的反应不同。

2. 不要跟外国人讲文字游戏或一语双关的笑话。

关于笑话
About Jokes

People of every country enjoy humor, and they all have their funny stories, but explaining complicated jokes to business people who don't share your culture can be very tricky. Here are a few tips and traps:

1. Do remember that each culture reacts differently to jokes.
2. Don't tell foreigners a joke that depends on word play or punning.

---

outstretch 伸展，伸出。cement 巩固。flirtation 调情。conservatism 保守。tricky 棘手的。punning 双关语。

3. Do be careful about the subject of your joke. It could be taken seriously in a culture different from your own.

4. Do be informed about the sensitive issues in the country where you are visiting.

5. Do ask to hear a few local jokes. They will give you a sense of what's considered funny.

6. Do tell jokes; everyone enjoys a good laugh.

3. 注意笑话的主题。

4. 知晓到访国家的敏感话题。

5. 要求听当地的笑话。

6. 要给对方讲笑话。

知识产权
Intellectual Property Rights

Intellectual property is a general term that describes inventions or other discoveries that have been registered with government authorities for the sale or use by their owners. Such terms as *patent, trademark, copyright* fall into the category of intellectual property.

You can obtain information about patents and trademarks from the World Intellectual Property Organization (WIPO) at www.wipo.int or the U.S. Patent Office by going to its Web site at www.ustpo.gov, calling (800) 786-9199, faxing 571-273-3245, e-mailing USPTOinfo@ USPTO.gov, or writing:

知识产权是基于创造性智力成果和工商业标记依法产生的权利的统称，是指对智力劳动成果依法所享有的占有、使用、处分和收益的权利。知识产权包括专利、商标和版权。

Patent and Trademark Office
Crystal Plaza 3, Room 2C02
Division of Patents and Trademarks
Washington, DC 20231

The booklet titled *General Information on Patents* can be ordered from the Government Printing Office online at www.uspto.gov/ web/offices, or you can call 1-800-786-9199, fax 571-273-3245, or e-mail usptoinfo@ustpo.gov. Table 3.1 is a summary of the basic elements of intellectual rights in the United States.

---

intellectual property 知识产权。patent 专利。trademark 商标。copyright 版权。

表 3.1 知识产权

Table 3.1 Intellectual Property Rights

	Patents	Copyrights	Trade and Service Marks	Trade Name	Trade Dress	Trade Secrets
Duration (years)	14–17 years	Life + 50 years	As long as in use	As long as in use	As long as in use	Until public disclosure
How	Apply to patent office	By original creation in permanent form	By use	By use	By use	By security measures
Requirements	Useful/novel	Non-functional original creation	Fanciful and distinguishing	Non-confusion with others	Fanciful, non-functional	Not known
Prevents	Manufacturer use or sale	Copying or adapting	Confusing or misleading use	Confusing or misleading use	Confusing or misleading use	Disclosure
Protects	Utility and design attributes	Authorship	Reputation and goodwill	Goodwill	Reputation	Info for competitive advantage
Examples	Product/mechanism/ process/style	Label design/ operating manual	Coca-Cola	Computer Land, Inc.	Container shape	Formula
Legal costs	$1,500–$3,000	$10–$100	$100–$400			

专利注册
Patent Registration

You should recognize that patent registration in the United States does not protect your product in a foreign country. In general, protection in one country does not constitute protection in another. The rule of thumb is to apply for and register all intellectual property rights in each country where you intend to do business. Registration can be expensive; therefore, several multilateral organizations have been formed that make registration possible for all member countries.

你应该认识到，在美国的专利注册并不能保护你在国外的产品。

注册费是很昂贵的，因此，形成了许多多边组织以便为所有成员国完成注册。

共同体专利
The Community Patent

The *community patent*, also known as the European community patent or EC patent, is a patent measure being debated within the European Union. It would allow individuals and companies to obtain a unitary patent throughout the European Union. The community patent should not be confused with European patents, which are granted under the European Patent Convention. European patents, once granted, become a bundle of nationally enforceable patents in the designated states.

共同体专利，也称为欧共体专利，是在欧盟中备受争议的专利标准。

The community patent is intended to solve granting and enforcement by providing a patent right that is consistent across Europe. This fulfills one of the key principles of the internal market in that the same market conditions exist wherever in Europe trade is carried out—different patent rights in different countries distort this principle.

共同体专利致力于解决在欧洲授予和执行专利保护保持一致性的问题。

In view of the difficulties in reaching an agreement on the community patent, other legal agreements have been proposed outside the European Union legal framework to reduce the cost of translation (of patents when granted) and litigation, namely the London Agreement and the European Patent Litigation Agreement (EPLA).

欧洲专利公约
European Patent Convention

The Convention on the Grant of European Patents of October 5, 1973, commonly known as the *European Patent Convention* (EPC), is a multilateral treaty instituting the European Patent Organization and providing an autonomous legal system according to which European

1973 年 10 月 5 日制订的《欧洲专利公约》是多边条约，据此建立了欧洲专利组织，为授予的专利提供独立的法律体系。

---

patent registration 专利注册。community patent 共同体专利。grant 授予。enforcement 执行。autonomous 独立的。

patents are granted. Once granted, a European patent becomes equivalent to a bundle of nationally enforceable, nationally revocable patents, except for the provision of a time-limited, unified, postgrant opposition procedure. See www.epo.org/patents/law/legal-texts/html/epc/1973/e/ma1.html

现在不存在适用整个欧盟的专利。从 20 世纪 70 年代起，就存在关于建立欧盟通用专利的讨论。

There is currently no single European Union–wide patent. Since the 1970s, there has been concurrent discussion toward the creation of a community patent in the European Union. In May 2004, however, a stalemate was reached, and the prospect of a single European Union–wide patent is receding.

《欧洲专利公约》是独立于欧盟的，其成员国与欧盟的不同，瑞士、列支敦士登、土耳其、摩纳哥以及冰岛是欧洲专利公约的成员国，但不是欧盟的成员国；而马耳他是欧盟的成员国却不是欧洲专利公约的成员国。

The EPC is separate from the European Union, and its membership is different: Switzerland, Liechtenstein, Turkey, Monaco, and Iceland are members of the EPO but are not members of the EU, while the opposite is true for Malta. The EPC provides a legal framework for the granting of European patents via a single, harmonized procedure before the European patent office. A single patent application may be filed at the European patent office in Munich, at its branches at The Hague or Berlin, or at a national patent office of a contracting state, if the national law of the state so permits. This last provision is important in countries such as the United Kingdom, in which it is an offense for a U.K. resident to file a patent application for inventions in certain sensitive areas abroad without obtaining clearance through the U.K. patent office first.

专利权合作条约

The Patent Cooperation Treaty

《专利权合作条约》为填写专利申请国际保护提供了统一的程序。

The *Patent Cooperation Treaty* (PCT) provides a unified procedure for filing patent applications to protect inventions internationally. A single filing results in a single search accompanied by a written opinion (and optionally a preliminary examination), after which the examination (if provided by national law) and grant procedures are handled by the relevant national or regional authorities. The PCT does not lead to the granting of an "international patent," which does not exist.

《专利权合作条约》并不意味"国际专利"的授权，因为这种授权是不存在的。

The states party to the PCT constitute the International Patent Cooperation Union. As of May 24, 2006, there were 132 contracting states.

---

concurrent 同时存在的。Liechtenstein 列支敦士登。patent cooperation treaty 专利权合作条约。unified 统一的。

商标注册
Trademark Registration

Trademark registration is less costly and time consuming than patent registration.

商标注册与专利注册相比，既不昂贵也不耗时。

1. The International Convention for the Protection of Industrial Property, better known as the Paris Union, is 90 years old and covers patents as well as trademarks. Under this convention six-month protection is provided a firm, during which time the trademark can be registered in the other member countries.
2. The Madrid Arrangement for International Registration of Trademarks has 22 members, but it offers the advantage that registration in one country qualifies as registration in all other member countries.

交　流
Communications

Although nothing substitutes for personal contact when developing an international marketing structure, this may not always be possible. Therefore, the tone of initial written communications is critical. It often makes the difference between a profitable long-term arrangement and a lost opportunity.

在拓展某种国际营销结构时，什么都替代不了人际关系，但人际关系也不是万能的。因此，最初的书面交流风格至关重要。

介绍信、传真和邮件
The Introductory Letter, Facsimile (Fax), or E-mail

Your introductory letter, fax, or e-mail most often can be written in your language, your potential buyers (or sellers) language, or in English. With the exception of Latin America, English has become the language of international business, but use simple words. If your communication must be translated and transmitted into a foreign language, make sure that you have it translated back to English by a third party before sending it. However proficient a person is in the other language, funny things can happen in translation.

你的介绍信、传真或电子邮件常常是用你使用的语言、你潜在客户使用的语言或英语书来写的。

如果你的书信必须要翻译成外国语言，在发出之前要请第三方将你所翻译的书信再翻译成你使用的语言（英语）。

    From the beginning establish your company's favorable reputation and explain the relationship that you seek. Describe the product you want to market (export) or to purchase (import). Propose a personal

personal contact 人际关系。tone 风格。facsimile 传真。

meeting and offer the buyer a visit to your firm during the person's next visit to your country. Ask for a response to your letter. Figure 3.2 shows a sample letter of introduction.

后续交流
Follow-Up Communications

科技的进步产生了更多的交流方式，包括快递服务在内的多种方式都可以用于交流。选择好的交流方式能够带来更好的结果。成功的进出口业务依赖于可靠的双向沟通。

As technology improves, more alternative forms of communications, including express delivery services, have become available, and choosing the best alternative may result in the competitive difference. Successful importing/exporting depends on reliable two-way communication. It is critical in establishing and running an import/export marketing network.

电 话
Telephone

言语是传递想法和接收反馈的最快方式。电话通信允许有即时反馈——对即时发现的问题和出现的机会进行快速回复。

尽管国际长途迅速而有效，但是如果有很多话要说，费用就会很高。

Speech is the fastest way to convey ideas and receive answers. Voice communications allow for immediate feedback—quick response to fast-breaking problems or opportunities. Most countries can be dialed directly, and the rates for international telephone service depend on the time of day. While international telephone can be expeditious, it can be expensive if you have a lot to say.

传 真
Facsimile

传真一直是商务通信中发展最为迅速的工具之一。

Facsimile (fax), or telecopier service, remains one of the fastest growing means of business communication. The advantage of fax is that any image of up to $8\frac{1}{2}$ by 14 inches can be transmitted directly to the receiving unit. Letters, pictures, contracts, forms, catalog sheets, drawings, and illustrations—anything that would reproduce in a copy machine—can be sent.

On a historical note, facsimile is not new. It was invented over a century ago, in 1842, by Alexander Bain, a Scottish clockmaker. His device used a pendulum that swept a metal point over a set of raised metal letters. When the point touched a letter, it created an electrical charge that traveled down a telegraph wire to reproduce on paper the series of letters the pendulum had touched. Wire service photos were

---

express delivery services 快递服务。two-way communication 双向沟通。fast-breaking 迅速展开的。expeditious 迅速完成的。

图 3.2 介绍信样例
Figure 3.2 Sample Letter of Introduction

Our Company, Inc.
Hometown, U.S.A.

Ref:
Date:

XYZ Foreign Co.
2A1 Moon River
Yokohama, Japan

Gentlemen:

Our Company, Inc., markets a line of highway spots. When secured to the centerline of highway, these spots provide for increased safety for motorists. We believe that these spots might interest foreign markets, especially the Japanese market. Our major customers include highway contractors and highway departments of the states of ABC and DEF.

Our Company, founded in 1983, has sales of $1.5 million. Further details are given in the attached brochure. The attached catalogs and specification sheets give detailed information about our products.

We are writing to learn whether: (1) XYZ Foreign Co. has a requirement to purchase similar products for use in Japan; and (2) XYZ Foreign Co. would be interested in representing Our Company in Japan.

Don't hesitate to telephone if you need further details. We look forward to meeting with representatives of XYZ Foreign Co. about our highway spots.

Sincerely,

W. T. Door
President

transmitted by fax as early as 1930. The U.S. Navy used them aboard ship during World War II for the transmission of weather data.

最早的传真机是老爷机而且十分昂贵，发送一页纸需要花费 10 多分钟以及 18 000 多美元的成本。现在，专用传真终端只需花费 60 美元。

The earliest fax machines were clunkers and very expensive, taking more than 10 minutes to send a single page and costing more than $18,000. Today, dedicated facsimile terminals cost as little as $60. Their speed equates favorably to telex. Fax transmits over ordinary voice phone networks. Several private bureaus manage faxes as a worldwide service. There is no effective proof of delivery of a fax document.

尽管大多数公司还能够接收和发送传真，但这项技术在互联网的世界中显得越来越过时了。

Although most businesses still maintain some kind of fax capability, the technology appears increasingly dated in the world of the Internet.

互联网
Internet

It wasn't that long ago that the Internet was just a public, amorphous collection of computer networks—a technofad made up of blending a few personal computers and citizen's band radio enthusiasts.

现在互联网是发展最快的，也成为最佳的交易场所。

Today the Internet is the fastest growing and most exciting place to do business (see Chapter 4). New cross-indexing software and imaginative services are connecting the home computer masses to electronic commerce through Web servers and high-speed circuits into the World Wide Web.

将买卖双方联系在一起的概念以及无纸化办公降低了交易成本。

This concept of linking buyers and sellers and elimination of paperwork will drive down the cost of transactions. The Internet has become the low-cost alternative to faxes, express mail, and other communications channels such as 1-800 telephone sales. Most international

大多数跨国公司都有自己的网页，而且将其制作成多种语言。

businesses have their own Web pages in more than one language. There are programs that will translate from one country's language to another.

网络覆盖了所有国家，而且最有趣的一点是，没有人能够完全控制和拥有网络。

The Internet knows no international boundaries—internauts are logging on from Bangkok to New York's Broadway. The network extends to all countries, and the most interesting part of it is nobody owns the Internet. The Internet is not guided by a single company or institution. The internet protocol (IP) allows any number of computer networks to link up and act as one.

On another historical note, the Internet is also not new. Its beginning was in the late 1960s when the Pentagon (American Defense

---

clunker 老爷机。dedicated 专用的。drive down 降低。

Department) asked computer scientists to find the best way for an unlimited number of computers to communicate—without relying on any single computer to be traffic cop. That way the system would not be vulnerable to nuclear attack. The outcome was the decision to fund experimental packet-switching communications using a transmission and control/internet protocol (TCP/IP) technology called ARPAnet that quickly expanded to dozens of universities and corporations. Programs were written to help people exchange e-mail and tap into remote databases. In 1983 ARPAnet was split into two networks, ARPAnet and Milnet, and the Pentagon mandated TCP/IP as the standard protocol. These two networks evolved into the Internet.

结果就是筹建包交换实验通信网络，该网络使用了传输和控制协议技术，被称为阿帕网，这种网络迅速蔓延至大学和企业中。

1983 年，阿帕网分成了两个网络，阿帕网和军用网。美国国防部将网络传输控制协议作为标准协议。

HOT TIP

Though print lacks speed (compared to voice), it provides written documentation that can be read and reread at the reader's pace and schedule.

电　报
Cables and Telexes

International mailgrams, telegrams, or cables can still be sent anywhere mail goes. These forms of communication require a complete mailing address, including any postal codes.

国际电报服务能够向任何地方传递信息。这种交流方式需要完整的邮件地址，包括邮政编码。

Cables are sent electronically to the major city nearest the recipient. There, the message may be telephoned and mailed, mailed only, or (in a few locations) delivered by messenger. Cables don't offer proof of delivery that a telex message does, and because of the extra handling, cables are significantly more expensive than telex messages. But a cable can be sent to anyone, anywhere.

电报通过电子方式传输到接收终端附近的主要城市。

There are still some telex terminals in government and business offices around the world. Their advantage is they can receive information automatically, even when unattended.

世界各地的政府部门和商务部门仍有接收电报的终端。它们的优势是，即便在没人的时候也可以自动接收信息。

---

packet-switching 包交换。TCP 网络传输控制协议。protocol 协议。telex 电报。mailgram 邮递电报。recipient 接收者。

交流工具
Communications Equipment

电子数据传输在 20 世纪 90 年代迅猛发展。21 世纪，数据在进出口商、代理商、分销商和客户之间的流动一定会更简单、更快速地流动。

Electronic data transmission grew rapidly throughout the 1990s. In the new century data must flow easily and quickly back and forth among the importer/exporter and agencies, distributors, and customers. Electronic mail is now commonly delivered over international phone lines. Practically any computer can be interfaced with a modem via a cable, ordinary telephone, satellite, or microwave to any another computer or word processor anywhere in the world so long as the receiving country does not restrict or prohibit transborder data flows.

HOT COMMUNICATIONS TIPS

1. Write out your message and check it by reading it aloud.
2. Some situations in international business can be frustrating, so take care not to lose your temper and send a "zinger" that you'll regret later. Develop a cordial and professional style, and stick to it at all times. Try to draft replies in the morning when you are fresh. Whenever possible, let a second party read each message.
3. Send messages earlier in the day and earlier in the week to avoid the heavy calling periods and possible delay of your message.

保持短信的简洁，但要避免可能不被理解的缩写。

4. Keep your messages brief, but avoid abbreviations that might not be understood.
5. Try to reply to every fax/telex/Internet message the same day it is received, even if only to give a date when a more complete reply will be sent. Keep in mind the differences in time zones between countries.
6. Use "ATTN: Name" rather than "Dear Name." Also, almost all fax/Internet messages, by custom, end with "Regards," "Best regards," or occasionally "Cordially."

旅 行
Travel

国际间的不信任是进出口贸易通往成功的障碍。

Mistrust across international borders can be a barrier to a successful import/export business. Therefore, visiting the country and the people

electronic data transmission 电子数据传输。abbreviation 缩写。mistrust 不信任。

who offer goods for your importation or the agents or distributors who market your export products is essential. These personal contacts remind us that we have more in common with people from other nations than differences. Travel to exotic places is not only fun, but it is a tax deductible expense of international trade as well.

这些人际关系提醒我们人与人之间的共性大于个性差别。到外国旅行不仅是为了开心，它也是国际贸易中的一种避税方式。

HOT TIP

The Internal Revenue Service will look closely at travel expenses to make sure that you are actually doing business and not indulging your love of travel. For this purpose keep good records during your travels and make sure you profit from your trips.

计划旅行
Planning a Trip

You alone know your itinerary, how long you can stay in each place, and what you expect to accomplish, so lay out your own trip before turning it over to a travel agent. Make certain your local arrival time allows for time changes and scheduled business meetings. Also, allow time for rest prior to negotiating.

一定要了解你的预定行程，将在每个地方呆多久以及要完成的任务。在移交给旅行社负责之前，要设计好自己的行程。

After you have planned out your trip, take it to the travel agent for booking. Allow three to five days and expect some changes. You may need to go through country B in order to get to country C.

外国旅行信息
Foreign Travel Information

Terrorism is a major concern to traveling traders, but it should not keep you from your work. To stay alert to any possible danger areas in the world, contact the Citizens Emergency Center, Office of American Citizen Service & Crisis Management at the U.S. Department of State, Washington, DC, at 202-647-5225. See www.travel.state.gov for important information on traveling abroad.

恐怖主义是旅行贸易商关心的主要问题，但这并不能阻止你要进行的工作。

---

exotic 外国的。deductible 可扣除的。terrorism 恐怖主义。

五项旅行小贴士
Five Traveling Tips

1. 轻装旅行。通常到达后要通过海关的移民检查站。做好打开行李和接受检查的准备，并且保持微笑！

2. 去大多数国家最好坐商务舱；商务舱比经济舱更舒服，比头等舱更便宜。

3. 除非你对一国的酒店很熟悉，否则你最好还是入住国际知名的酒店。

4. 即使为你提供的食物是世界上最好的，也要少吃，并且只能引用无菌水。

5. 为调整时差做好准备。

1. Travel light. The usual arrival sequence is immigration followed by customs. Be ready to open your luggage and sometimes declare each item. Smile!

2. Request business class to most countries; it's more comfortable than coach and less expensive than first class.

3. Unless you are familiar with the better hotels in a country, you are usually better off staying at one that is internationally recognized. Most major travel companies, agents, or your local library can give you the names of the best hotels.

4. Are you a bit overweight? Now is the time to drop a few pounds. The food may be the best in the world, but eat light and drink only sterilized water.

5. Plan for the changing time zones. Think ahead and determine the local time of arrival for the plane you have booked. Remember that time is reckoned from Greenwich, England, and watches are normally set to a particular zone time. Time is changed near the crossing of the boundary between zones, usually at a whole hour. If you know the time zone, you can calculate the local time. Figure 3.3 depicts international time zones as they appear at noon Eastern standard time.

护照和签证
Passports and Visas

护照是用于识别公民国籍的旅行证件，公民的国籍为护照的签发国。

签证是出境者想要访问的国家的官方认可。

A *passport* is a travel document that identifies the holder as a citizen of the country from which it is issued. In the United States, the Department of State issues passports. You can apply at your local U.S. post office. Although these may change, the cost for Americans 16 years of age and older is $92 which includes a passport fee of $50, a security surcharge of $12, and an execution fee of $30. For those younger than 16, the passport fee is $40 plus the other fees, totaling $82. You should allow about two to three weeks for processing.

The *visa* is an official endorsement from a country a person wishes to visit. You must receive it before entry into that country is permitted. Some nations don't require a visa. Check with your travel agent or the

---

arrival sequence 到达顺序。business class 商务舱。coach 经济舱。sterilized water 无菌水。endorsement 认可。

图 3.3 国际时区

Figure 3.3 International Time Zones

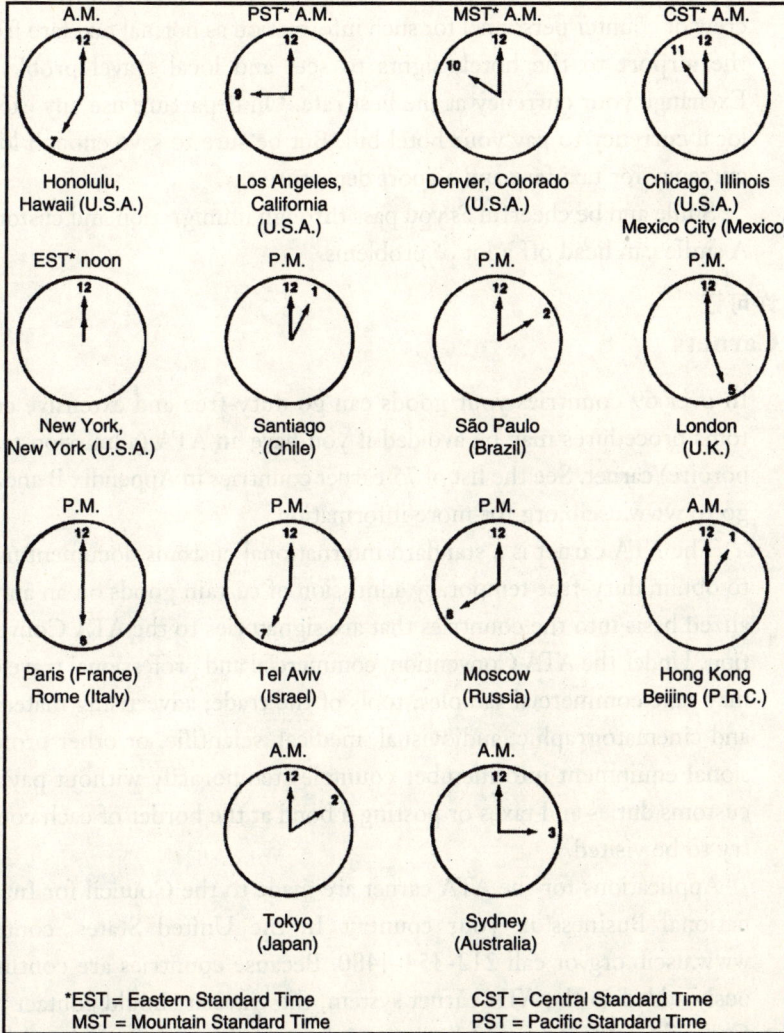

A.M.	PST* A.M.	MST* A.M.	CST* A.M.
Honolulu, Hawaii (U.S.A.)	Los Angeles, California (U.S.A.)	Denver, Colorado (U.S.A.)	Chicago, Illinois (U.S.A.) Mexico City (Mexico)
EST* noon	P.M.	P.M.	P.M.
New York, New York (U.S.A.)	Santiago (Chile)	São Paulo (Brazil)	London (U.K.)
P.M.	P.M.	P.M.	A.M.
Paris (France) Rome (Italy)	Tel Aviv (Israel)	Moscow (Russia)	Hong Kong Beijing (P.R.C.)
	A.M.	A.M.	
	Tokyo (Japan)	Sydney (Australia)	

*EST = Eastern Standard Time   CST = Central Standard Time
MST = Mountain Standard Time   PST = Pacific Standard Time

consul or embassy for the country you're planning to visit. You may prefer to give your passport and three photos to a visa service and let the service make the rounds of embassies. Count on waiting a week or more for the completion of this service.

Fares and Gratuities 费用和小费

刚到一个陌生的国家时，向航空公司的工作人员或前台人员询问从机场到酒店的出租车费用、观光地点以及当地的旅游问题。在最合适的汇率水平兑换货币。

On arrival in a country you have never visited before, ask the airline crew or counter personnel for such information as normal taxi fare from the airport to the hotel, sights to see, and local travel problems. Exchange your currency at the best rate. On departure use any excess local currency to pay your hotel bill. But be sure to save enough local currency for taxi fare and airport departure tax.

在通过海关时保持微笑，一个微笑往往能解决很多问题。

Smile and be cheerful as you pass through immigration and customs. A smile can head off a lot of problems.

许可证
Carnets

如果你有 ATA 单证册，那么你的货物可以在 70 多个国家免税并避免繁杂的海关手续。

In over 69 countries your goods can go duty-free and extensive customs procedures may be avoided if you have an ATA (admission temporoire) carnet. See the list of 75 carnet countries in Appendix B and/or go to www.uscib.org for more information.

ATA 单证册是用于获取 ATA 条约签约国对特定商品年税豁免权的标准国际海关文件。

The ATA carnet is a standard international customs document used to obtain duty-free temporary admission of certain goods on an annualized basis into the countries that are signatories to the ATA Convention. Under the ATA Convention, commercial and professional travelers may take commercial samples; tools of the trade; advertising material; and cinematographic, audiovisual, medical, scientific, or other professional equipment into member countries temporarily without paying customs duties and taxes or posting a bond at the border of each country to be visited.

因为很多国家都陆续加入了 ATA 单证册系统，旅行者应该与国际商务委员会保持联系，以便能随时了解目标访问国是否在 ATA 单证册系统中。

Applications for the ATA carnet are made to the Council for International Business in your country. In the United States, contact www.uscib.org or call 212-354-4480. Because countries are continuously added to the ATA carnet system, the traveler should contact the Council for International Business to learn if the country to be visited is included on the list. The list of over 97 nations and territories where the ATA carnet can be used (current as of 2008, www.ATAcarnet.com) may be found in Appendix B. The fee charged for the carnet depends on the value of the goods to be covered. A bond, letter of credit, or bank guarantee of 40 percent of the value of the goods is also required to cover duties and taxes that would be due if goods imported into a

---

gratuity 小费。counter personnel 前台工作人员。signatory 签约国。council for international business 国际商务委员会。

foreign country were not paid by the carnet holder. Typical processing fees are:

Shipment Value	Basic Processing Fee
Under $5,000	US$120
$5,000–14,999	US$150
$15,000–49,999	US$175
$50,000–199,999	US$200
$200,000–499,999	US$225
$500,000 and over	US$250

Further information can be found in the informative book published by the council titled *Carnet: Move Goods Duty-Free through Customs*.

If you don't get a carnet, check your samples at the airport with customs, but allow plenty of time to get them before the next flight.

The next chapter is intended to vault you into the cyber world. Read it and incorporate Internet sales into your project.

如果你得不到许可证，就需要让机场的海关人员检查你的样品，而且要在下次航班前给检查留出足够的时间。

下一章将带你进入网络世界。

CHAPTER 4

SELLING WITH E-COMMERCE

使用电子商务进行销售

This is one of the most important chapters of this book. Why? Because the Internet has redefined modern business!

Every day virtually every newspaper and television station in every country tells the story of how millions of computer users tap the global network for unparalleled access to communications, research information, and trade.

每一天，各个国家几乎所有报纸和电视台都在报道这样的故事：成千上万的电脑用户如何利用全球网络，接触到前所未有的沟通渠道、研究信息和贸易机会。

In its many forms, *e-commerce* may be defined as any commercial transaction carried out, facilitated, or enabled by the exchange of information electronically. The true value of the Internet and the World Wide Web that resides therein is that it is borderless.

电子商务可以定义为，通过电子信息交换来实施、促进或促成的商业交易。

Think of countries as if they were lakes without connecting canals; now with the Internet, people from one lake can swim easily to another lake where they can experience food, wares, and culture they could never before access.

互联网和商业
The Internet and Your Business

The potential of the Internet for international e-commerce has been more than realized—big cross-border business is being conducted over

互联网在国际电子商务中的潜力得到了充分发挥——通过网络而进行的大宗跨界交易每天都在发生。

---

redefine 重新定义。tap 利用。commercial transaction 商业交易。borderless 无国界的。canal 运河。potential 潜力。

the Web. The benefit to business is the capability to bring customers, vendors, and suppliers closer together and thus maximizing results. It promotes economies of scale, reduces operational costs, and improves customer service by enabling businesses to communicate directly with the client.

背 景
Background

Once the exclusive province of government and university researchers, the Internet has become an information nirvana for the common business person and is growing at a rate of about 10 to 20 percent each month.

如今你可以通过打开网页浏览器，进入栩栩如生的网络中去，游走于成千上万个网页之间——从出售太阳镜到兜售橡皮泥，应有尽有。

Created in 1989 at CERN, a huge Swiss research laboratory, the Web began simply as a project to link scientists worldwide. But its intuitive, easy-to-use hypertextual design caused the Web to spread beyond its original user community. By accessing the Web with a browsing program, you can now tap a graphic environment in which you move between millions of Web sites that offer everything from sunglasses to Silly Putty. Most Web pages integrate images, sounds, and text to advertise their products and services.

微软公司创始人比尔·盖茨曾说过："网络代表了无摩擦的资本主义。"

In the 1950s the world sold things on Main Street; in the 1980s it was the mall; in the 1990s it was the superstore; but in the 2000s it is and will be at www.com. Why? Because, as Bill Gates, the founder of Microsoft, says, "The Net represents frictionless capitalism." (For a listing of Internet terms, see the glossary at the back of the book.)

全球营销机会
The Global Marketing Opportunity

No supranational organization or head of state has been able to bring the world together, but the Web is uniting the world. Because there is no president or king of the Internet, small businesses can sell anywhere in the world.

互联网的明显优势在于，能够越过供应链的中间环节——即传统商业中的经销商、零售商和店面——直接到达消费者。

The obvious advantage of the Internet is the ability to bypass the middle of the supply chain—that is, the many distributors, wholesalers, and storefronts of traditional business—to reach directly to the consumer. Now, customers (users and buyers) can be served directly, just like the old direct-mail marketing process but without the high cost

---

nirvana 天堂。CERN 欧洲核子研究中心。intuitive 凭直觉的。Silly Putty 橡皮泥。
supranational 超国家的（指涉及不止一个国家）。bypass 绕过，避开。distributor 经销商。storefront 店面。

of printing and postage. More importantly, the Internet knows no boundaries—it can reach the potential customer in every nook and cranny of the world, wherever a person can surf the Web.

网络商人
The Cyber Trader

In 1998 there were $6.1 billion in consumer purchases were conducted over the Internet and about $15.6 billion in business-to-business sales. In 2001 the increase was 800 percent stronger, moving to more than $25 billion in consumer purchases and more than $200 billion in business-to-business sales. Yet today e-commerce is only 1 percent of total U.S. gross domestic product (GDP) and only 0.02 percent of total retail sales. Internet sales are expected to grow exponentially—in 2007, 1.319 billion people were using this method of communication.

1998 年，有价值 61 亿美元的消费品买卖以及约 156 亿美元的企业间交易是通过网络进行的。

不断变化的竞争
The Changing Competition

The Web is also changing competition. Online businesses have an easier time locking in their customers with plenty of room for further growth. Consider geography, for example. As retailers expand, they must build storefronts and organize distribution networks, settling for smaller and smaller markets and having already hit the larger ones. The online competitor has the advantage because the business has instant reach. Costs of acquiring a customer in another city or country are the same as finding one locally.

网络正在改变竞争方式。在线企业更容易锁定顾客，并且具有更大的增长空间。

Price is another way that the online business wins in the ever-changing competitive world. An online seller can undercut the non-Web player. In fact, some are even offering products and services for free while gaining their income through outside advertising.

价格是在线企业在瞬息万变的竞争中制胜的另一种手段。

开始着手
Getting Started

Getting your business on the Web requires the least amount of financial capital; it simply requires what is known as a *virtual office*—that is, a computer or television, proper software, and a modem. This virtual

将你的企业搬到网上只需花费极少的财务资金。你所需要的只是一间虚拟办公室——即一台电脑或电视，合适的软件以及一台调制解调器。

---

every nook and cranny 各个地方。consumer purchase 消费品购买。business-to-business 企业对企业（电子商务）。exponentially 指数的。undercut 削价竞争，以低于（竞争对手）的价格做生意。virtual 虚拟的。

换句话说，你的生意不再取决于一个店面或一张办公桌——你的网站就是你的店铺。

在万维网占据一席之地的第一步，便是设计一个由主页和若干辅助信息页构成的网站（如图4.1所示）。

office, which could be in the back room of your business, in your home, or on your lap when you're traveling, provides you with the adaptability and flexibility to enter your business environment on an equal footing with the largest companies. In other words, your business is no longer tied to a physical storefront or a desk—your Web page is your storefront. As long as you can plug into a telephone or cable line (or connect to a satellite), you can do business. You can even get faxes through your e-mail system by using services such as efax.com

The first step in obtaining a presence on the World Wide Web is the designing of a Web site, which is made up of a home page and several supplemental pages of information (see Figure 4.1). The home page is to the rest of your Web site as a book cover is to its contents. Because your business is international, you should consider allowing the user

图 4.1　典型的主页

Figure 4.1 Typical Home Page

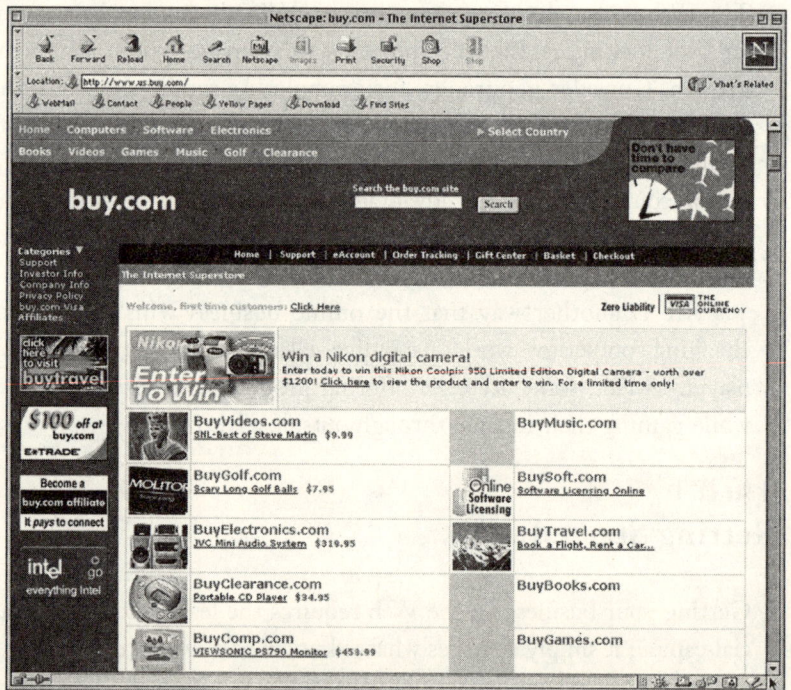

---

adaptability 适应性。flexibility 灵活性。on an equal footing 处于平等地位，平等地。plug into 接通。home page 主页。supplemental 辅助性的。

to click on a choice of languages—maybe English, French, Italian, Mandarin, and Hindi. Similarly, an early decision will be how many and which countries should you have a home page presence. For instance, Dell Computers has crossed national boundaries by having Web sites all over the world.

创办主页
Home Page Presence

The home page design should be bold and visual but lean and mean, so that it can quickly capture attention yet be understood at a glance and lead the reader to the other pages of the site. Keep the home page simple. Don't clutter, and make it easy to navigate. The prospective customer who gets lost or confused while reading is quickly gone. Use your home page to make a few essential points like who you are, what you offer, and what's on the rest of the pages. Don't be too commercial. Internet protocol dictates that you offer some free information and entertainment first. Then you can ask for the sale.

主页设计既要醒目直观，又要简明精炼，能够迅速吸引读者的注意力，让其对网站内容一目了然，并引导读者进入网站的其他页面。

利用你的主页说明几个要点，诸如你是谁，提供什么产品，网页还有什么其他内容。

No matter what you are selling, there are already many sites devoted to the same products or services. Know your competitors by searching them out. Learn what they have emphasized and what is working for them.

All too many businesses rush into this project without thinking it through. It is essential to plan ahead by identifying and honing your key messages and organizing them in a logical structure, developing a prototype page design, testing it on representative users, and refining it through successive iterations. Even after your Web site is up and running, revisit it often—keep it fresh by giving users something new and a reason to return.

太多数企业并未考虑清楚，就盲目启动了项目。预先计划是至关重要的，你可以提前确定和推敲想传达的关键信息，将它们按照逻辑结构组织好，设计出页面原型；然后，对代表性用户进行测试，最后通过多次重复这一过程进一步改进页面设计。

KEYS TO SITE DESIGN

- Start slowly
- Place emphasis on content
- Make it easy for consumers to get around (navigate)
- Avoid using too many graphic elements

Mandarin 普通话。Hindi 印地语。lean 精炼的。clutter 凌乱摆放。navigate 浏览。Internet protocol 互联网通信协议。hone 推敲。prototype 原型。iteration 反复。

- Be entertaining
- Make your site graphically pleasing
- Reach sight-impaired readers
- Design for the overseas market by incorporating multiple languages
- Add pages to your site
- Accept credit cards
- Give payment options
- Make it easy to order
- Provide a shopping cart
- Provide links

博　客
Blogging

博客是网络日志的通用缩写，即条目（如日志或日记）根据张贴时间，以倒序方式由新到旧排列的一类网站。

一篇博客通常会综合文字、图像以及与话题相关的其他博客、网页和媒体链接。

博客可以寄存在专门的博客托管服务器，也可以通过博客软件，如 WordPress、blogger、LiveJournal，或者常规的网站托管服务器如 Dream-Host 来运行。

Blog is the contraction universally used for Weblog, a type of Web site in which entries are made (such as in a journal or diary) and displayed in reverse chronological order.

They often provide commentary or news on a particular subject, such as food, politics, or business. A typical blog combines text, images, and links to other blogs, Web pages, and other media related to the topic. Most blogs are primarily textual although some focus on photographs (photoblog), videos (vlog), or audio (podcast) and are part of a wider network of social media.

Early blogs were simply manually updated components of common Web sites. However, the evolution of tools to facilitate the production and maintenance of Web articles posted in chronological fashion made the publishing process feasible to a much larger, less technical population. Ultimately, this resulted in the distinct class of online publishing that produces blogs we recognize today. For instance, the use of some sort of browser-based software is now a typical aspect of blogging. Blogs can be hosted by dedicated blog hosting services, or they can be run using blog software, such as WordPress, blogger or LiveJournal, or they can run on regular Web hosting services, such as DreamHost.

---

contraction 缩写。textual 文本的。manually 手动地。feasible 可行的。dedicated 专门用途的。

While the great majority of blogs are noncommercial, full-time bloggers have struggled to find a way to make a profit from their work. The most common and simplest method is to accept targeted banner advertising. One form of advertising for bloggers is to promote merchandise from other sites. They receive a commission when a customer buys the item after following a blog link.

对于博客写手来说，推销来自其他网站的商品是一种营销方式。当有顾客通过点击博客链接购买了该商品时，博客写手就可以从中得到佣金。

HISTORICAL NOTE

According to Wikipedia, the term *Weblog* was coined by Jorn Barger on December 17, 1997. The short form, *blog*, was coined by Peter Merholz, who jokingly broke the word *Weblog* into the phrase *we blog* in the sidebar of his blog Peterme.com in April or May of 1999. This was quickly adopted as both a noun and verb ("to blog," meaning "to edit one's Weblog or to post to one's Weblog").

创建自己的主页
You Can Create Your Own Web Site

Can you design your own Web site? Of course you can! Many people do. Learning HTML code is not difficult (see Figure 4.2); neither are FrontPage or DreamWeaver softwares. What is difficult is designing a Web page that captures the attention of customers. The technology of design is easy enough to learn, but the art of getting attention is not, so you might want to consider getting professional help.

设计的技术容易掌握，但赢得关注的技巧却不简单，所以你可能需要考虑获得一些专业帮助。

SOFTWARE GUIDE

There are many software tools available to allow you to get your e-commerce project off the ground. Here is a list of some Internet

有许多软件工具可以帮助你开展电子商务项目。

---

banner advertising 旗帜广告（最常见的网络广告形式，通常置于页面顶部，最先映入网络访客眼帘）。merchandise 商品。commission 佣金。coin 创造（新词语）。

software products; however, neither quality nor rank is implied—be aware the market is changing rapidly so these may not be around next year.

Oracle Applications, (650) 506-7000, www.oracle.com
Peoplesoft, (800) 380-7638, www.peoplesoft.com
MySap.com, (610) 355-2500, www.sap.com
Broadbase EPM, (650) 614-8301, www.broadbase.com
BroadVision One-to-One, (650) 261-5900, www.broadvison.com
Commerce Exchange, (212) 301-2500, www.interworld.com
E-Speak and Chai Appliance Platform, (650) 857-1501
The Kana Platform, (650) 298-9282, www.kana.com
NetCommerce Family, (800) 772-2227, www.ibm.com
Spectra and ColdFusion, (888) 939-2545, www.altaire.com
Sun-Netscape Alliance, (650) 254-1900, www.netscape.com
GoLive from Adobe, (800) 833-6687, www.adobe.com
Homesite, (888) 939-2545, www.allaire.com
FrontPage 2000, (800) 426-9400, www.microsoft.com
WebLogic, (800) 817-4BEA, www.beasys.com
Oberon E-Enterprise, (800) 654-1215, www.oberon.com
Enfinity, (800) 736-5197, www.intershop.com
Infranet, (408)343-4400, www.portal.com
Quickbooks Internet Gateway, (650) 944-6000, www.quicken.com
e-BIZ, (888) 4LUXENT, www.e-bixinabox.com

寻求外援
Or You Can Get Someone Else to Do It

你所需要的是找一位现代网络高手，帮助你设计从第一眼印象，到商品陈列，再到握手达成协议的整个在线交易流程。

Too many firms turn the task of creating a Web site over to a marketing director of the old school who never got past e-mail. What you need is a modern Internet geek who can design an entire online transaction from first look to showroom tour to a final handshake deal.

还有一些人来自大广告公司，他们既拥有多年从业经验，又能快速运用网络技术这种现代通信手段。

Like any other new endeavor, in every city there are people who specialize in Web page strategy and design. Many of these are recent college students who focused their training in this specialty. Others are affiliated with major advertising companies who have the advantage of the ad firm's years of experience and adapt it to the Web technology of modern communications.

geek 网络高手，电脑玩家。showroom 展销厅。endeavor 努力，尝试。specialize in 擅长。affiliated 隶属于。

HOT TIP

A *domain name* is what people type into search engines to find Web sites. Most companies use several domain names and aliases such as "Your-company.com" and others like "international business"—those appropriate to what people might type into a search engine to find your specialty or industry. The trick is to get your domain name to the top of the search engine list.

域名，即人们输入搜索引擎中并凭此找到网站的依据。

图 4.2   超文本标记语言（HTML）示例

Figure 4.2 Example of HTML

Partial List of HTML Markup Tags

Markup Tags	Use of Tag
<A HREF="pagename.htm"> ... </A>	Create a link to another document
<A HREF="http://www.abc.com"> ... </A>	Create a link to another Web site
<A HREF="MAIL TO:you@xyz.com"> ... </A>	Create a link in order to send an e-mail message
<B> ... </B>	Boldface text
<BLOCKQUOTE> ... </BLOCKQUOTE>	Indents text from the left and right margins
<BODY> ... </BODY>	Encloses the body of the HTML document which is displayed by the browser
 	Creates a line break without extra space
<CENTER> ... </CENTER>	Centers text
<FONT COLOR = "X"> ... </FONT>	Allows use of different font colors e.g., <FONT COLOR = "red">
<FONT FACE = "X"> ... </FONT>	Allows use of different font styles e.g., <FONT FACE = "arial">
<FONT SIZE = "X"> ... </FONT>	Allows change of font size in running text e.g., <FONT SIZE="+2">
<H1> thru <H6> ... </H1> thru </H6>	First- through sixth-level headings
<HEAD> ... </HEAD>	Encloses the heading of the HTML document
<HR>	Creates a horizontal rule line
<HTML> ... </HTML>	Encloses the entire HTML document
<I> ... </I>	Italic text
<IMG SRC="xxx">	Used to insert an in-line image, e.g., <IMG SRC="pic.gif">
<LI>	Used to create list items
	Used in place of a space to create a nonbreaking space so line doesn't overflow line
<OL> ... </OL>	Used to create a numbered or ordered list
<P>	Creates a line break with extra space before start of next text block
<PRE> ... </PRE>	Retains the spacing that is keyed in the text within the tags
<TITLE> ... </TITLE>	Indicates the title of the HTML document
<U> ... </U>	Underlined text
<UL> ... </UL>	Used to create a bulleted or unordered list
<!-- ... -->	Used to insert nondisplayed comments in the HTML document

Note: For a complete listing of HTML codes, check the following Web site: http://www.willcam.com/cmat/html/crossname.html

(Continued)

---

domain name 域名。alias 别名。trick 诀窍。

图 4.2　超文本标记语言（HTML）示例（接上页）

Figure 4.2　(Continued)

Sample of Markup Tags

```
<HTML>
<HEAD>
<TITLE>My Home Page</TITLE></HEAD><BR>
<BODY>
<FONT SIZE="+2"><B><I>Welcome to...</B></I></FONT><BR>
<FONT SIZE="+3"><B><I>My Home Page</B></I></FONT><P>
<IMG SRC="4bird.gif"><P><P><P>
<FONT SIZE="+1">I'm<B>glad</B>you are visiting my home page.
<BR><BR>
<H1>Example of first-level heading</H1>
<H3>Example of third-level heading</H3><P>
<!--This comment will not print on the Web page-->
Following are list items:<BR>
<UL>
<LI>List item #1<BR>
<LI>List item #2<P>
</UL>
<PRE>      A PRE tag allows you to control placement
</FONT></PRE><P>
Send an e-mail message to:
<A HREF="mailto:me@my-isp">me@my-isp</A>
<BR><BR></FONT>
<HR>
<CENTER>
<FONT SIZE="2">Copyright &#169 1996-97.companyname
</CENTER>
</BODY>
</HTML>
```

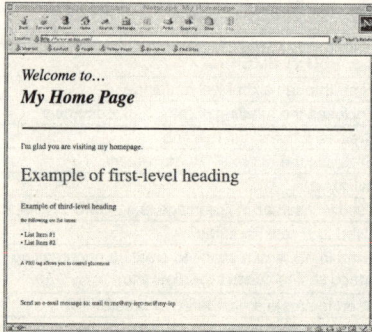

Essential Web Page Tags

```
<HTML>
<HEAD>
    Between the HEAD tags you put the title, meta
    tags, and other nonprinting information
<TITLE>Title of your page goes here</TITLE>
</HEAD>
<BODY>
    Between the BODY tags is where you put all
    information that will be visible on your Web page.
</BODY>
</HTML>
```

推广网页

Getting Out There

拥有一个网站是一回事，让顾客知道它的存在并能够找到它是另外一回事。

It is one thing to have a Web site; it's another that customers know it exists and how to find it. First of all, put your Web site and e-mail addresses on your brochures, flyers, trucks, ships, billboards, ads, stationery, and business cards. Next get your Web site address listed in an Internet business directory such as www.directory.net. There are many such directories, and many do not charge for inclusion. Another is to join a virtual mall—a group of Internet businesses using the metaphor of a shopping mall. Last but not least, be certain to get your address on as many search engines as possible.

搜索引擎
Search Engines

Search engines compile lists for consumers who surf for a product. The trick is to get your address as high on the search engine list as possible. Because engines use different criteria, there are several strategies. First in importance is your domain name. For instance the term "international business" will bring domain names such as internationalbusiness.com or international-business.com or internationalbusiness.org to the top of the list. If your business domain name just used the initials of your company, you will find yourself near the bottom of the list. The right strategy is to use several domain names. The second trick is giving the right title of your Web pages. A title such as "ABCD company discount sunglasses" will come up closer to the top than just the company name. The next criterion is the HTML document. Sunglass.html will get you closer to the top than 1234.doc or abbreviated names.

搜索引擎为上网搜寻产品的顾客汇集了名录。窍门就在于让你的网址在搜索引擎列表中要尽量靠前。

第二个窍门是给你的网页取一个恰当的名字。

TOP SEARCH ENGINES

37.com (searches 37 search engines at once)
google.com
Altavista.com
Infoseek.com
Excite.com
aol.com/netfind
hotbot.com

---

brochure 宣传册。directory 工商名录。charge 收费。metaphor 比喻。compile 汇集。initials（全名的）首字母。abbreviated 缩写的。

lycos.com
webscrawler.com
yahoo.com

寻找外国市场
Finding Foreign Markets

全世界有超过 2 亿的在线用户，其中 1 亿分布在美国和加拿大。

There are more than 200 million online users worldwide; over 100 million are in the United States and Canada. Even so, the potential market is phenomenal because everyone who has a computer or television set is getting on the Net.

Finding foreign buyers continues to be a market research problem. As always, start with the country or region. But where to look? Try the following databases:

STAT-USA/Internet. A service of the U.S. Department of Commerce, this is the site for the U.S. business, economic, and trade community. It provides authoritative information from the federal government. It includes access to the National Trade Data Bank (NTDB) for country and market research. (http://www.stat-usa.gov/)

Strategis. This is a Canadian government trade assistance site which has international trade information and statistics that can be turned into a graphic presentation of the top 10 markets for most products. Follow the international and trade links. (http://www.strategis.ic. gc.ca/engdoc/main.html)

The Central Intelligence Agency. The CIA Fact Book is one of the best sources of basic information on any country. (http://www.odci. gov/cia/ciahome.html)

The SBA Office for International Trade. Extensive links and training resources can be found at http://www.sbaoniine. sba.gov/OIT/info/Iinks.html.

Michigan State University, Center for International Business and Education Research (CIBER). International Business Resources on the WWW. It has one of the best and most extensive sites for international markets, trade leads, and hotlinks on all aspects of global markets. (http://ciber.bus.msu.edu/busres.htm)

---

phenomenal 非凡的。authoritative 权威的。statistics 统计数据。Central Intelligence Agency（美国）中央情报局。SBA（美国）小企业管理局。extensive 大量的。hotlink 热链接。

Tradeport. This is one of the most extensive international trade resources on the Internet. A free site with market information, guidance, and resource listing as well as trade leads and international events in the southern California area. (http://www.tradeport.org)

寻找国外买家
Finding Foreign Buyers

Of course there are over 400 trade lead sites: the United Nations (www.un.org) and the World Trade Centers Association (www.wtca.org) have lead services. To reach over 2 million traders, try these resources:

NEOS—National Export Offer Service. A comprehensive site for links and access to foreign buyers, directories, and guidance resources. (http://www.exportservices.com)

Europages. Contains information on 500,000 companies in 30 countries. Excellent place to search for companies to contact, by product or service search as buyers or for market research. (http://www.europages.com)

Clear Freight. Follow the trade lead links section for an extensive set of contacts and go back to the main page for freight forwarder information. (http://www.clearfreight.com)

Global Electronic Commerce Korea. Great site with links to many other countries with company directories. Try EC Links for an extensive list of other areas and trade lead sites. (http://www.commerce. ktnet.co.kr)

Beaucoup. A search engine directory that also lists country-specific searches and several directories in each country. (http://www.beaucoup.com)

Europeonline. A central access site to all countries in Europe in local languages and English, for business, financial, and general information. Access to European Union info and europages. (http://www.europeonline.com)

Trade Show Central. A free Internet service providing information on more than 50,000 trade shows, conferences, and seminars; 5,000 service providers; and 8,000 venues and facilities around the world. (http://www.tscentral.com/)

---

comprehensive 详尽的，全面的。 freight forwarder 货运代理。 European Union 欧盟。 trade show 贸易展览。

政府采购
Government Procurement

自从世贸组织对政府采购投标以法律形式进行规定后，政府采购便面临来自全球的竞争。

Ever since the World Trade Organization formalized opportunities for bidding, government procurement competition has become worldwide. Here are a few valuable addresses:

www.wto.org/

www.arnet.gov

www.texas-one.org/market/newposts.html

www.financenet.gov/financenet/sales/saleint.html

www.Jetro.go.jp

www.govcon.com

www.sbaonline.sba.gov

产品定价和营销
Pricing and Marketing Your Product

任意定价的日子已经远去。由于互联网提供了世界性的开放，没有实质内容的定价已经一去不复返。

Gone are the days of arbitrary pricing. Because the Internet offers worldwide openness, pricing without substance is gone forever. You must continually check the market and competition and provide additional services and features as necessary to maintain your price. Places to search are www.price.com or mysimon.com.

营销技巧
Marketing Techniques

互联网是一个由创造力主宰的地方。

The Internet is a place where creativity reigns. Here are some techniques that have been evolving as the Web has grown from childhood to adolescence:

- Set up a chat area or a blog
- Sell advertising on your page
- Create contests for your customers

---

formalize 使正式化。bidding 投标。arbitrary 任意的。reign 主宰，支配。

- Build customer lists
- Offer a free catalog
- Offer coupons
- Provide information
- Publish a newsletter
- Sell access to your products and services
- Upload your annual report

沟通交流
Communications

If you don't have an e-mail address, you may as well pack up and move to the South Pole. In today's business world, an e-mail address is a must.

E-mail is currently being used 10 to 1 over postal services, and the rate of change is growing. Business contracts are being negotiated between nations via e-mail routinely. This author recently negotiated book contracts with a London publisher by e-mail.

目前电子邮件的使用数量是邮政服务的十倍，并且还在持续增长。

付款方式
Getting Paid

Yes, you can ask for cash, you can take checks, PayPal, or accept credit cards, but the world's standard method of payment for big sales is still the documentary letter of credit (see Chapter 6 for a more complete discussion). The Internet is able to combine technology with standard business systems to continue to use the letter of credit as an easy, trustworthy payment method.

你可以要求现金支付，也可以用支票、贝宝或信用卡支付，但世界上大宗交易的标准支付方式仍然是使用跟单信用证。

Internet technologies available include: document management software, document imaging, electronic mail, interactive forms within Web browsers, and password security protocols. One source of good information about this subject is www.AVGTSG.com, a company that specializes in payment solutions relating to the Internet.

互联网技术包括：文档管理软件、文档影像、电子邮件、互动形式的网页浏览器以及密码安全协议。

---

catalog 商品名录。coupon（购物）优惠券。annual report 年报。pack up 收拾行李。negotiate 协商。routine 常规的。letter of credit 信用证。interactive 互动的。

保持联系
Keeping in Touch

国际贸易中的一切变化如此
之快，以至于大多数商务人
士都发现很难跟上节奏。

Things are changing so fast in international trade that most business people find it difficult to keep up. However, here are several publications that seem to keep up with the trends:

www.baidu.com

www.alibaba.com

www.taobao.com

www.AliPay.com

www.tradeport.com

www.aaatrading.com

www.exporter.com

www.worldtrademag.com

www.exporttoday.com

www.AVGTSG.com

www.pangaea.net

www.tradecompass.com

www.euromktg.com

www.fedex.com

www.dhl.com

www.bankamerica.com

www.worldbank.com

www.merklerweb.com/imall/imall/htm

未来如何
What About the Future?

Eliminating cultural differences is one of the goals of Internet trade. Some people can't get past their feelings about differences and therefore they don't trade with foreigners.

A text-based system suitable for smaller businesses with the same rules for everyone is needed. However, it should be one that would allow

建立一个基于本文、适合小
企业、规则统一的体系是必
要的。

---

keep up with the trend 紧跟时代潮流。eliminate 消除。

us to close a deal quickly, but not before we can check on performance and financial background. A corollary, and most important, the system must be secure.

Are you familiar with the Chinese Web site Alibaba.com (essentially a Chinese manufacturer's business directory)? This company has been growing at a phenomenal rate since about 2001 (along with others such a FITA, Europages, and tradeleads.com).

Alibaba is somewhat different from sites in other countries because it is continually finding new ways of leveraging technology to enhance its overall value proposition. Alibaba recently struck a deal with Microsoft to begin implementing real-time communications (essentially like MSN instant messenger) in its platform so that as buyers find potential suppliers, they can instantly form a dialogue. This essentially breaks new ground for the future of trade on the Internet—not because of where Alibaba is now but because of where it will be going. It signals a new paradigm in international trade.

阿里巴巴与其他国家的网站有所不同，它总是在找寻新方法来利用科技提升公司的整体价值主张。

这从根本上开拓了未来网上贸易的新天地——不是因为阿里巴巴现在身处哪里，而是它未来要去往何方。这标志着国际贸易的一个新范式。

电子商务法
E-commerce Law

The laws governing e-commerce are constantly changing. This author does not claim to be an expert in this area but encourages those participating in this important area of world business to become familiar with the latest methods. Here are a few sources you may find useful:

euro.ecom.cmu.edu/resources/elibrary/ecllinks.shtml

www.bakernet.com/ecommerce

www.knowthis.com/legal/internetlaw.htm

www.mbc.com/ecommerce/ecom_overview.asp

www.denniskennedy.com/resources/technology-law-central/ecomlaw.aspx

www.weblaw.co.uk

The next chapter further expands the concepts related to both import and export, developing the fundamentals needed to "complete the transaction," namely, financing, avoiding risk, shipping, and documentation.

---

corollary 必然的结果。leverage 利用。value proposition 价值主张（即公司通过其产品和服务向消费者提供的价值）。real-time 实时的。paradigm 范式。fundamentals 基本原则。documentation 单据。

推荐读物
Further Readings

Alfonsi, Benjamin, "Web globalization," IEEE Distributed Systems Online, Vol. No. 1, 2005.

Bishop, Mark, *How to Build a Successful International Web Site*, Coriolis Group Books, 1997. An excellent detailed instruction manual for creating an international Web site, including software for language editing and information on international search engines.

Block, David, "*Globalization, Transnational Communication and the Internet,*" Institute of Education, London University, 2003.

Clarke, George R. G., and Scott J. Wallsten, "Evidence from Industrial and Developing Countries," World Bank Policy Research Working paper 3215, February 2004.

Cronin, Mary, *Doing More Business on the Internet*, Wiley, 1995.

Easton, Jaclyn, *Striking It Rich.com—Profiles of 23 Incredibly Successful Websites You've Probably Never Heard Of*, McGraw-Hill, 1998. A very exciting collection of accounts of a wide variety of Web sites and how they achieved success. This book contains the mistakes, ideas, and insights of different online businesses and provides a great understanding of what it takes to achieve success. Her active Web site contains updates on the subjects and keeps the book from being outdated.

Ellsworth, Jill, and Matthew Ellsworth, *The Internet Business Book*, John Wiley, 1994.

Emery, Vince, *How to Grow Your Business on the Internet* (3rd Ed.), Coriolis Group Books, 1996. A most comprehensive discussion of the best Internet business strategies, marketing strategies, and many aspects of online business, based on actual experience and several years of active participation in the field. Also has an active Web site.

Gilster, Paul, *The Internet Navigator*, John Wiley, 1993.

Lundquist, Leslie Heeter, *Selling Online for Dummies*, IDG Books Worldwide, 2000. A basic instruction manual for setting up business online and developing a Web site and the tools to enhance business results. Also comes with a package of software tools and tips.

Resnick, Rosalind, and Dave Taylor, *The Internet Business Guide* (2nd Ed.), Sams Publishing, 1995.

Schwartz, Evan, *Webonomics: Nine Essential Principles for Growing your Business on the World Wide Web*, Broadway Books, 1998. An excellent analysis about what works online and what does not work. Contains fundamental insights into Internet business, global or otherwise. Schwartz also publishes an e-mail newsletter for readers and subscribers.

Smith, Bud, and Frank Catalano, *Marketing Online for Dummies*, IDG Books Worldwide, 1998. A comprehensive guide to marketing strategies online and includes a software package with many tools.

CHAPTER 5

COMPLETING A SUCCESSFUL TRANSACTION

成功达成交易

In Chapter 2 you learned the basics of start-up. Chapter 3 led you through the concepts of planning and negotiating a transaction. Then Chapter 4 explained how to compete using e-commerce. This chapter covers the remaining commonalties, that is, paying for the goods and physically moving them from one country to another.

Now, are you ready for the steps needed to complete an import or export transaction? They are:

本章包括共性知识篇的剩余部分，即有关商品付款和将商品从一国运输到另一国的内容。

1. Financing
2. E-banking
3. Avoiding risk
4. Letters of credit
5. Physical distribution (packing and shipping)
6. Documentation

融 资
Financing

To start, expand, or take advantage of opportunities, all businesses need new money sooner or later. By *new money* we mean money that we have not yet earned but that can become the engine for growth.

新注入资金指的是尚未挣得、但可能拉动增长的新资金。

For the importer, financing offers the ability to pay for the overseas manufacture and shipment of foreign goods destined for the domestic market. For the exporter, financing could mean working capital to pay for international travel and the marketing effort. New money can also be loans to foreign buyers so that buyers can purchase an exporter's goods.

融资使进口商有能力支付海外制造费用，以及将商品从国外运往国内市场的费用。对出口商而言，融资可能意味着获得支付国际旅行和营销方面的运营资本。

If the homework phase is done well and purchase orders for the product(s) are in hand, there is plenty of currency available—banks or factors are waiting to assist.

银 行
The Bank

Commercial banking is the primary industry that supports the financing of importing and exporting. Selection of a banking partner is an essential part of the teamwork required for international trade success. When shopping for a bank, look for the following:

商业银行是支持进出口融资的主要机构。选择银行伙伴是国际贸易取得成功必不可少的一部分。

1. A strong international department
2. E-banking
3. Speed in handling transactions (does it want to make money on your money—called the *float*?)
4. The bank's relationship with overseas banks (that is, does it have corresponding relationships with banks in the countries in which you wish to do business?)
5. Credit policy

HOT TIP

In the import/export industry there is a saying: "Walk on two legs." This means that you should choose carefully and then work closely with a good international bank and a customs broker/freight forwarder.

在进出口行业中有一种"两条腿走路"的说法。这意味着你应当谨慎选择，与信誉良好的国际银行和报关行／货运代理紧密合作。

---

destined for 运往（某处）。working capital 运营资本。factor 保理商。commercial bank 商业银行。float（货币汇率）浮动。

电子银行
E-banking

Electronic banking (e-banking) is an umbrella term for the process by which customers perform banking transactions electronically without physically visiting an institution. The following terms all refer to one form or another of electronic banking:

电子银行是一个大概念，指的是顾客通过电子手段进行银行交易，而不用亲自去银行的过程。

- Personal computer (PC) banking
- Internet banking
- Virtual banking
- Online banking
- Home banking
- Remote electronic banking
- Phone banking

Personal computer banking, Internet, or online banking are the most frequently used designations. It should be noted, however, that the terms used to describe the various types of electronic banking are often used interchangeably.

个人电脑银行、互联网银行或在线银行是几个最常用的名称。

This form of banking enables customers to execute transactions from a computer via a modem. The bank typically offers the customer a proprietary financial software program that allows the customer to perform financial transactions from his or her home computer. The customer then dials into the bank with his or her modem, downloads data, and runs the programs that are resident on the customer's computer.

Currently, many banks offer banking systems that allow customers to obtain account balances and credit card statements, pay bills, and transfer funds between accounts.

目前，很多银行系统允许顾客查看账户余额和信用卡账单以及进行还款、转账等操作。

The alternative method is often called Internet banking. You enter your personal account on the bank's Web site with a coded personal identification number (PIN). Internet banking uses the Internet as the delivery channel by which, for example, we transfer funds, pay bills, view checking and savings account balances, pay mortgages, and purchase financial instruments and certificates of deposit. An Internet banking customer accesses his or her accounts from a browser—software that runs Internet banking programs resident on the bank's World Wide

互联网银行顾客通过浏览器进入其账户，浏览器所运行的银行软件位于银行万维网

---

designation 名称。execute 实施。proprietary 专营的。resident 存在。

的服务器，而非用户的个人计算机上。

Web server, not on the user's PC. A true Internet bank is one that provides account balances and some transactional capabilities to retail customers over the World Wide Web. Internet banks are also known as virtual, cyber, Net, interactive, or Web banks.

Online currencies such as PayPal and Internetcash have increased e-commerce sales to just under $16 billion per quarter in 2006, from about $6 billion in 1999.

Paypal 和 Internetcash 是这样运作的：消费者通过提供银行卡或信用卡信息为账户充值，然后就可以向任何有电子邮件的人转账了。经由 Paypal 和 Internetcash 的钱可以通过支票撤回或转至银行账户。

PayPal and Internetcash work like this: A consumer funds an account by providing his or her bank or credit card information. The consumer can then send funds to anyone with an e-mail address. Funds from PayPal or Internetcash can be withdrawn by check or transferred to a bank account.

一些网络银行没有设立实体网点。在某些情况下，网络银行并不局限于国内交易，还可以进行大宗资产的即时交易。

Some Internet banks exist without physical branches. In some cases, Web banks are not restricted to conducting transactions within national borders and have the ability to conduct transactions involving large amounts of assets instantaneously. According to industry analysts, electronic banking provides a variety of attractive possibilities for remote account access, including:

- Availability of inquiry and transaction services around the clock
- Worldwide connectivity
- Easy access to transaction data, both recent and historical
- Direct customer control of international movement of funds without intermediation of financial institutions in customer's jurisdiction

银行融资形式
Forms of Bank Financing

国际贸易贷款分为两类：担保贷款和无担保贷款。

Loans for international trade fall into two categories: secured and unsecured.

担保融资
Secured Financing

通过抵押物进行的融资即为

Banks are not high risk takers. To reduce their exposure to loss, they often ask for collateral. Financing against collateral is called *secured*

---

withdraw 撤回。instantaneously 瞬间。around the clock 昼夜不停。intermediation 金融机构中介费用。jurisdiction 管辖权。collateral 抵押物。

financing and is the most common method of raising new money. Banks will advance funds against payment obligations, shipment documents, or storage documents. Most common of these is advancement of funds against payment obligations or documentary title. In this case, the trader pledges the goods for export or import as collateral for a loan to finance those goods. The bank maintains a secure position by accepting as collateral documents that convey title such as negotiable bills of lading, warehouse receipts, or trust receipts.

担保融资，这是最常见的一种筹资方式。银行将提前履行给付义务，预付运输单据或仓储单据。

Another popular method of obtaining secured financing is the *banker's acceptance* (BA). This is a time draft presented to a bank by an exporter. This differs from what is known as a *trade acceptance* between buyer and seller in which a bank is not involved. The bank stamps and signs the draft "accepted" on behalf of its client, the importer. By accepting the draft, the bank undertakes and recognizes the obligation to pay the draft at maturity and has placed its creditworthiness between the exporter (*drawer*) and the importer (*drawee*). Banker's acceptances are negotiable instruments that can be sold in the money market. The BA rate is a discount rate generally two to three points below the prime rate. With the full creditworthiness of the bank behind the draft, eligible BAs attract the very best of market interest rates. The criteria for eligibility are:

另外一种通用的担保融资方式为银行承兑汇票。这是一种由出口商递交给银行的远期汇票。

银行承兑汇票之后，就承担并承认了在到期日支付汇票的义务，并在出口商（开票人）和进口商（受票人）之间建立起信用。

1. The BA must be created within 30 days of the shipment of the goods.
2. The maximum tenor is 180 days after shipment.
3. It must be self-liquidating.
4. It cannot be used for working capital purposes.
5. The credit recipient must attest to no duplication.

Shipping documents. Commercial invoices, bills of lading, insurance certificates, consular invoices, and related documents.
Draft. The same as a "bill of exchange." A written order for a certain sum of money to be transferred on a certain date from the person who owes the money or agrees to make the payment

承运收据，商业发票、海运提单、保险凭证、领事发票以及相关单据。

汇票，债务人或同意支付的一方（汇票受票人）在某一确定日期，向债权人（汇票

advance 预付（金）。pledge 抵押。banker's acceptance（B/A）银行承兑汇票。time draft 远期汇票。trade acceptance 贸易承兑。maturity 到期。drawer 开票人。drawee 受票人。discount rate 贴现率。prime rate（银行的）最低贷款利率。tenor 票期，合约期。self-liquidating 能迅速变现的。

开票人）支付一定金额的书
面支付命令。另见词汇表中
"定期汇票"、"跟单汇票"、
"即期汇票" 和 "远期汇票"。

(the drawee) to the creditor to whom the money is owed (the
drawer of the draft). See glossary for "date draft," "documentary
draft," "sight draft," and "time draft."

无担保贷款
Unsecured Financing

事实上，无担保贷款只针对
那些在所在银行有良好信用
状况，或拥有长期贸易经验
的进出口商。

In truth, *unsecured financing* is only for those who have a sound credit
standing with their bank or have had long-term trading experience. It
usually amounts to expanding already existing lines of working credit.
For the small importer/exporter unsecured financing will probably be
limited to a personal line of credit.

保理商
Factors

保理商指的是以折扣价（通
常是账款总额的 5% 至 8%）
购买应收账款的代理商。银
行承担了 95% 代收账款业
务，其余 5% 的保理工作通
过私人专家完成。保理商通
过托收获利，并且能为卖方
提供现金流的来源，尽管数
额比企业亲自托收要低。

A *factor* is an agent who will, at a discount (usually 5 to 8 percent of the
gross), buy receivables. Banks do 95 percent of factoring; the remainder is done by private specialists. The factor makes a profit on the collection and provides a source of cash flow for the seller, albeit less than
if the business had held out to make the collection itself.

For example, suppose you had a receivable of $1,000. A factor might
offer you a $750 advance on the invoice and charge you 5 percent on
the gross of $1,000 per month until collection. If the collection is made
within the first month, the factor would keep only $50 and return $200.
If it takes two months, the factor would keep $100 and return only
$150, and so on.

进口商从中获得的好处是，
可以用现金再订购海外产
品。制造商的收益在于获得
现金流，用于扩大生产或制
造新产品。

The importer benefits from having the cash to reorder products from
overseas. For a manufacturer, the benefit can be cash flow available for
increased or new production.

其他私人融资渠道
Other Private Sources of Financing

The United States has several major private trade financing institutions,
all in competition to support your export programs.

---

credit standing 信用状况。line of credit 信贷额度。receivables 应收账款。collection 托收。reorder 再订购。

私人出口融资公司（PEFCO）
Private Export Funding Corporation (PEFCO)

The Private Export Funding Corporation (PEFCO) was established in 1970 and is owned by about 60 banks, 7 industrial corporations, and an investment banking firm. PEFCO operates with its own capital stock, an extensive line of credit from the U.S. government's EXIM Bank, and the proceeds of its secured and unsecured debt obligations. It provides medium- and long-term loans, subject to EXIM Bank approval, to foreign buyers of U.S. goods and services. PEFCO generally deals in sales of capital goods with a minimum commitment of about $1 million—there is no maximum. Contact: PEFCO, 280 Park Ave. (4-West), New York, NY 10017; phone: (212) 916-0300; fax: (212) 286-0304; e-mail: info@pefco.com; www.pefco.com

私人出口融资公司通过自身股本、美国政府进出口银行提供的贷款，以及从担保贷款和无担保贷款中获取的收益来运营。

海外私人投资公司（OPIC）
Overseas Private Investment Corporation (OPIC)

The Overseas Private Investment Corporation (OPIC) is a private, self-sustaining institution whose purpose is to promote economic growth in developing countries. OPIC's programs include insurance, finance, missions, contractors' and exporters' insurance programs, small contractors' guarantee programs, and investor information services. For more information: OPIC, 1615 M Street NW, Washington, DC 20527; phone: (202) 336-8400; fax: (202) 408-9859; www.opic.gov

海外私人投资公司经营的项目包括保险、融资、出访考察、承包商和出口商保险、小型承包商担保以及投资人信息服务。

政府渠道
Government Sources

Many nations are short on foreign exchange, and what they have is earmarked for priority national imports and to service large international credit commitments. Nevertheless, there are probably more sources of competitive financing available today to support exporting than at any other time in history. The major complaint is that not enough firms are taking advantage of the programs.

许多国家外汇短缺，只能将现有外汇投入国家重点进口和大宗国际信贷中。

小企业管理局（SBA）
Small Business Administration (SBA)

All nations support the growth of small business. For example the U.S. government has a Small Business Administration (SBA), which guarantees that small companies that can show reasonable ability to pay

以隶属美国政府的小企业管理局为例，该局确保具备合理偿还能力的小企业以不高

---

capital stock 股本。proceeds 收益。subject to 以某事物为条件，取决于某事物。
self-sustaining 自给的。insurance 保险。guarantee 担保。earmark 指定款项的用途。

于银行最低贷款率 4.25% 的利率，获得为期十年的流动资金贷款。

小企业管理局的出口周转信用额度担保项目，为生产或购买商品销往外国市场的小企业提供出口前融资，并帮助其进入或开发国外市场。

进出口银行针对已找到销路，但买方未能在所在国找到融资途径的出口商，为其提供贷款、担保和保险等形式的小企业信贷支持。

项目包括中长期贷款和担保，最高可涵盖出口交易金额的 85%，偿还期限为一年或一年以上。

国际开发总署是美国国会的下属分支机构，主要为欠发

can get 10-year working capital loans for not more than prime plus 4.25 percent. The maximum maturity may be up to 25 years, depending on the use of the loan proceeds. Interest rates can be negotiated between borrowers and lenders, subject to SBA maximums pegged at prime rate. The SBA's export revolving-line-of-credit guarantee program provides pre-export financing for the manufacture or purchase of goods for sale to foreign markets and to help a small business penetrate or develop a foreign market. The maximum maturity for this financing is 18 months. The SBA, in cooperation with the Export–Import Bank, participates in loans of between $200,000 and $1 million.

进出口银行
Export–Import (EXIM) Bank

For those exporters who have found a sale, but the buyer can't find the financing in her or his own country, the Export–Import (EXIM) Bank has funds available to provide credit support in the form of loans, guarantees, and insurance for small businesses. The Export–Import Bank of the United States is a federal agency to help finance the export of U.S. goods and services. Rates vary but are available for a 5- to 10-year maturity period.

Programs include medium- and long-term loans and guarantees that cover up to 85 percent of a transaction's export value with repayment terms of one year or longer. Long-term loans and guarantees are provided for over seven years but not usually more than 10 years. The Medium-Term Credit Program has more than $300 million available for small businesses facing subsidized foreign competition. The Small Business Credit Program also has funds available, with direct credit for exporting medium term goods; competition is not necessary. The EXIM Working Capital Program (EWCP) guarantees the lender's repayment on short-term capital loans for exports with 0- to 10-year repayment periods. Web site contact can be made at www.exim.gov.

国际开发总署
The Agency for International Development (AID)

This organization, a subordinate division of the U.S. State Department, provides loans and grants to less-developed countries for both

---

peg 使（价格）固定或维持在某水平。revolving line of credit 周转信用额度。penetrate 进入。subsidized（政府）补贴的。repayment 偿还款。

developmental and foreign policy reasons. Under the AID Development Assistance Program funds are available at rates of 2 and 3 percent over 40 years. The AID Economic Development Fund also has funds at similar interest rates. Generally, these funds are available through invitations to bid through the *Commerce Daily Bulletin*, a publication available from the Government Printing Office, Washington, DC 20402; phone: (202) 712-0600; fax (202) 216-3524; e-mail: inquiries@ usaid.gov; Web site: www.usaid.gov.

达国家提供贷款和拨款，致力于推动其发展和外交。

国际开发合作总署
The International Development Cooperation Agency (IDCA)

This organization sponsors a Trade and Development Program (TDP), and loans funds on an annual basis so that friendly countries can procure foreign goods and services for major development projects. Often, these funds support smaller firms in subcontract positions.

国际开发合作总署资助了贸易与发展计划（TDP），并且每年对友好国家提供贷款，使之能够采购外国商品和服务，用于重大发展项目。

规避风险
Avoiding Risk

Doing business always involves some risk, so you should expect across-border business to be no different. A certain amount of uncertainty is always present in doing business across international borders, but much of it can be hedged, managed, and controlled. All major exporting countries have arrangements to protect exporters and the bankers who provide their funding support. Avoiding and/or controlling risks in global trade is an everyday occurrence for importers and exporters. Understanding the instruments available for avoiding risk is not difficult but is vital. There are essentially four kinds of risks:

风险永远与商业并存，跨境贸易也不例外。

了解一些可行的规避风险的手段并不困难，却至关重要。

- *Commercial risks.*   Not being paid; non-delivery of goods; insolvency or protracted default by the buyer; competition; and disputes over product, warranty, and so forth.
- *Foreign exchange risks.*   Foreign exchange fluctuations.
- *Political risks.*   War, coup d'état, revolution, expropriation, expulsion, foreign exchange controls, or cancellation of import or export licenses.

Commerce Daily Bulletin 每日商务公报。subcontract 分包，转包。hedge 增值，保值。insolvency 破产，无力偿还。default 违约（尤指未偿还债务）。warranty 保单。fluctuation 变动。coup d'etat（法语）政变。expropriation 没收，征收。

- *Shipping risks.* Risk of damage and/or loss at sea or via other transportation.

Most risks allow for a method of avoidance. Of course, there is no insurance for such problems as disputes over quality or loss of markets resulting from competition, but there are management instruments for three aspects of risk: not being paid, loss or damage, and foreign exchange exposure.

规避商业风险
Avoidance of Commercial Risk

一旦货物发出，卖方应确保买方将按时付款。目标在于至少能够将对方不支付的风险降到最低。另一方面，买方需要确认卖方按时发货，且货物确实与订单所述相同。

规避风险的两个关键措施是检查买方的信用评级和声誉，以及拟定销售合同。

The *seller* would like to be certain that the buyer will pay on time once the goods have been shipped. The goal is to at least minimize the risk of nonpayment. On the other hand, the *buyer* wants to be certain the seller will deliver on time and that the goods are exactly what the buyer ordered.

These concerns are most often heard from anyone beginning an import/export business. Mistrust across international borders is natural; after all, there is a certain amount of mistrust even in our own culture. Two keys to risk avoidance is a check of the buyer's credit rating and reputation, as well as a well-written sales contract. In Chapter 3 you learned that an early step in the process of international trade is to gain contract agreement with your overseas business associate. This should include the method of payment.

付　款
Getting Paid

根据大多数商务人士跨国经营的经验，海外坏账率很少超过销售额的 0.5%。这是因为在海外市场中，良好的资信状况需要通过长期的及时付款才能建立起来。

付款方式按照卖方风险从高到低依次为：记账赊销、寄售、银行汇票（远期汇票和

Ensuring prompt payment worries exporters more than any other factor. The truth is that the likelihood of a bad debt from an international customer is very low. In the experience of most international business people, overseas bad debts seldom exceed 0.5 percent of sales. The reason is that in overseas markets, credit is still something to be earned as a result of having a record of prompt payment. Use common sense in extending credit to overseas customers, but don't use tougher rules than you use for your domestic clients.

The methods of payment, in order of decreasing risk to the seller are: open account, consignment, bank drafts (time draft, sight draft),

---

instrument 手段。mistrust 不信任。credit rating 信用评级。prompt 及时的。extend 提供。consignment 寄售。

authority to purchase, letter of credit, and cash in advance. Table 5.1 summarizes and compares the various methods of payment in order of decreasing risk to the exporter and increasing risk to the importer. Other useful methods that enable paperless trading between companies are Electronic Data Interchange, or EDI (www.EDI.com); Swift (www.swift.com); and Bolero (www.bolero.net).

即期汇票），委托付款，信用证和交货前付现款。

记账赊销
Open Account
The *open account* is a trade arrangement in which goods are shipped to a foreign buyer without guarantee of payment. Though the riskiest, many firms that have a long-standing business relationship with the same overseas firm use this method. Needless to say, the key is to know your buyer and your buyer's country. You should use an open account when the buyer has a continuing need for the seller's product or service. Some experienced exporters say that they deal only in open accounts. But they

记账赊销指的是在没有支付保函的情况下，将商品提前运送给国外买家的支付方法。

表 5.1   不同支付方式的比较
Table 5.1 Comparison of Various Methods of Payment

(In order of decreasing risk to exporter and increasing risk to importer)

Method	Goods Available to Buyers	Usual Time of Payment	Exporter Risk	Importer Risk
Open account	Before payment	As agreed	Most: relies on importer to pay account	Least
Consignment	Before payment	After sold	Maximum: exporter retains title	Minor inventory cost
Time draft	Before payment	On maturity of draft	High: relies on importer to pay draft	Minimal check of quantity/ quality
Sight draft	After payment	On presenting draft to importer	If unpaid, goods are returned/ disposed	Little if inspection report required
Authority to purchase	After payment	On presenting draft	Be careful of recourse	Little if inspection report required
Letter of credit	After payment	When documents are available after shipment	None	None if inspection report required
Cash	After payment	Before shipment	Least	Most

---

paperless trading 无纸贸易。needless to say 不用说。time draft 远期汇票。sight draft 即期汇票。

always preface that statement by saying that they have close relationships and have been doing business with those overseas clients for many years. An open account can be risky unless the buyer is of unquestioned integrity and has withstood a thorough credit investigation. The advantage of this method is its ease and convenience, but with open-account sales, you bear the burden of financing the shipment. Standard practice in many countries is to defer payment until the merchandise is sold, sometimes even longer. Therefore, among the forms of payment, open-account sales require the greatest amount of working capital. In addition, you bear the exchange rate if the sales are quoted in foreign currency. Nevertheless, competitive pressures may force the use of this method.

记账赊销付款方式的优势在于简单、便捷，但选择这种方式意味着你要承担运费。

HOT TIP

Relationships between buyer and seller make the difference by reducing mistrust. Make an effort to meet and get to know your trading partner.

买卖双方的关系对减少彼此间的不信任有影响。应努力去认识和了解你的贸易伙伴。

寄 售
Consignment
The seller (consignor) retains title to the goods during shipment and storage of the product in the warehouse or retail store. The consignee acts as a selling agent, selling the goods and remitting the net proceeds to the consignor. Like open-account sales, consignment sales can also be risky, and they lend themselves to only certain kinds of merchandise. Great care should be taken in working out this contractual arrangement. Be sure it is covered with adequate risk insurance.

在运输、仓储和零售期间，卖方（发货人）对货物保有所有权。收货人充当销售代理的角色，即负责销售商品并将净收益汇给发货人。

银行汇票、远期汇票和即期汇票
Bank Drafts, Time Drafts, and Sight Drafts
Payment for many sales is arranged using one of many time-tested banking methods. *Bank drafts* (bills of exchange), *time drafts*, and *sight drafts* are each useful under certain circumstances.

Bank Drafts   Bank drafts are simply written orders that activate payment either at sight or at "tenor," which is a future time or date. A bank

简单来说，银行汇票指的是在见票时，未来某一时间或

---

preface 以……为开端。integrity 诚信。credit investigation 信用调查。defer 延期，推迟。consignor 发货人。consignee 收货人。remit 汇款。time-tested 久经考验的。

draft is a check, drawn by a bank on another bank, used primarily where it is necessary for the customer to provide funds payable at a bank in some distant location. The exporter who undertakes this payment method can offer a range of payment options to the overseas customer.

合约到期日，起动支付的书面命令。

Time (Date) Draft   This is an acceptance order drawn by the exporter on the importer (customer), payable a certain number of days after "sight" (presentation) to the holder. Think of it as nothing more than an IOU, or promise to pay in the future.

远期汇票指由出口商开具，要求进口方（客户）在"见票"若干天后承兑的汇票。

Documents such as negotiable bills of lading, insurance certificates, and commercial invoices accompany the draft and are submitted through the exporter's bank for collection. When presented to the importer at the bank, the importer acknowledges that the documents are acceptable and commits to pay by writing "accepted" on the draft and signing it. The importer normally has 30 to 180 days depending on the draft's term to make payments to the bank for transmittal.

其他需由出口方银行提交、托收时与汇票一起出具的单据包括可转让提单、保险凭证和商业发票。当单据由银行呈递给进口方时，进口方便承认了票据的可承兑性，并在汇票上签署"承兑"字样，即承诺在汇票到期时付款。

Sight Draft   This is similar to the time draft except that the importer's bank holds the documents until the importer releases the funds. Sight drafts are the most common method employed by exporters throughout the world. Sight drafts are nothing more than a written order on a standardized bank format requesting money from the overseas buyer. While this method costs less than the letter of credit (defined below), it has greater risk because the importer can refuse to honor the draft.

即期汇票与远期汇票类似，唯一的不同在于，在进口方放款之前，即期汇票将由进口方银行持有。

Bill of lading. A document that provides the terms of the contract between the shipper and the transportation company to move freight between stated points at a specified charge.

Commercial or customs invoice. A bill for the goods from the seller to the buyer. It is one method used by governments to determine the value of the goods for customs valuation purposes.

At sight. Indicates that a negotiable instrument is to be paid upon presentation or demand.

提单，提单为承运人和托运公司之间以特定运价、在指定地点间运输货物提供了合同条款依据。

商业发票或关税发票，由卖方向买方开具的货物票据。这是政府在关税估价时用来判断货物价值的一种凭据。

即期，即期或见票即付意味着可流通票据在见票时或对方要求时应立即支付。

IOU 借据。bill of lading 提单。commercial invoice 商业发票。transmittal 传送。honor 兑现。shipper 托运人。customs valuation 关税估价。negotiable instrument 可流通票据。

委托购买证明确了出口商可以向进口商方银行开具跟单汇票的银行。这种支付方式的问题在于，进口商若不支付汇票，银行可向出口商行使追索权。如果出口商同意这种支付方式，建议在委托购买证和汇票上具体说明"无追索权"。

远期汇票、即期汇票和委托购买证的主要风险在于买方可以拒绝付款或者选择收货。而要求对方凭单付款可以规避这种风险。

信用证是久经时间考验的一种支付方式，即若能确保所有单据与信用证条款完全一致，进口方银行将付款给出口方的凭证。

几乎所有跟单信用证都依循《商业跟单信用证统一惯例》运作，该惯例得到了 156 个国家银行业的认可。

委托购买证
Authority to Purchase

This method is occasionally used in the Far East. It specifies a bank where the exporter can draw a documentary draft on the importer's bank. The problem with this method is that if the importer fails to pay the draft, the bank has "recourse" to the exporter for settlement. If an exporter consents to this method, it is suggested that the authority to purchase specify "without recourse" and so state on drafts.

The major risk with the time, sight, and authority to purchase methods is that the buyer can refuse to pay or to pick up the goods. The method of avoidance is to require cash against documents. Unfortunately, this method is slow because banks are slow in transferring funds because they want to use the time float (short-term investment of bank money) to earn interest. Using a wire transfer can get around this.

信用证（L/C）
Letters of Credit (L/C)

Ideally an exporter would deal only in cash, but in reality, few business people are initially able or willing to do business under those terms. Because of the risk of non-payment resulting from insolvency, bankruptcy, or other severe deterioration, procedures and documents have been developed that help to ensure that foreign buyers honor their agreements.

The most common form of collection is payment against a *letter of credit* (L/C). The L/C is the time-tested method in which an importer's bank guarantees that if all documents are presented in exact conformity with the terms of the L/C, it will pay the exporter. The procedure is not difficult to understand, and most cities have banks with persons familiar with L/C's mechanics.

This method is well understood by traders around the world, is simple, and is as good as your bank. Internationally the term *documentary credits* is synonymous with the term *letter of credit*. They involve thousands of transactions and billions of dollars every day in every part of the world. They are almost always operated in accordance with the Uniform Customs and Practice for Documentary Credits of the International Chamber of Commerce, a code of practice that is recognized by banking communities in 156 countries. A *Guide to Documentary Operations*, which includes all the standard forms, is available from ICC Publishing Corporation, Inc., 156 Fifth Avenue, Suite 417, New York,

---

documentary draft 跟单汇票。recourse 追索权。cash against document 凭单付款。wire transfer 电汇。deterioration 损耗。documentary credit 跟单信用（证）。

NY 10010; phone: (212) 206-1150; fax: (212) 633-6025; e-mail pub@ iccwbo.org; Web address: www.iccbooks.com.

An L/C is a document issued by a bank at the importer's or buyer's request in favor of the seller. It promises to pay a specified amount of money upon receipt by the bank of certain documents within a specified time or at intervals corresponding with shipments of goods. It is a universally used method of achieving a commercially acceptable compromise. Think of a letter of credit as a loan against collateral wherein the funds are placed in an escrow account. The amount in the account depends on the relationship between the buyer and the buyer's bank.

信用证是开证银行根据进口商或买方要求开立，有利于保护卖方的一种付款单据。

Typically, if you don't already have an account, the bank will require 100 percent collateral. With an account, the bank will establish a line of credit against that account. For instance, if you have $5,000 in your account and the transaction is expected to cost $1,000, your account will be reduced to $4,000 and the line of credit will be established as $1,000.

通常情况下，买方若没有银行账户，银行将要求其提供100%的抵押物；如果有账户，银行将依此为其建立信贷额度。

Commercial letter of credit charges are competitive, so you should comparison shop. Typically they are like those shown in Table 5.2.

表 5.2   典型信用证的资费情况

Table 5.2 Typical Letters of Credit Charges

Type of Credit	Typical Charges
Import and domestic	⅛ of 1% of transaction with a minimum of $75 to $100
	Amendments: ⅛ of 1% flat, minimum $70
	Payment fee: ¼ of 1% flat, minimum $90 per draft
	Acceptance fee: Per annum fee (360-day basis), minimum $75 for each draft accepted
	Discrepancy fee: $40
Export	Advising: $60
	Confirmation: Subject to country risk conditions, minimum $75
	Amendments: $55
	Assignment of proceeds/transfers: ⅛ of 1% of the transaction with a minimum of $75
	Discrepancy fee: $45
	Payment/negotiation: ⅒ of 1%, minimum $85–$95.
Standby letters	Issuance fee: An annual percentage (360-day basis) based on credit risk considerations, minimum $250
	Amendment fee: Risk-related fee is charged, minimum $250
	Payment fee: ¼ of 1% flat, minimum $90 per draft
Collections—documentary	Incoming: sight, $75; time, $95
	Outgoing: sight, $75; time, $95

escrow account 托管账户。comparison shop 边比较，边采购。amendment 改正。discrepancy（票据）不符。standby letter 备用信用证。

备用信用证，顾名思义，指的是当支付未在特定期间（通常是30~60天）内完成时，所需启用的信用证。

信用证的支付分为即期和远期两种。即期信用证意味着，当提交单据符合规章时，开证行（即买方银行）在出具和不出具汇票的情况下，都会进行支付。

信用证可分为可撤销信用证和不可撤销信用证两类。可撤销信用证意味着，开证行不需提前提醒或通知卖方，可在任何时间修改或取消信用证。不可撤销，即非经双方一致同意，不得修改或取消信用证条款。

Standby L/Cs   Sometimes when dealing with an open account, the exporter requires a *standby L/C*. This means just what the name implies; the L/C is not to be executed unless payment is not made within the specified period, usually 30–60 days. Bank handling charges for standby L/Cs are usually higher than those for a commercial (import) L/C.

Issuing, Confirming, and Advising Banks   Letters of credit are payable either at *sight* or on a *time* draft basis. Under a sight L/C, the *issuing* (buyers) bank pays, with or without a draft, when it is satisfied that the presented documents conform to the conforms. An *advising* bank (most often the *confirming* or seller's bank) informs the seller or beneficiary that an L/C has been issued. Under a time (acceptance) L/C, once the associated draft is presented and found to be in exact conformity, the draft is stamped "accepted" and can then be negotiated as a "banker's acceptance" by the exporter, at a discount to reflect the cost of money advanced against the draft.

Once the buyer and the seller agree that they will use an L/C for payment and they have worked out the conditions, the buyer or importer applies for the L/C to his or her international bank. Figure 5.1 is an example of a letter of credit application.

Types of L/Cs   There are two types of letters of credit: revocable and irrevocable. *Revocable credit* means that the document can be amended or canceled at any time without prior warning or notification of the seller. *Irrevocable* simply means that the terms of the document can be amended or canceled only with the agreement of all parties.

Confirmation means that the U.S. bank guarantees payment by the foreign bank.

Using the application as its guide, the bank issues a document of credit incorporating the terms agreed to by the parties. Figure 5.2 is an example of an L/C.

Figure 5.3 shows the three phases of documentary credit in their simplest form. In Phase I, your (*issuing*) bank notifies the seller through an *advising* bank or the seller's (*confirming*) bank that a credit has been issued. In Phase II, the seller then ships the goods and presents the documents to the bank, at which time the seller is paid. Phase III is the settlement phase in which the documents are then transferred to the buyer's bank, whereupon the buyer pays the bank any remaining

---

issuing bank 开证行。conforms 惯例，规章。advising bank 通知行。revocable credit 可撤销信用证。irrevocable 不可撤销的。confirmation 保兑。

图 5.1　开立信用证申请

Figure 5.1 Request to Open a Letter of Credit (L/C)

To:　Importer's international bank

　　　　　　　　　　　　　Request to open documentary
　　　　　　　　　　　　　credit (commercial letter of
　　　　　　　　　　　　　credit and security agreement)

　　　　　　　　　　　　　Date _____

　　Please open for my/our account a documentary credit (letter of credit)
in accordance with the undermentioned particulars.
　　We agree that, except so far as otherwise expressly stated, this credit
will be subject to the Uniform Customs and Practice for Documentary
Credits, ICC Publication #290.

　　We undertake to execute the Bank's usual form of indemnity.

Type of Credit: Irrevocable, i.e., cannot be canceled without
　　　　　　　　　　　　　　　　beneficiary's agreement.
　　　　　　　　　　Revocable, i.e., subject to cancellation.
Method of Advice:　[ ] Airmail　　[ ] E-mail/FAX, short details
　　　　　　　　　　[ ] E-mail/FAX, full details
Beneficiary's bank: _____

In favor of beneficiary: Company name and address.

Amount or sum of:

Availability: Valid until_____in_____for negotiation/date
　　　　　　　　　　　　　　　　place acceptance/payment.

This credit is available by drafts drawn at _____ sight/
accompanied by the required documents.

Documents　　Invoice in three copies.
required:　　 Full set "clean on board" bills of lading to order of
　　　　　　　 shipper, blank endorsed. In case movement of goods
　　　　　　　 involves more than one mode, a "Combined
　　　　　　　 Transport Document" should be called for.

　　　　　　　 Negotiable Marine and War risk insurance for %
　　　　　　　 (usually 110%) of invoice value covering all risks.

(Continued)

图 5.1（接上图）
Figure 5.1 (Continued)

Certificate of Inspection

Other
Documents: Certificate of origin issued by Chamber of Commerce
              in three copies.

Packing List

Quantity and
description
of goods

Price per unit:

Terms and
relative port
or place: CIF/C&F/FOB/FAS/_____
Place _____

Dispatch/
Shipment   From _____ to _____

Special
Instructions
(if any):

monies in exchange for the documents. Thus, on arrival of the goods, the buyer or importer has the proper documents for entry.

信用证特殊的中介用途
Special Middleman Uses of Letters of Credit

There are three special uses of commercial letters of credit for the import/export middleman: transferable, assignment of proceeds, and back-to-back L/Cs. Figure 5.4 compares the risks involved with using each method.

Transferable L/C   Figure 5.5 shows pictorially how the *transferable L/C* works. The buyer opens the L/C, which states clearly that it is transferable, on behalf of the middleman as the original beneficiary who in turn transfers all or part of the L/C to the supplier(s). The transfer must be made under the same terms and conditions as those in the

对于进出口中间商而言，有三种特殊用途的商业信用证：可转让信用证、款项让渡和背对背信用证。

买方开具信用证时，必须清楚标明可转让字样，中间商有权作为原信用证受益人，向供应商转让信用证的所有金额或部分金额。

---

certificate of inspection 检验证书。middleman 中间商，经纪人。transferable L/C 可转让信用证。

图 5.2　信用证样例
Figure 5.2 Sample Letter of Credit (L/C)

Name of issuing bank	Documentary Credit No. _____
Place and date of issue	Place and date of expiration
Applicant	Amount
	Credit available with [ ] Payment [ ] Acceptance [ ] Negotiation
Shipment from _____ Shipment to _____	Against presentation of documents detailed herein
	[ ] Drawn on _____ Bank

Invoice in three copies

Full set "clean on board" bills of lading to order of shipper, blank endorsed. In case movement of goods involves more than one made, a "Combined Transport Document" should be called for.

Negotiable Marine and War risk insurance for _____% (usually 110%) of invoice value covering all risks.

Certificate of Inspection

Certificate of origin issued by Chamber of Commerce in three copies.

Packing List

Documents to be presented within _____ days after date of issuance of the shipping document(s) but within the validity of the credit.

We hereby issue this Documentary Credit in your favor.

                              Issuing Bank

original L/C with the following exceptions: amount, unit price, expiration date, and shipping date. In this instance the buyer and supplier are usually disclosed to each other.

    Assignment of Proceeds   The *assignment of proceeds* method is shown in Figure 5.6; Figure 5.7 shows a typical letter of assignment.

---

clean on board bill of lading 清洁已装船提单。expiration date 到期日。disclose 公开。assignment of proceeds 款项让渡。

图 5.3 信用证运作的三个阶段
Figure 5.3 The Three Phases of a Letter of Credit (L/C)

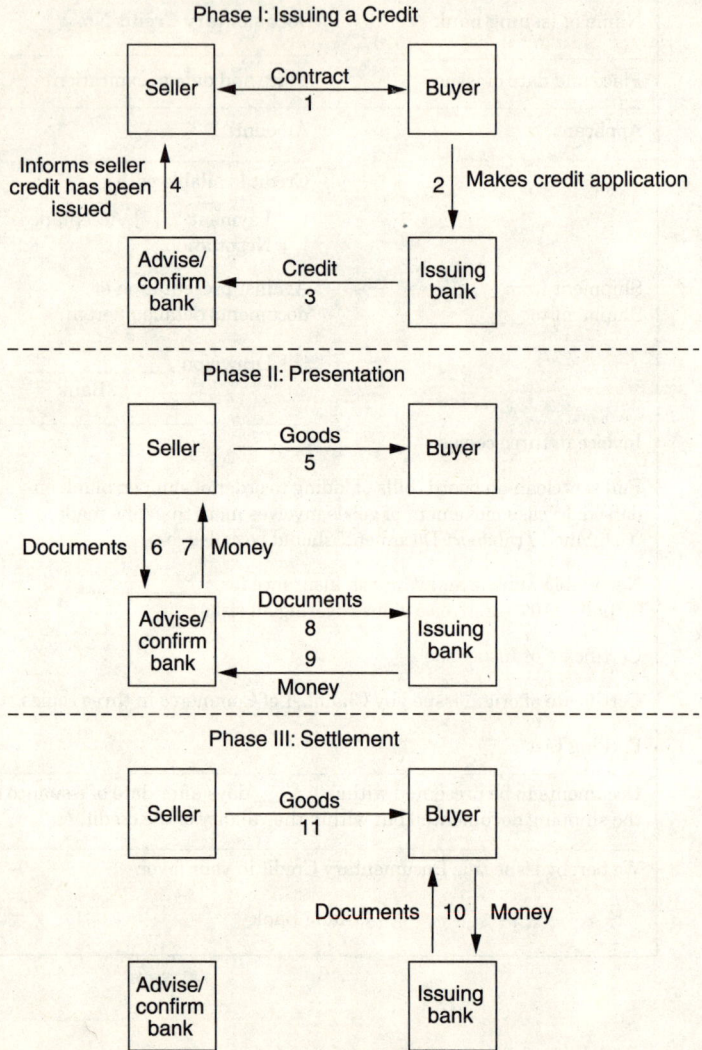

Phase I: Issuing a Credit

Phase II: Presentation

Phase III: Settlement

需要注意的是，所有信用证的款项都是可以转让的。在款项让渡的例子中，买方开具信用证，依赖中间商遵照信用证要求履行义务，受益人才能获得相应款项。中间商单据若出现任何出入，信用证款项都不能予以支付。

Note that the proceeds of all letters of credit may be assigned. In this instance the buyer opens the L/C as the beneficiary and relies on the middleman to comply so that the beneficiary can be paid. Any discrepancy in middleman documents will prevent payment under the L/C.

图 5.4　三种用途的风险比较

Figure 5.4 Comparison of Risks

	Assignment of Proceeds	*Transferable L/C*	*Back-to-Back L/C*
Risk to middleman	Supplier relies on middleman to comply with L/C	Middleman relies on supplier to comply with L/C	Supplier's performance must satisfy both L/Cs
Risk to middleman's bank	None	Minimal	Supplier does not comply with master L/C
Disclosure	Buyer and seller are not disclosed	Buyer and seller are disclosed	Buyer and seller are not disclosed (with third-party documents)

图 5.5　可转让信用证

Figure 5.5 Transferable Letter of Credit (L/C)

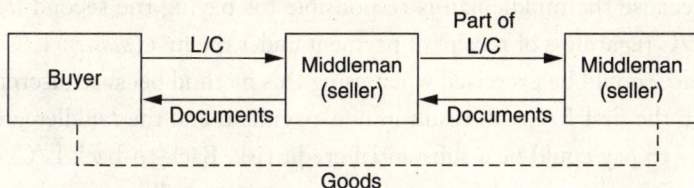

- L/C must state that it is transferable.
- Original beneficiary transfers all or part of L/C to supplier(s).
- Transfer must be made under the same terms and conditions with the following exceptions:
  Amount
  Unit price
  Expiration date
  Shipping date
- Buyer and supplier are usually disclosed to each other.

The middleman instructs the advising bank to effect payment to the supplier when the documents are negotiated. In this way, buyers and sellers are not disclosed to each other.

Back-to-Back Letters of Credit When using the *back-to-back* method shown in Figure 5.8, the middleman must have a line of credit

单据议付后，中间商即命令通知银行履行付款。在这种方式下，买卖双方当事人不直接接触。

采用如图 5.8 所示，使用背对背信用证时，中间商必须拥

图 5.6 款项让渡

Figure 5.6 Assignment of Proceeds

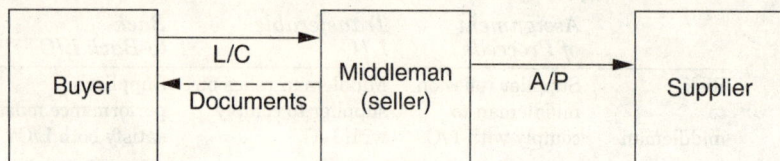

- Supplier relies on middleman to comply with L/C so that he or she can be paid. Discrepancy in middleman's documents will prevent payment under L/C.
- Middleman instructs advising bank to effect payment to supplier when documents are negotiated.
- Buyer and seller are not disclosed to each other.
- Proceeds of all letters of credit can be assigned.

有银行信贷额度，因为不管第一信用证（又称原信用证）是否得到支付，中间商都有责任支付第二信用证（又称备用信用证）。

because the middleman is responsible for paying the second (*backing*) L/C regardless of receipt of payment under the first (*master*) L/C. Great care should be exercised when using this method because discrepancies on the first L/C will result in non-payment, and the middleman's ability to pay could be a substantial credit risk. Back-to-back L/Cs should be issued on nearly identical terms and must allow for third-party documents.

Cash in Advance

大多数国外商人都会争取在收到货物之后再付款，他们认为亲眼见到货物才是最保险的。

This method of getting paid is the most desirable, but the foreign buyer usually objects to tying up his or her capital. On the grounds that seeing the merchandise is the best insurance, most foreign business people try not to pay until they actually receive the goods. Furthermore, the buyer may resent the implication that he or she may not be creditworthy.

避免坏账
Avoiding Bad Credit

预防坏账比纠正坏账更容易。如果出现付款问题，要与客户企业保持沟通、合作，

Pick your customer carefully. Bad debts are more easily avoided than rectified. If there are payment problems, keep communicating and

tie up 占用。resent 憎恶。rectify 纠正、改正。

图 5.7　典型的信用证转让书

Figure 5.7 Typical Letter of Assignment

ASSIGNMENT OF PROCEEDS

Gentlemen:

Here is Letter of Credit No. _____ issued by _____ in favor of _____ _____ for an amount in excess of $ _____ expiring _____.

Our drafts and documents in terms of this credit will be presented by us to your office. We authorize and direct you to pay to _____ the sum of $ _____ from the proceeds of these drafts, in consideration of value received.

These instructions are irrevocable and shall continue under any extension of this Letter of Credit. Please acknowledge receipt of these instructions directly to _____ by forwarding them a copy of this letter.

Sincerely yours,

_____

Signature verified:

_____
Name of Bank

_____
Authorized Signature

The above assignment has been duly noted on our records.

_____
International Banking Department, The Bank of San Diego
Authorized Signature

working with the firm until the matter is settled. Even the most valued customers have financial problems from time to time. If nothing else works, request that your department of industry or commerce or the International Chamber of Commerce begin negotiations on your behalf.

一起致力于问题的解决。

图 5.8 背对背信用证

Figure 5.8 Back-to-Back Letter of Credit (L/C)

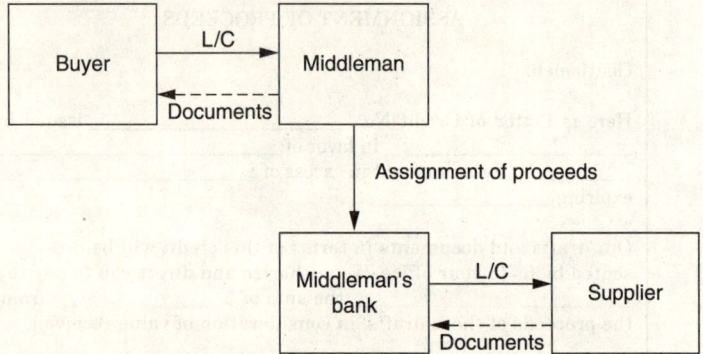

- Requires credit line for middleman.
- Middleman is responsible for paying the second (backing) L/C regardless of receipt of payment under first (master) L/C.
- Substantial credit risk in that discrepancies on the first L/C will result in nonpayment.
- L/Cs are issued on nearly identical terms.
- Middleman's ability to pay is a key consideration.
- L/C must allow third-party documents.

及时准确的信息是良好财务决策的基础。有两类国际资信信息需要关注：（1）进口商支付款项的能力和意愿；（2）其他国家允许使用可兑换货币进行支付的能力和意愿。

Information that is current and accurate is the food for good financing decisions. Basically two types of international credit information exist: (1) the ability and willingness of importing firms to make payment and (2) the ability and willingness of foreign countries to allow payment in a convertible currency.

There are several ways to obtain credit information about companies and their countries.

Information about Domestic Firms
- Commercial banks
- Commercial credit services, such as Dun & Bradstreet
- Trade associations

Information about Foreign Firms
- National Association of Credit Management (NACM)
- Foreign credit specialists in the credit departments of large exporting companies

convertible currency 可兑换货币。

- Commercial banks, which check buyer credit through their foreign branches and correspondents
- Commercial credit reporting services, such as Dun & Bradstreet
- Consultations with the EXIM Bank and the Foreign Credit Insurance Association (FCIA)
- The U.S. Commerce Department's *World Trade Directory Reports*

Information about Foreign Countries
- World Bank
- Chase World Information Corporation
- The magazine *Institutional Investor*
- National Association of Credit Management (NACM)

避免运输风险
Avoiding Shipping Risks

Marine cargo insurance is an essential business tool for import/export and most startup traders are advised to work closely with a freight forwarder. Generally, coverage is sold on a warehouse-to-warehouse basis (i.e., from the sender's factory to the receiver's platform). Coverage usually ceases a specific number of days after the ship or plane is unloaded. You purchase policies on a per-shipment or "blanket" basis. Freight forwarders usually have a blanket policy to cover clients who do not have their own policy. Most insurance companies base cargo insurance on the value of all charges of the shipment including freight handling, and so on, plus 10 percent to cover unseen contingencies. Rates vary according to product, client's track record, destination, and shipping method.

海洋运输货物保险是进出口必不可少的商业工具，建议大多数刚入行的贸易商最好与货运代理紧密合作。

大多数保险公司基于所有运输货物的价值进行货运承保，包括货物搬运和装卸等，外加百分之十的未知意外险。保险费根据产品、客户业绩记录、到达目的地和运输方式而定。

Ocean cargo insurance costs about $0.50 to $1.50 per $100 of invoice value. Air cargo is usually about 25 to 30 percent less.

避免政治风险
Avoiding Political Risk

No two national export credit systems are identical. However, there are similarities, the greatest of which is the universal involvement of government through the export credit agency concerned and of the commercial banking sector in the workings of the system.

---

correspondent 代理行。institutional investor 机构投资者。coverage（承保）范围。blanket policy 统保单。contingency 偶然事故。

所有进出口银行与商业银行合作，向出口商提供很多安排，如帮助出口商向商业银行提供信贷担保，获得出口融资等。

Most countries have export/import banks. In the United States, EXIM Bank serves by providing credit support in the form of loans, guarantees, and insurance. All EXIM Banks cooperate with commercial banks in providing a number of arrangements to help exporters offer credit guarantees to commercial banks that finance export sales. The Overseas Private Investment Corporation (OPIC) and the Foreign Credit Insurance Association (FCIA) also provide insurance to exporters, enabling them to extend credit terms to their overseas buyers. Private insurers cover the normal commercial credit risks; EXIM Bank assumes all liability for political risk.

To contact the FCIA: write FCIA, Marketing Department, 11th Floor, 40 Rector Street, New York, NY 10006 or FCIA, 125 Park Avenue, New York, NY 10006; phone: (212) 885-1500; fax: (212) 885-1535.

商业银行主要在进出口银行提供的出口担保贷款中起中介作用。

The programs available through OPIC and FCIA are well advertised and easily available. Commercial banks are essentially intermediaries to the EXIM Bank for export guarantees on loans (beginning at loans of up to 1 year and ending at loans of up to 10–15 years). FCIA offers insurance in two basic maturities: (1) a short-term policy of up to 180 days and (2) a medium-term policy from 181 days up to 5 years. You may also obtain a combination policy of those maturities. In addition, FCIA has a master policy providing *blanket protection* (one policy designed to provide coverage for all the exporter's sales to overseas buyers).

避免外汇风险
Avoiding Foreign Exchange Risk

When the dollar is strong—as it was in the early 1980s—traders prefer to deal in the dollar. When the dollar is weak, traders begin to deal in other currencies. Of course the dollar is as good as gold because it is a politically stable currency that is traded internationally. Because of its stability, it has become the vehicle currency for most international transactions.

美元凭借其稳定性，成为大多数国际交易中的标准支付货币。

So long as exporters deal only in their currency, there is no foreign exchange risk. However, the strength and popularity of currencies is cyclical, and the dollar is not always the leader. Often, an exporter is faced with the prospect of pricing products or services in currencies other than dollars. Importers must buy foreign currency to pay for products and services from risk-avoiding foreign suppliers demanding

---

vehicle currency（国际）支付货币，周转货币。cyclical 周期的，循环的。

payment in their own currency. In the current era of floating exchanges rates, there are risks resulting from exposure whenever there are cash flows denominated in foreign currencies.

Exposure is the effect on a firm or an individual if there is a change in exchange rates.

Hedging or *covering* is the use of the forward foreign exchange market to avoid foreign currency risk.

The *forward* or *future exchange rate* is the rate that is contracted today for the delivery of a currency at a specified date in the future at a price agreed upon today.

Successfully managing currency risk is imperative. No longer can an importer/exporter speculate by doing nothing and then pass the foreign exchange losses on to customers in the form of higher prices. The best business decision for an importer/exporter is to hedge or cover in the forward market when there is risk of exposure. To do otherwise is to be a speculator, not a business person. Use the forward rate for the date on which payment is required. This avoids all foreign exchange risk, is simple, and is reasonably inexpensive. The cost of a forward contract is small—the difference between the cost of the spot market (today's cost of money) and the cost of the forward market. Major international banks and brokerage houses can help you arrange a foreign exchange forward contract. Spot and forward markets are quoted daily in the *Journal of Commerce* and the *Wall Street Journal*.

对于一个进口商或出口商而言，在面临外汇风险时，最佳的商业方案就是，利用期货交易对外汇套期保值。

远期合约的成本很小——即现货市场成本（现今货币成本）与远期市场成本之差。

代理商 / 分销商协议
Agency/Distributor Agreements

Chapter 3 explores your relationship with overseas distributors. A manufacturer or importer/exporter will seldom agree to meet all a distributor's conditions. Most are negotiable, and a firm that is not internationally known may have to concede to more demands than others in a more

---

denominate 支配，控制。exposure 外汇风险。hedge 套期保值。forward exchange rate 远期外汇汇率。negotiable 协商。

favorable position. The following five tips may help to avoid risk in doing business with distributors:

1. ***Put the agency agreement in writing.*** The rights and obligations resulting from a written agreement require no extraneous proof and are all that is necessary to record or prove the terms of a contract in most countries.

2. ***Set forth the benefit to both parties in the agreement.*** Well-balanced agreements should not place an excess of profitless burden on one of the parties. Performance of the agreement may be impossible to enforce against a party who has no apparent benefit from it.

3. ***Give clear definition and meaning to all contract terms.*** Many English terms that are spelled similarly in the foreign language have entirely different meanings. Require that the English version prevail when there is doubt. To avoid conflict use INCOTERMS (see Chapter 2).

代理商合同应当包含双方权责描述，代理关系性质和持续时间，以及合约可能终止的原因。

4. ***Expressly state the rights and obligations of the parties.*** The agency contract should contain a description of the rights and duties of each party, the nature and duration of the relationship, and the reasons for which the agreement may be terminated.

如果当地法律允许的话，应在合同中说明可能发生的法律纠纷所属的司法管辖范围。在适当的时候，可提请仲裁。

5. ***Specify a jurisdictional clause.*** If local laws will allow, specify in the contract the jurisdiction that will handle any legal disputes that may arise. Where possible, use arbitration. Basic arbitration rules and principles are generally the same anywhere. Clauses in the contract should contain identification of the arbitration body or forum. Model arbitration clauses may be obtained from the American Arbitration Association, 140 West 51st Street, New York, NY 10020; phone: (212) 484-4000; fax: (212) 765-4874. You may also contact the U.S. Council for International Business, 1212 Avenue of the Americas, New York, NY 10036; phone: (212) 354-4480; fax: (212) 575-0327; e-mail: info@uscib.org; Web site:WWW.uscib.org.

物流（包装和运输）
Physical Distribution (Shipping and Packing)

物理运输常称做物流，指的是将商品从一国制造商运送至另一国客户的手段。

Physical distribution, often referred to as *logistics*, is the means by which goods are moved from the manufacturer in one country to the customer

---

extraneous 外部的，外来的。prevail 普遍存在。jurisdiction 司法权。arbitration 仲裁。logistics 物流。

in another. This section discusses two vital aspects for which the importer/exporter should have an appreciation: shipping and packing.

运 输
Shipping

An import/export business can directly arrange its own land, ocean, and air shipping of international cargo. Inland transportation is handled in much the same way as a domestic transaction, except that certain export marks must be added to the standard information shown on a domestic bill of lading. Also the inland carrier must be instructed to notify the ocean or air carrier.

国内运输与国内交易的处理方式基本一样，唯一的区别是需要在国内提单的标准信息上添加某些出口标记。

水路运输
Water Transportation

There are three types of ocean service: conference lines, independent lines, and tramp vessels. An *ocean conference* is an association of ocean carriers joined together to establish common rates and shipping conditions. Conferences have two rates: the regular tariff and a lower contract rate. You can obtain the contract rate if you sign a contract to use conference vessels exclusively during the contract period. *Independent lines* accept bookings from all shippers contingent on the availability of space. They are often less expensive than conference rates. An independent usually quotes rates at about 10 percent lower than a conference carrier in situations where the two are in competition. *Tramp vessels* usually carry only bulk cargoes and do not follow an established schedule; rather, they operate on charters.

海运航线分为三类：班轮航线、独立航线和不定期航线。班轮公会是海运承运人共同达成统一运输费率和运输条件的联盟。

Regardless of the type of carrier you use, the carrier will issue a booking contract, which reserves space on a specific ship. Unless you cancel in advance, you may be required to pay even if your cargo doesn't make the sailing. You must be insured with ocean marine insurance. An insurance broker or your freight forwarder can arrange this for you.

Marine insurance. Insurance that will compensate the owner of goods transported on the seas in the event of loss that would not be legally recovered from the carrier. Also covers air shipments.

Inland 国内的。 contingent 取决于。 tramp vessel 不定期航线。 charter 包租（船）。 marine insurance 海运保险。

航空运输
Air Transportation

Air freight continues to grow as a popular and competitive method for international cargoes. The growth has been facilitated by innovation in the cargo industry. Air carriers have excellent capacity, use very efficient loading and unloading equipment, and handle standardized containers. The advantages are (1) the speed of delivery, which gets perishable cargoes to the place of destination in prime condition; (2) the ability to respond to unpredictable product demands; and (3) the rapid movement of repair parts.

航空运输的优势在于：(1) 传输速度快，可以将易腐烂的货物在最佳状态下运输到目的地；(2) 能够响应难以预测的产品需求；(3) 快速运送修理部件。

Air freight moves under a general cargo rate or a commodity rate. A special unit load rate is available when approved air shipping containers are used.

陆路运输
Land Transportation

Transportation over land has become less regulated and, therefore, more competitive and efficient. The largest import/export market (NAFTA) can be served directly by road and rail. Importers and exporters look primarily to land transportation to move their goods to the nearest port of departure or as one leg of a sea, land, or air combination often referred to as *intermodalism*.

联 运
Intermodalism

The movement of international shipments via container using sequential transportation methods is the system of the future. The concept makes use of the most efficient and cost-effective methods to move goods.

通过集装箱连续运输来实现国际输送，是物流体系的未来。

Load Center This concept stimulated the sophistication of today's intermodal world. As ships grew to hold more containers, they became more expensive to operate. One way to reduce costs was to hold down the number of port calls. In order to fill the ships at fewer ports, the cargo has to be funneled into these load centers. The simplification and organization of movements of cargo has become the fair-haired child of transportation specialists. An entirely new set of terms has developed around the concept.

Bridges A *microbridge* is the routing of a container to or from anywhere in the United States to or from any port. A *minibridge* moves a container that originates or terminates in a U.S. port other than the

---

capacity 承载量。perishable 易腐烂的。prime 最佳的，最理想的。NAFTA 北美自由贸易协定。leg 一站。intermodalism 多式联运。sequential 连续的。sophistication 复杂。funnel 集中。microbridge 微桥运输。

one where it enters or leaves the country. A *land bridge* off-loads a container at any U.S. port, ships it cross-country by rail, and then reloads aboard a vessel for final movement to a foreign destination. *RO/RO* refers to the roll-on/roll-off capability of containerized cargo, which is the foundation of intermodalism.

RO/RO 指的是集装箱货物的滚装能力，这构成了联运的基础。

An example of intermodalism might be a container of goods originating in Europe but destined for Japan. It could be rolled off a ship by truck and then onto a train in Newport News, Virginia (RO/RO), where it would be joined by another container trucked in from Florida, (minibridge) also destined for Japan. The containers would then be moved across the United States (land bridge) then rolled off the train and onto a ship in Long Beach, California, which would complete the movement to Tokyo. Figure 5.9 illustrates the intermodal concept.

HOT TIP

If the details of transportation and all the new-fangled ideas are not for you, then see your nearest freight forwarder (discussed in Chapter 7).

图 5.9　联运的概念

Figure 5.9 Intermodal Concept

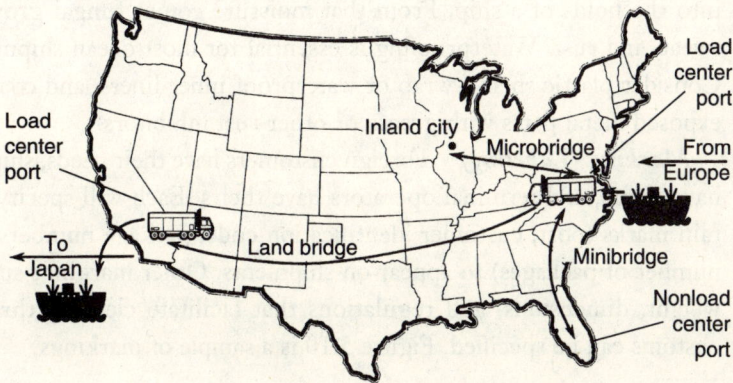

---

land bridge 陆桥。destined 开往，去往。new-fangled 新产生的。

跨国海运中的包装和唛头
Packaging and Marking for Overseas Shipment

Whether importing or exporting, your product(s) must travel thousands of miles undamaged. Your package must be protected from breakage, dampness, careless storage, rough handling, thieves, and weather. Insurance might cover the loss, but lost time and the ill will of your overseas trading partner are a high price to pay. It has been estimated that as much as 70 percent of all cargo loss could be prevented by proper packaging and marking.

据估计，恰当的包装和唛头可以规避高达百分之七十的货物损失。

An excellent source for all aspects of packing and packaging is the *Modern Packaging Encyclopedia*, published annually by McGraw-Hill, New York.

Breakage   Ocean shipments are often roughly loaded by stevedores using forklifts, slings, nets, and conveyors. During the voyage, rough water and storms can cause loads to shift and sometimes crash into other containers. Even small packages sent through the mail can be squeezed, thrown, or crushed.

Assume the worst when packaging for overseas delivery. Use stronger and heavier materials than you would for domestic shipments. On the other hand, don't over pack—you pay by weight and volume. For large ocean shipments consider standardized containers that can be transferred from truck or rail car without being opened.

Pilferage (Theft)   Use strapping and seals and avoid trademarks or content descriptions.

Moisture and Weather   The heat and humidity of the tropics as well as rainstorms and rough weather at sea can cause moisture to seep into the holds of a ship. From that moisture comes fungal growths, sweat, and rust. Waterproofing is essential for most ocean shipments. Consider plastic shrink-wrap or waterproof inner liners, and coat any exposed metal parts with grease or other rust inhibitors.

防水对于大多数海运来说至关重要。可以考虑使用塑料收缩胶膜或防水里衬，以及在任何暴露在外的金属上涂抹油脂或其他防锈剂。

Marking (Labeling)   Foreign customers have their needs, shippers have theirs, and terminal operators have theirs. Each will specify certain marks (port, customer identification code, package numbers, and number of packages) to appear on shipments. Other markings such as weight, dimensions, and regulations that facilitate clearing through customs can be specified. Figure 5.10 is a sample of markings.

---

ill will 敌意。stevedore 装卸工，码头工人。forklift 叉式升降机。sling 吊索。seep 渗透。fungal 霉菌的。inhibitor 抑制剂。clearing 报关。

图 5.10　唛头示例
Figure 5.10 Example of Markings

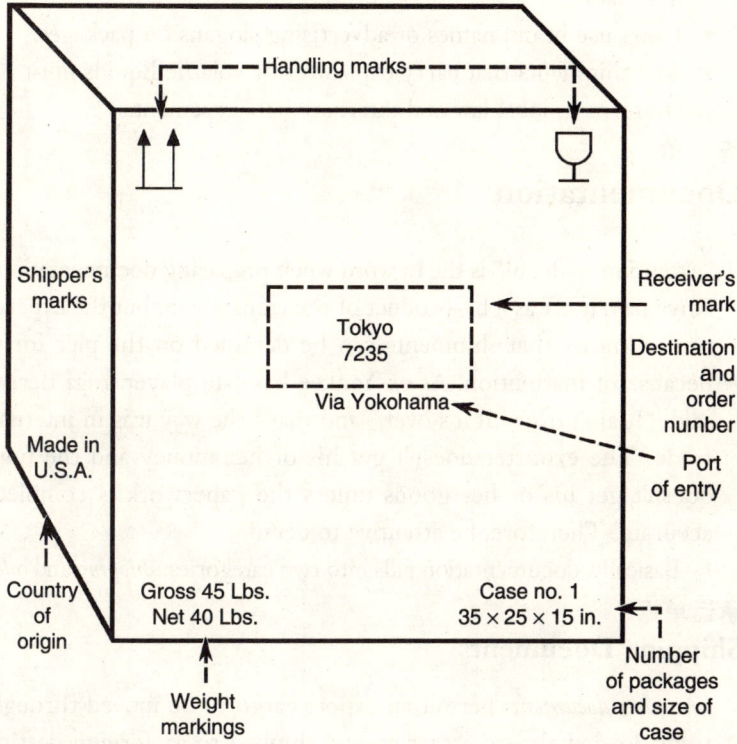

Handling marks

Shipper's marks

Receiver's mark

Tokyo
7235

Via Yokohama

Destination and order number

Port of entry

Made in U.S.A.

Country of origin

Gross 45 Lbs.
Net 40 Lbs.

Case no. 1
35 × 25 × 15 in.

Number of packages and size of case

Weight markings

船运唛头一览表
Checklist for Shipping

- Write your customer's name and address or shipping code on the package.
- Use black waterproof ink for the stencils.
- Include port of exit and port of entry on your label.
- Don't forget to include package and case number.
- Include dimensions (inches and metric).
- Mark exports "Made in U.S.A." and so on, so that the package will get through customs in most foreign countries.
- Express gross and net weight in pounds and/or kilograms.

---

stencil 模板。dimension 体积，尺寸。

- Don't forget cautionary markings such as, "this side up" or "handle with care" in both the language of origin and the language of destination.
- Don't use brand names or advertising slogans on packages.
- Any shipments that carry explosives or volatile liquids must conform to local law and international agreements.

备 单
Documentation

"注重细节"是准备单证时的经验之谈。新手可能对此不以为然，认为细节不过是交易的副产品，但有经验的贸易商都知道，运送的货物可能会因为细节上的疏忽，而被扣留在码头长达数周。

"Attention to detail" is the byword when preparing documentation. The naïve pass it off as a by-product of the transaction, but the experienced trader knows that shipments can be detained on the pier for weeks because of inattention. As ex-Yankee baseball player Yogi Berra once said, "It ain't over 'til it's over," and that's the way it is in international trade. The exporter doesn't get his or her money and the importer doesn't get his or her goods unless the paperwork is complete and accurate! Therefore, be attentive to detail.

Basically, documentation falls into two categories: *shipping* and *collecting*.

承运单据
Shipping Documents

承运单据是出口货物通过海关，装上运输工具，运往国外目的地的凭据。

Shipping documents permit an export cargo to be moved through customs, loaded aboard a carrier, and shipped to its foreign destination. These documents are:

- Export licenses
- Packing lists
- Bills of lading
- Export declarations

托收单据
Collection Documents

托收单据是收取货款时需提交给进口商（使用汇票的情况下），或进口商银行（使用信用证的情况下）的单据。

Collection documents are those needed for submission to the importer (in the case of a draft) or to the importer's bank (in the case of an L/C) in order to receive payment. These are:

- Commercial invoices
- Consular invoices

---

this side up 此面向上。handle with care 小心轻放。explosive 易爆物品。volatile 易挥发的。byword 常常挂在嘴边的话。detain 扣留。

- Certificates of origin
- Inspection certificates
- Bills of lading

When endorsed by the shipper, you can use the bill of lading for sight draft or for L/C shipments. Other documents sometimes required for collection are manufacturing and insurance certificates and dock or warehouse receipts. Keep in mind that customs house brokers and freight forwarders are specialists in documentation as well as in physical distribution.

Collection. The procedure whereby a bank collects money for a seller against a draft drawn on a buyer abroad, usually through a correspondent bank.

托收，托收是卖方开具以国外买方为付款人的汇票，委托出口地银行，通常是由卖方在进口地的代理行来收取货款的一种结算程序。

单　据
The Documents

This section describes the various documents in detail and provides samples of each.

Certificate of Origin

The *certificate of origin* is a document that certifies to the buyer the country in which the goods were produced. A recognized chamber of commerce usually performs the certificate of origin of the merchandise. Some countries require a separate certificate, sometimes countersigned by a chamber of commerce and possibly even visaed by the resident consul at the port of export. These statements are required to indicate preferential rates of import duties such as "most favored nation." Often, as little as 35 percent of a nation's materials and/or labor can qualify it for favorable duties. Some nations require special forms, while others accept a certification on the shipper's own letterhead. See Figure 5.11 for an example of a certificate of origin.

原产地证明是向买方证明货物生产国家的单据。

---

customs house 海关。broker 经纪人。chamber of commerce 商会。

图 5.11   原产地证明

Figure 5.11 Certificate of Origin

Our Company, Inc.

Hometown, Wherever

Date _____

Your Company

Hometown, Wherever

Point of Origin Declaration

For the purpose of positively identifying certain components as

being manufactured in _____ and therefore qualifying for
                        (Country)

entry under _____.
              (Tariff code identification)

Component(s) description: _____

_____

Part number: _____

_____

The manufacturer _____ warrants and repre-

sents that the articles supplied to _____

_____
                          (Company)

and described above are articles of _____.
                                    (Country)

The articles were manufactured at _____
                                  (Address of location of plant)

_____.

Authorized signature and date

_____

Title

Following is a checklist for a certificate of origin that can be used as a guide:

- The letter or form should originate from the address of the manufacturer of the product.

- A responsible and knowledgeable person within the manufacturing company (an *officer* of the corporation) must sign the letter.
- The letter or form will not be accepted if it is from an outside sales office or distributor. It cannot be signed by a salesperson.
- The letter should clearly state where the product in question was manufactured.

商业发票
Commercial Invoice

The *commercial invoice* is a bill that conforms in all respects to the agreement between the importer and the exporter. It could have the exact terms of the pro forma invoice first offered in response to a quotation, or it could differ in those terms that were the result of final negotiations. In any case there should be no surprises for the importer. The commercial invoice should (1) itemize the merchandise by price per unit and any charges paid by the buyer, and (2) specify the terms of payment and any marks or numbers on the packages. See Figure 5.12.

商业发票，根据出口方与进口方达成的协议所列出的清单。

领事发票
Consular Invoice

This invoice is not required by all countries. It is obtained from the commercial attaché or through the consular office of the country in question in the port of export. When required, it is in addition to a commercial invoice and must conform in every respect to that document, as well as to the bill of lading and any insurance documents. Its purpose is to allow clearance of your shipment into the country that requires it. See Figure 5.13.

Commercial attaché. The commercial expert on the diplomatic staff of his or her country's embassy or large consulate in a foreign country.

商务专员，是一个国家在驻外国大使馆或较大领事馆里所设的负责外交事务方面的商务专家。

制造证书
Certificate of Manufacture

This document certifies that the goods ordered by the importer have been produced and are ready for shipment. For example, it might be used in those cases in which the manufacturer has moved ahead in

---

pro forma invoice 形式发票。itemize 详细列出。 commercial attaché 商务专员。consular office 领事馆。

图 5.12　商业发票

Figure 5.12 Commercial Invoice

XYZ Foreign Co.
2A1 Moon River
Yokohama, Japan

Purchase Order:
Invoice Number: 00012
Invoice Date:

Sold To: Our Company, Inc.　　　　Ship To: Our Company, Inc.
　　　　Hometown, U.S.A.　　　　　　　　Hometown, U.S.A.

Forwarding Agent:

Via:　　　　　　　　　　　　　　　Country of Origin: Japan

Quantiy	Part No.	Description	Price Each	Total Price
10	A2Z	Machines	$100.00	$1,000.00

Inland freight, export packing and forwarding fees　　$ 100.00

Free alongside (FAS) Yokohama　　　　　　　$1,100.00
Estimated ocean freight　　　　　　　　　　$ 100.00
Estimated marine insurance　　　　　　　　$ 50.00

Packed in 10 crates, 100 cubic feet
Gross weight 1,000 lbs.
Net weight　　900 lbs.
Payment terms: Confirmed irrevocable letter of credit confirmed by a
U.S. bank. Shipment to be made two (2) weeks after receipt of firm order.
Additional conditions of sale: XYZ Foreign Co. to provide:
Certificate of Origin
Consular Invoice
Certificate of Manufacture
Insurance Certificate
Inspection Certificate

production with only a down payment, thus allowing the importer to avoid allocation of the full amount too far in advance. Generally, invoices and packing lists are forwarded to the importer with the certificate of manufacture. See Figure 5.14.

图 5.13 领事发票

Figure 5.13 Consular Invoice

FACTURA COMERCIAL

No. de la Factura...... .... Lugar (Ciudad) .... Fecha: Día. .... Mes........ Año........
(Commercial Invoic #) Place (City) Date: Day Mo. Year

INTERVIENEN	Nombre de la Cía. o del Agente autorizado	Número (No.)	DOMICILIO (Address)		
			Calle (Street)	Ciudad (City)	Tel. (Phone)
Vendedor o refmitente (Seller or shipper)					
Comprador (Buyer)					
Consig. a Destinatario (Consigned to)					
Agente o Gestor Agent-Broker					

Lugar y Puerto de Embarque Port of Loading	Lugar y Puerto de Destino Port of Unloading	Fecha de Embarque Date of Shipment	Nombre del Buque o Cía. Aérea Transp. Vessel/Airline Name

CONDICIONES DE VENTA: FOB - CIF   SEGURO (Insurance) :

Cantidad y Número de Bultos	PESO		Detalle descriptivo de la mercadería, indicando marca, lugar de fabricación, clase o tipo del producto, series, números, etc. y cualquier otra información adicional relacionada. (Denomination and details of each article: quantity, quality, measure, merch. origin, etc.)	Precio de la Mercadería (Merchandise Price)
	Kilogramos	Libras		

(Continued)

131

图 5.13 领事发票（接上页）

Figure 5.13 Consular Invoice (Continued)

El agente autorizado que firma la presente, declara bajo juramento que todos los datos declarados en la presente factura, son exactos y verdaderos y que los precios pagados o por pagarse, son los reales y convenidos, que no existe convenio o arreglo alguno que permita la alteración o modificación de éstos, ni tampoco de su cantidad o calidad.

Firma del Agente, Vendedor o
Despachante autorizado. Fecha.

Importe mercad. .... U$S
Merch. Price

Transporte .... U$S

Otros (other) .... U$S

SUB-TOTAL .... U$S

Tasa Consular, Fee U$S

IMPORTE TOTAL U$S

The.............................
A recognized Chamber of Commerce under the laws of the State of California has examined the manufacturer's invoice or shipper affidavit concerning the origin of the merchandise and according to the best of its knowledge and belief, finds that the products named originated in the United States of North America.

Authorized Officer.......................... Date............

CONSULADO DE LA REPUBLICA ARGENTINA

Espacio para Certificacion Consular

FACTURA COMERCIAL No.

Certifico que la firma que aparece en este

documento y dice ....

es auténtica y pertenece al funcionario des-

cripto.

Los Angeles, Calif.

Número de orden ....

No. del arancel..............................

Der. percib. U$S.

Depositado en el Banco

图 5.14　制造证书
Figure 5.14 Certificate of Manufacture

DATE:

REFERENCE:　ACCOUNT NAME AND ADDRESS
　　　　　　 PURCHASE ORDER NO. AND/OR
　　　　　　 CONTRACT NO.

BANK NAME AND LETTER OF CREDIT NO:

MERCHANDISE DESCRIPTION:

CERTIFICATE OF RECENT MANUFACTURE

WE HEREBY CERTIFY THAT THE HEREIN DESCRIBED MER-
CHANDISE IS OF RECENT MANUFACTURE, IN THIS CASE
NOT OLDER THAN ＿＿ YEAR(S) FROM THIS DATE.

NAME AND ADDRESS OF MANUFACTURER:

BY: ＿＿＿＿＿＿＿＿＿＿＿＿＿＿
　　　　(Original signature)

出口许可证
Export Licenses

Export licensing procedures are described in detail in Chapter 7 as one of the six topics unique to exporting. These licenses are of two basic varieties: general and validated. *Validated licenses* require careful attention because they apply to products that the government wants to control closely for either strategic or economic reasons. The commodity control list (CCL) sets forth items such as certain weapons, technologies, and high-tech products. Export administration regulations set forth all licensing requirements for commodities under the jurisdiction of the Office of Export Administration (OEA), International Trade Administration. Once it has been determined that a license is needed, the Application for Export License must be prepared and submitted to the OEA. See Figure 7.1 in Chapter 7.

许可证有两种基本类型：普通许可证和有效许可证。有效许可证需要多加注意，因为它们是应用于政府出于策略或经济原因而紧密控制的产品。货物控制单中包括某些武器、技术和高科技产品等。

validated license 有效许可证。commodity control list（CCL）货物控制单。

保险凭证
Insurance Certificates

保险凭证提供承保范围说明书，也可以是合同、定购单或商务发票的约定，以获得赔偿金。

Insurance certificates provide evidence of coverage and may be a stipulation of a contract, purchase order, or commercial invoice in order to receive payment. These indicate the type and amount of coverage and identify the merchandise in terms of packages and identifying marks. You should make certain that the information on this certificate agrees exactly with invoices and bills of lading. See Figure 5.15.

检验证书
Inspection Certificates

检验证书是保护进口人免遭诈骗、错误或质量问题的证明文件。

These are documents that protect the importer against fraud, error, or quality performance. The inspection is most often conducted by an independent firm, but it is sometimes accomplished by the shipper. An affidavit that certifies the inspection is often required under terms of a letter of credit. For example, a Taiwanese firm wanted to import used diesel generators from the United States. That company insisted that an independent engineer certify satisfactory operation of each generator, at specifications, prior to shipment. See Figure 5.16.

装箱单
Packing Lists

装箱单为装船时所开具，详细列出了所装载的货物。

A packing list accompanies the shipment and describes the cargo in detail. It includes the shipper, the consignee, measurements, serial numbers, weights, and any other data peculiar to the shipment. When correctly completed, it is placed in a waterproof bag or envelope with the words, "Packing List Enclosed" and attached to the outside of the container. See Figure 5.17.

托运人出口申报
Shippers Export Declaration

托运人出口申报由出口商或货运代理人向美国政府提交（其他国家可能也有相似要求）。

The shipper's export declaration (SED) is prepared by the exporter or freight forwarder for the U.S. government (other countries may have a similar requirement). It is a data collection document required on all exports in excess of $2,500. It is prepared for purposes of providing statistical information to the Bureau of Census and to indicate the

---

stipulation 规定，说明书。fraud 诈骗。shipper 托运人。

图 5.15 海上保险凭证

Figure 5.15 Certificate of Marine Insurance

CERTIFICATE OF MARINE INSURANCE

No. 573951

(globe logo) International Cargo & Surety Insurance Company

* $ _____
(sum insured)

This is to Certify, That on the _____ day of _____ this Company

insured under Policy No. _____ made for

for the sum of _____ Dollars,

on _____

*(Amounts in excess of $1,000,000.00 cannot be insured under this Certificate)

Valued at sum insured. Shipped on board the S/S or M/S _____ and/or following
steamer or steamers

at and from _____
(Initial Point of Shipment)   (Port of Shipment)

to _____ , via _____
(Port of Places of Destination)

and it is understood and agreed, that in case of loss, the same

is payable to the order of _____ on surrender of the Certificate which
conveys the right of collecting any such loss as fully as if the property were covered by a special policy direct to the holder hereof, and free from
any liability for unpaid premiums. This certificate is issued subject to the standard International Cargo & Surety Insurance Company open cargo policy,
which is incorporated herein by reference. To the extent that any terms or conditions in this certificate are inconsistent with the standard policy, the
standard policy shall govern the rights and duties of all parties subject to the contract of insurance. Copies of the standard policy are available, upon
request, from International Cargo & Surety Insurance Company, 1501 Woodfield Road, Schaumburg, Illinois 60173.

SPECIAL CONDITIONS

Merchandise shipped with an UNDER DECK bill of lading insured—
Against all risks of physical loss or damage from any external cause, irrespective of percentage, excepting those excluded by the
F.C.& S and S.R.& C.C. Warranties, arising during transportation between the points of shipment and of destination named herein

SAMPLE

ON DECK SHIPMENTS (with an ON DECK bill of lading) and/or shipments of used merchandise insured:
Warranted free of particular average unless caused by the vessel being stranded, sunk, burnt, on fire or in collision, but including
risk of jettison and/or washing overboard, irrespective of percentage.

MARKS & NUMBERS		
	SCHEDULE B CODE (commodity)	SCHEDULE C-E CODE (country)

TERMS AND CONDITIONS—SEE ALSO BACK HEREOF

WAREHOUSE TO WAREHOUSE This insurance attaches from the time the goods leave the Warehouse and/or Store at the place named in the Policy for the commencement of the transit and continues
during the ordinary course of transit, including customary transhipment if any, until the goods are discharged overside from the overseas vessel at the final port. Thereafter the insurance continues whilst
the goods are in transit and/or awaiting transit until delivered to final warehouse at the destination named in the Policy or until the expiry of 15 days (or 30 days if the destination to which the goods
are insured is outside the limits of the port) whichever shall first occur. The time limits referred to above to be reckoned from midnight of the day on which the discharge overside of the goods hereby
insured from the overseas vessel is completed. Held covered at a premium to be arranged in the event of transhipment, if any, other than as above and/or in the event of delay in excess of the above
time limits arising from circumstances beyond the control of the Assured

(Continued)

135

图 5.15 海上保险凭证（接上页）

Figure 5.15 Certificate of Marine Insurance (Continued)

NOTE – IT IS NECESSARY FOR THE ASSURED TO GIVE PROMPT NOTICE TO THESE ASSURERS WHEN THEY BECOME AWARE OF AN EVENT FOR WHICH THEY ARE "HELD COVERED" UNDER THIS POLICY AND THE RIGHT TO SUCH COVER IS DEPENDENT ON COMPLIANCE WITH THIS OBLIGATION.

PERILS CLAUSE Touching the adventures and perils which the Company is contented to bear, and takes upon itself, they are of the seas, fires, assailing thieves, jettisons, barratry of the master and mariners, and all other like perils, losses and misfortunes (illicit or contraband trade excepted in all cases), that have or shall come to the hurt, detriment or damage of the said goods and merchandise, or any part thereof.

SHORE CLAUSE Where this insurance by its terms covers while on docks, wharves or elsewhere on shore, and/or during land transportation, it shall include the risks of collision, derailment, overturning or other accident to the conveyance, fire, lightning, sprinkler leakage, cyclones, hurricanes, earthquakes, floods (meaning the rising of navigable waters), and/or collapse or subsidence of docks or wharves, even though the insurance be otherwise F.P.A.

BOTH TO BLAME CLAUSE Where goods are shipped under a Bill of Lading containing the so-called "Both to Blame Collision" Clause, these Assurers agree as to all losses covered by this insurance, to indemnify the Assured for this Policy's proportion of any amount (not exceeding the amount insured) which the Assured may be legally bound to pay to the shipowners under such clause in the event that such liability is asserted the Assured agree to notify these Assurers who shall have the right at their own cost and expense to defend the Assured against such claim.

MACHINERY CLAUSE: When the property insured under this Policy includes a machine consisting when complete for sale or use of several parts, then in case of loss or damage covered by this insurance to any part of such machine, these Assurers shall be liable only for the proportion of the insured value of the part lost or damaged, or at the Assured's option, for the cost and expense, including labor and forwarding charges, of replacing or repairing the lost or damaged part; but in no event shall these Assurers be liable for more than the insured value of the complete machine.

LABELS CLAUSE In case of damage affecting labels, capsules or wrappers, these Assurers, if liable therefor under the terms of this policy, shall not be liable for more than an amount sufficient to pay the cost of new labels, capsules or wrappers, and the cost of reconditioning the goods, but in no event shall these Assurers be liable for more than the insured value of the damaged merchandise.

DELAY CLAUSE: Warranted free of claim for loss of market or for loss, damage or deterioration arising from delay, whether caused by a peril insured against or otherwise, unless expressly assumed in writing hereon.

AMERICAN INSTITUTE CLAUSES: This insurance, in addition to the foregoing, is also subject to the following American Institute Cargo Clauses, current forms:

1. CRAFT, ETC.	4. GENERAL AVERAGE
2. DEVIATION	5. EXPLOSION
3. WAREHOUSING & FORWARDING CHARGES,	6. BILL OF LADING, ETC.
PACKAGES TOTALLY LOST LOADING, ETC.	7. MARINE EXTENSION CLAUSES

8. INCHMAREE
9. CONSTRUCTIVE TOTAL LOSS
10. CARRIER
11. S.R. & C.C. ENDORSEMENT
12. WAR RISK INSURANCE
13. SOUTH AMERICA 60 DAY CLAUSE

PARAMOUNT WARRANTIES: THE FOLLOWING WARRANTIES SHALL BE PARAMOUNT AND SHALL NOT BE MODIFIED OR SUPERSEDED BY ANY OTHER PROVISION INCLUDED HEREIN OR STAMPED OR ENDORSED HEREON UNLESS SUCH OTHER PROVISION REFERS SPECIFICALLY TO THE RISKS EXCLUDED BY THESE WARRANTIES AND EXPRESSLY ASSUMES THE SAID RISKS:

F.C. & S. (a) Notwithstanding anything herein contained to the contrary, this insurance is warranted free from capture, seizure, arrest, restraint, detainment, confiscation, preemption, requisition or nationalization, and the consequences thereof or any attempt thereat, whether in time of peace or war and whether lawful or otherwise; also warranted free, whether in time of peace or war, from all loss, damage or expense caused by any weapon of war employing atomic or nuclear fission and/or fusion or other reaction or radioactive force or matter or by any mine or torpedo, also warranted free from all consequences of hostilities or warlike operations (whether there be a declaration of war or not), but this warranty shall not exclude collision or contact with aircraft, rockets or similar missiles or with any fixed or floating object (other than a mine or torpedo), stranding, heavy weather, fire or explosion unless caused directly (and independently of the nature of the voyage or service which the vessel concerned or, in the case of a collision, any other vessel involved therein, is performing) by a hostile act by or against a belligerent power; and for the purposes of this warranty "power" includes any authority maintaining naval, military or air forces in association with a power.

Further warranted free from the consequences of civil war, revolution, rebellion, insurrection, or civil strife arising therefrom, or piracy.

S.R. & C.C. (b) Warranted free of loss or damage caused by or resulting from strikes, lockouts, labor disturbances, riots, civil commotions or the acts of any person or persons taking part in any such occurrence or disorder.

This Certificate is issued in Original and Duplicate, one of which being accomplished the other to stand null and void. To support a claim local Revenue Laws may require this certificate to be stamped.

Not transferable unless countersigned

Countersigned _____

ADDITIONAL CONDITIONS AND
INSTRUCTIONS TO CLAIMANTS ON REVERSE SIDE

OM18

President *Secretary*

Kenneth J. Khong

SAMPLE ORIGINAL

图 5.16　检验证书
Figure 5.16 Inspection Certificate

DATE:

REFERENCE:　　ACCOUNT NAME AND ADDRESS
　　　　　　　PURCHASE ORDER NO. AND/OR
　　　　　　　CONTRACT NO.

BANK NAME AND LETTER OF CREDIT NO.

MERCHANDISE DESCRIPTION:

　　　　　INSPECTION CERTIFICATE

WE HEREBY CERTIFY THAT THE HEREIN DESCRIBED MER-
CHANDISE HAS BEEN INSPECTED AND FOUND TO BE OF
HIGHEST QUALITY AND IN GOOD WORKING ORDER.

　　　　　PORTER INTERNATIONAL INC.

BY: _____
　　　　　(Original signature)

---

proper authorization to export. It is the basis for measuring the volume and type of exports leaving a country. The document requires complete information about the shipment, including description, value, net and gross weights, and relevant license information, thus closing the licensing information loop back to the OEA. See Figure 5.18.

提　单
Bills of Lading

A *bill of lading* is a contract between the owner of the goods (exporter) and the carrier. It is both evidence that the shipment has been made, and the receipt for the goods that have been shipped. Figure 5.19 is a bill of lading for an air carrier, called an air waybill. Figure 5.20 is an ocean bill of lading. While e-commerce has not yet reached the bill of lading process, it is getting close and will soon be a reality. Several ship

提单是货主（出口商）与承运人之间的合同。它既是装船完毕的证明，也是货物已经运送的收据。

---

bill of lading 提单。

图 5.17 装箱单
Figure 5.17 Packing List

To XYZ Foreign Co.   Date: _____
    2A1 Moon River
    Yokohama, Japan

Gentlemen:

Under your order No. <u>123</u> the material listed below was
shipped <u>1/1/18</u> via <u>Truck and vessel</u>

To <u>Yokohama</u>

Via: _____

Shipment consists of: Marks:

___ Cases ___ Packages   XYZ Foreign Co.
                          2A1 Moon River
___ Crates ___ Cartons   Yokohama, Japan

___ Bbls ___ Drums   Made in U.S.A.

___ Reels   #7235
                          _____

                          _____

Package Number	Weights (Lbs or Kilos)	Dimensions	Quality	Contents
	Gross Legal Net	Ht. Wth. Lth.		
7235	45	40 35 25 15		Toys

lines have already automated part of the process, and there are indica-
tions that a system to replace paper bills of lading with electronic
communications will soon be marketed.

记名提单
Straight Bills of Lading
These are nonnegotiable bills that consign the goods to an importer or
other party named on the document. Once consummated, the seller

记名提单是将货物运给进口
商或证明文件上所列出的其
他方的票据，不可转让。

consign 把……交付给。

图 5.18 托运人出口申报

Figure 5.18 Shipper's Export Declaration

U.S. DEPARTMENT OF COMMERCE — BUREAU OF THE CENSUS — INTERNATIONAL TRADE ADMINISTRATION

SHIPPER'S EXPORT DECLARATION

FORM **7525-V** (3-19-85)

OMB No. 0607-0018

1a. EXPORTER (Name and address including ZIP code)

ZIP CODE

2. DATE OF EXPORTATION

3. BILL OF LADING/AIR WAYBILL NO.

b. EXPORTER EIN NO.

c. PARTIES TO TRANSACTION
☐ Related   ☐ Non-related

4a. ULTIMATE CONSIGNEE

b. INTERMEDIATE CONSIGNEE

NONE

5. FORWARDING AGENT

Porter International, Inc.
P.O. Box 41-A
San Ysidro, California 92173

6. POINT (STATE) OF ORIGIN OR FTZ NO.

7. COUNTRY OF ULTIMATE DESTINATION

MEXICO

8. LOADING PIER/TERMINAL

9. MODE OF TRANSPORT (Specify)
TRUCK

10. EXPORTING CARRIER
Truck Lic.:

11. PORT OF EXPORT
San Diego, (S. Y.), California

12. FOREIGN PORT OF UNLOADING

13. CONTAINERIZED (Vessel only)
☐ Yes   ☐ No

(Continued)

139

图 5.18 托运人出口申报（接上页）

Figure 5.18 Shipper's Export Declaration (Continued)

14. SCHEDULE B DESCRIPTION OF COMMODITIES. *(Use columns 15—19)*

MARKS, NOS. AND KINDS OF PKGS. (15)	D/F (16)	SCHEDULE B NUMBER (17)	QUANTITY — SCHEDULE B UNIT(S) (18)	SHIPPING WEIGHT (Pounds) (19)	VALUE (U.S. dollars, omit cents) (Selling price or cost if not sold) (20)

21. VALIDATED LICENSE NO./GENERAL LICENSE SYMBOL

22. ECCN *(When required)*

23. Duly authorized officer or employee

The exporter authorizes the forwarder named above to act as forwarding agent for export control and customs purposes.

24. I certify that all statements made and all information contained herein are true and correct and that I have read and understand the instructions for preparation of this document, set forth in the **"Correct Way to Fill Out the Shipper's Export Declaration."** I understand that civil and criminal penalties, including forfeiture and sale, may be imposed for making false or fraudulent statements herein, failing to provide the requested information or for violation of U.S. laws on exportation (13 U.S.C. Sec. 305; 22 U.S.C. Sec. 401; 18 U.S.C. Sec. 1001; 50 U.S.C. App. 2410).

Signature

Confidential-For use solely for official purposes authorized by the Secretary of Commerce (13 U.S.C. 301 (g)).

Title   **EXPORT CLERK**

Export shipments are subject to inspection by U.S. Customs Service and/or Office of Export Enforcement.

Date

25. AUTHENTICATION *(When required)*

THESE COMMODITIES LICENSED BY U.S. FOR ULTIMATE DESTINATION — MEXICO — DIVERSION CONTRARY TO U.S. LAW PROHIBITED.

图 5.19 航空运单（提单）

Figure 5.19 Air Waybill (Bill of Lading)

Shipper's Name and Address	Shipper's Account Number	Not negotiable **Air Waybill** (Air Consignment note) Issued by

Copies 1, 2 and 3 of this Air Waybill are originals and have the same validity

Consignee's Name and Address		It is agreed that the goods described herein are accepted in apparent good order and condition (except as noted) for carriage SUBJECT TO THE CONDITIONS OF CONTRACT ON THE REVERSE HEREOF. THE SHIPPER'S ATTENTION IS DRAWN TO THE NOTICE CONCERNING CARRIERS' LIMITATION OF LIABILITY. Shipper may increase such limitation of liability by declaring a higher value for carriage and paying a supplemental charge if required.

To expedite movement, shipment may be diverted to motor or other carrier unless shipper gives other instructions hereon.

Issuing Carrier's Agent Name and City	Accounting Information

Agent's IATA Code	Account No.	**SEE WARSAW NOTICE AND CONDITIONS OF CONTRACT ON REVERSE SIDE.**

Airport of Departure (Addr. of first Carrier) and requested Routing

By first Carrier	Routing and Destination			Currency	WT/VAL		Other		Declared Value for Carriage	Declared Value for Customs
					PPD	COLL	PPD	COLL		

Airport of Destination	Flight/Date	For Carrier Use only	Flight/Date	Amount of Insurance	INSURANCE - If Carrier offers insurance, and such insurance is requested in accordance with conditions on reverse hereof, indicate amount to be insured in figures in box marked amount of insurance.

Handling Information   These commodities licensed by the United States for ultimate destination .... Diversion contrary to United States law prohibited.

(Continued)

141

142

图 5.19 航空运单（提单）（接上页）

Figure 5.19 Air Waybill (Continued)

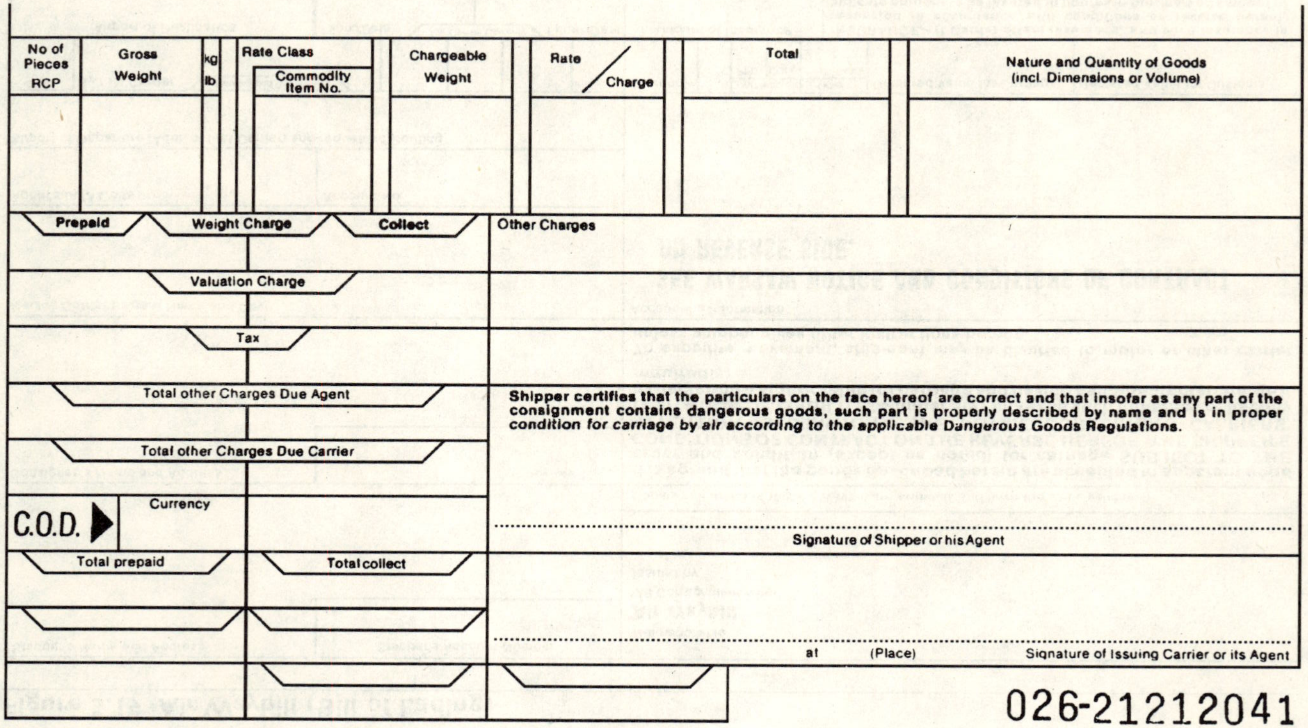

No of Pieces RCP	Gross Weight	kg / lb	Rate Class / Commodity Item No.	Chargeable Weight	Rate / Charge	Total	Nature and Quantity of Goods (incl. Dimensions or Volume)

Prepaid / Weight Charge / Collect — Other Charges

Valuation Charge

Tax

Total other Charges Due Agent

Total other Charges Due Carrier

Shipper certifies that the particulars on the face hereof are correct and that insofar as any part of the consignment contains dangerous goods, such part is properly described by name and is in proper condition for carriage by air according to the applicable Dangerous Goods Regulations.

Signature of Shipper or his Agent

Currency / C.O.D.

Total prepaid / Total collect

at _____ (Place) _____ Signature of Issuing Carrier or its Agent

026-21212041

图 5.20   海运提单

Figure 5.20 Ocean Bill of Lading

Shipper		B/L No.
		M132–11156

Consignee	BILL OF LADING
	COPY
	NON - NEGOTIABLE

Notify party	ALL TERMS, CONDITIONS AND EXCEPTIONS AS PER ORIGINAL BILL OF LADING

Pre-carriage by	Place of receipt KAOHSIUNG CY	"SUBJECT TO ALL THE TERMS AND CONDITIONS OF THE APPLICABLE TARIFF"

Ocean vessel Voy. No. AMERICA MARU 55227B	Port of loading KAOHSIUNG	

Port of discharge LOS ANGELES	Place of delivery TIJUANA CY	Final destination for the Merchant's reference

Container No. Seal No. Marks and Numbers	No. of Cont-ainers or pkgs.	Kind of packages; description of goods	Gross weight	Measurement
		''SHIPPER'S LOAD & COUNT''		
	3 CONTAINERS (677 CTNS)		9,014 KGS	120.32 M3
TIJUANA B.C. MEXICO VIA LOS ANGELES CA. MODEL: H260 C/NO. 1–235 MADE IN TAIWAN REPUBLIC OF CHINA –DO–BUT H667 C/NO.1	MODEL: C/NO. 1–441 MADE IN TAIWAN REPUBLIC OF CHINA	MODEL:H260,H670,H667 MODEL: JOB NO. & CODE NO. MODEL: JOB NO. CODE NO. MODEL: JOB NO. & CODE NO. ''FREIGHT COLLECT''		
	GSTU-8135538	C/S-480409 HS-41019 (192 C/T)		
	GSTU-8135939	C/S-480410 HS-41014 (192 C/T)		
	MOLU-2021646	C/S-480411 HS-41015 (293 C/T)		

*Total number of Containers or other packages or units received by the Carrier (in words)   THREE CONTAINERS ONLY

Freight and charges	Revenue tons	Rate	per	Prepaid	Collect
BOX RATE		(40'x3)	US $2,100.00/VAN (INCLUDING D.D.C.)		US$6,300.00
+ CY RECEIVING CHARGE			NT$900.00/VAN	NT$2,700.00	

Exchange rate	Prepaid at	Payable at TIJUANA	Place and date of issue TAIPEI TAIWAN
	Total prepaid in national currency	No. of original B(s)/L THREE/3	

LADEN ON BOARD THE VESSEL

Date   Signature   by

and/or the seller's bank loses title control because the goods will be delivered to anyone who can be identified as the consignee.

指示提单

Order Bill of Lading

指示提单是一种可以转让的票据。与记名提单不同，指示提单代表交易货物的所有权，它的原件必须在提交托收前背书。

This is a negotiable bill; unlike the straight bill, it represents the title to the goods in transit, and the original copy must be endorsed before it is presented to the bank for collection. In other words, the order bill can be used as collateral in financing—as documentation to discount or sell a draft. L/C transactions specify to whom the endorsement is to be made. Typically, they are made "in blank" or to the order of a third party, a bank, or a broker. *Air bills of lading* are usually "straight" (i.e., non-negotiable). Ocean shipping companies can issue "straight" or "to order."

清洁提单

Clean on Board

清洁提单意味着承运人接受货物，并将其全部装船。

To verify shipping performance, the carrier indicates the condition of the goods upon acceptance. You should prefer to ship on a bill of lading marked *clean on board*. That means that the carrier accepted the cargo and loaded it on board the vessel without exception.

不清洁提单

Foul Bill

不清洁提单指的是，装船时在提单上批注以标明货损。

A foul bill indicates an exception—that some damage is noted on the bill of lading. Discuss this with your carrier or freight forwarder to make sure that you have an opportunity to exchange any damaged goods and obtain a "clean" bill.

The next chapter explains, from A to Z, how to set up and build your company. It discusses how to decide on a name, how to go about getting start-up funds, and most importantly how to think through and write a business plan.

---

negotiable 可以转让的。title 所有权。endorse 背书。

CHAPTER 6

HOW TO SET UP YOUR OWN IMPORT/EXPORT BUSINESS

如何建立自己的进出口业务

"How do I start my own import/export business?"

That question is universal. The language might be different, but in any country in the world you will hear the same words. The answer depends on these questions: Have you done your homework? What is your product? Who will buy it? Is it profitable? Do you have contacts? Do you have a marketing plan?

By incorporating what you've learned in Chapters 2 through 5 about the fundamentals of import/export with the methods to be explained in this chapter, you should be ready to start your own import/export business.

通过第 2 章到第 5 章有关进出口基础的学习，你应该做好了启动进出口业务的准备。

The first part of this chapter describes the mechanics of start-up. The second part shows you how to develop a business plan so that you can raise capital and grow.

本章第二部分展示了，如何通过撰写商业计划书来筹集资金并谋求发展。

---

profitable 有利的。fundamental 基础的。mechanics 技巧。

启动的技巧
The Mechanics of Start-Up

The process for starting a small business is the same in any country in the world. You need capital, know-how, and management skills, but you do not need a fancy college degree. Anyone can operate a business.

启动资金
Start-Up Capital

In the initial stages of starting your own import/export business, the funds needed to support expenses will most likely come from your own pocket. While it is possible to begin an import/export business with as little as a few thousand dollars, many people underestimate the amount of capital needed to sustain the business through the early tough times.

金融资本的来源
Sources of Financial Capital

When your personal finances will not sustain the expenses of start-up until you reach breakeven and begin to show a profit, you must look for outside financial assistance. Unfortunately, banks are seldom the source of start-up capital. Why? Because banks seldom take risks. They generally expect a track record and collateral. Catch 22? Where can you go for financing? Most often, the best sources are relatives and/or friends— people who know you and believe in you. Even they may want a description of your intended business, so from the beginning you should develop a written plan for your business. It is not unusual that some people use their credit cards for initial funds. You may want to skip to the second part of this chapter immediately to learn how to write that plan. You can return to this section when you complete your business plan.

公司名称 / 标识
Business Name/Logo

Think of a name for your business. The company's name should reflect what your business does and be easily advertised by letter, fax, or over the Internet. For example, you can easily visualize the nature of the business called the "Southeast U.S.A. Furniture Import." It gives a more accurate picture of the company than would, "Kim Yee and Son." If the name you

虽然可以用尽可能少的钱来开展进出口业务，但是很多人都低估了在开始时的困难时期维系业务所需要的资金数额。

在达到收支平衡之前，财务状况还不足以支持你启动业务的需要时，你必须寻找外部融资援助。

---

uderestimate 低估。sustain 维持。breakeven 收支平衡点。catch 22 第 22 条军规，指不可逾越的障碍。

choose does not contain the owner's surname, a request to use a fictitious name, or DBA (doing business as) is required in most places. If the name of your business includes your last name, you might not be required to file a fictitious name approval. The cost for registering your fictitious name varies from country-to-country. In the United States, it is about $20.00. There is also a requirement to publish that name in a newspaper for several days. The U.S. cost for this is usually about $30 to $40.

企业组织
Business Organization

Next, decide how your business will be organized. The three common legal forms are sole proprietorship, partnership, and corporation. Most start-up import/export businesses begin as proprietorships or partnerships. They find little need to take on the extra paperwork and reporting requirements of a corporation in the beginning. Select the form of your business based on the intent, complexity, tax implications, and liability requirements of the business. If you're in doubt, consult a lawyer. Partnership agreements and incorporation papers can be expensive, ranging from as little as a few hundred dollars to several thousand.

有三种常见的商业组织形式：单一业主制、合伙制和股份公司制。

选择企业形式可以从业务的目的、复杂性、税务问题和责任要求等几方面来确定。

营业执照
Business License

Some countries require licenses to do international trade, but in the United States there is no licensing requirement; that is, there is no regulatory body that requires you to show special qualifications in order to present yourself as an importer or exporter. However, like any other business, you probably must meet local and state business licensing requirements. It is possible that the foreign country you are doing business with will require a license as well. Check with your freight forwarder.

在有些国家，从事国际贸易需要提供许证证，但是美国没有任何对许可证的要求，也就是说，没有任何监管部门要求提供可进口或出口的资质证明。

卖方许可证
Seller's Permit

Most nations and states have a sales tax. In order to ensure collection, a seller's permit is often required. These permits are usually state controlled, so as you begin your own import/export business, you should investigate your local laws.

销售许可证通常是由州政府控制，因此当你要开始进出口业务时，应该首先研究一下当地的法律。

---

proprietorship 单一业主制。complexity 复杂性。qualification 资格，资质 。fictitious 虚构的。

财务记录
Financial Records

Open a separate bank account in the name of your business. Keep accurate records, and pass all business income and expenses through your business account. Do not pay personal expenses from this account or otherwise mix personal income or expenses with business income and expenses. You may list personal "capital contributions" and "capital withdrawals," but keep these infrequent and in reasonably large sums—don't take out money in dribs and drabs.

个人花销不要从公司账户中支出，否则很容易将公司财政收支与个人收支混为一谈。

会 计
Accounting

From the beginning, learn to keep a simple set of books to feed into your Internal Revenue Service (IRS) forms at tax time. Keep a careful record (and all receipts) of all business expenses, and invoice all work on your company letterhead. At a minimum, you will need a general ledger organized into four sections: expenses, income, receivables (sales invoiced), and payables (bills received). For example, your expenses, like the cost of your trip to Hong Kong or Paris, should be listed chronologically, by month, down the left margin of the expense section. Across the page, the categories should correspond to tax categories. Check current IRS publications and tax software.

至少需要一个总账户，并将其分为四个部分：支出、收入、应收账款（销售票据），以及应付账款（已收票据）。

What kind of expenses should you expect in your own import/export business? Here are the most common ones:

- Stationery and business cards
- Telephone, answering machines, computer, calculator, copier, facsimile
- Internet Web site
- Rent, utilities, office furniture
- Inventory
- Business checking account
- Salaries and other staff expenses
- Travel

Table 6.1 offers an example of the categories of expenses shown in the expense section of your general ledger. The other sections of your ledger should be set up similarly.

---

letterhead 信笺抬头。receivable 应收账款。stationery 信笺，信封。facsimile 传真。
Internal Revenue Service 美国国内税务局。

表 6.1　费用类别

Table 6.1 Categories of Expenses

Date	Utilities	Telephone/ Fax	Travel Air	Travel Auto	Office Expense
January					
February					
March					

办　公
The Office

You can set up an office in your home or elsewhere. The location and outfitting will be determined by the volume and complexity of your firm. In the beginning, you may do business by letter and/or use e-mail and fax and part-time employees only occasionally. However, as your import/export business grows, you may need warehouse space for inventory and a larger office for a growing staff.

雇　员
Employees

As your office and trading staff grows, the complexity of paperwork and record keeping will also grow. Prior to hiring anyone, you must obtain an employer ID number from the IRS. You should also consider worker's compensation and benefits insurance.

商业保险
Business Insurance

Other kinds of business insurance that you should consider on a case-by-case basis are liability, disability, an FCIA (Foreign Credit Insurance Association) umbrella policy, and a customs bond.

一些你需要认真考虑的其他商业保险类别包括：债务保险、伤残保险、出口信用保险以及海关保税。

支持团队
Support Team

Early in the establishment of your import/export business, you should develop a relationship with your international support team. After a brief period of shopping around, settle on a long-term relationship with

货比三家之后，可以选择与国际银行、货运代理、海关

---

inventory 存货。compensation 赔偿。

经纪人、国际会计师和国际律师建立长期的合作关系。

(1) an international banker, (2) a freight forwarder, (3) a customs house broker, (4) an international accountant, and (5) an international attorney. Also, consider contacting the Small Business Administration (SBA) if you run into problems. Members of the SBA's Service Corps of Retired Executives (SCORE) are often available to provide free advice.

启动海外业务的十条诚律

The 10 Commandments of Starting an Overseas Business

业务的主要参与者不仅要能够直接合作并做出贡献，而且还需要拥有相应的国际业务经验。

在既定的时间周期里，应该把主要资源锁定在两到三个产品或目标上。

"两条腿走路"。除银行之外，找家好的货运代理或海关经纪。

经常与国际同仁进行有效沟通，考察海外市场并拜访海外制造商。

1. Limit the primary participants to people who not only can collaborate and contribute directly, but also are experienced in some form of international business.
2. Define your import/export market in terms of what is to be bought, precisely by whom, and why.
3. Concentrate all available resources on two or three products or objectives within a given time period.
4. Obtain the best information through your own industry.
5. Write down your business plan and work from it.
6. "Walk on two legs." Pick a good freight forwarder or customs house broker to walk alongside your banker.
7. Translate your literature into the language(s) of the country(ies) in which you will do business.
8. Use the services of the Departments of Commerce and Treasury.
9. Limit the effects of your inevitable mistakes by starting slowly.
10. Communicate frequently and well with your international contacts, and visit the overseas markets and manufacturers.

商业计划书

The Business Plan

In the beginning you may have only a notion of your plan tucked away in your head. As the concept of your business grows, it will be necessary to formalize your plan and stick to it. Putting out brush fires in order to maintain marginal survival is hardly a wise use of anyone's time.

---

attorney 律师。collaborate 合作。Departments of Commerce and Treasury 工商和财政部门。manufacturer 制造商。

The underlying concept of a business plan is to write out your thoughts. By raising and then systematically answering basic operational questions, you force self-criticism. Once it's on paper, others can read it and you can invite their opinions. Don't let your ego get in your way. Ask for constructive criticism from the most experienced people you can find. Often it is better to ask strangers because friends and relatives tend to want to shield you from hurt. Explain to your readers that you want to hear both the bad news and the good news. The more eyes that see the plan, the more likely you will (1) identify hazards while you still can act or avoid them and (2) spot opportunities while you can easily act to maximize them.

越多的人看到你的商业计划书，你就越有可能认识到其中的风险或及时采取行动规避风险；同时也越有可能看到机会并最大限度地利用机会。

The plan is nothing; planning is everything.
—*President (General) Dwight Eisenhower*

A business plan can be as brief as 10 pages and as long as 50. On average, they run about 20 pages. Every outline is usually about the same. Figure 6.1 suggests an outline format for your business plan.

如何展开一个商业计划
How to Begin the Business Plan

Stop everything and begin writing. The first draft of your plan will contain about 80 percent of the finished draft and can be finished in less than two days. One measure of the success of the process is the amount of pain it causes you. By looking at your business as an onlooker would, you may find that some of your vision, a pet project for instance, may have to be abandoned. Often, the process is done in eight steps:

计划书初稿应该完成整体计划的 80%，其余部分则可以在两天之内完成。

1. Define long-term objectives
2. State short-term goals
3. Set marketing strategies
4. Analyze available resources (personnel, material, etc.)
5. Assemble financial data
6. Review for realism
7. Rewrite
8. Implement

---

systematically 系统地，有条理地。constructive 建设性的。onlooker 旁观者。marketing strategy 营销策略。

图 6.1　商业计划纲要

Figure 6.1 Business Plan Outline

Cover Sheet: Name, principals, address, etc.

International Costumes, Inc.
Business Plan
Fiscal Year 20XX

Statement of Purpose:

Table of Contents: (corresponds to each exhibit)

   A. Executive summary
   B. Description of the business
   C. Product-line plan
   D. Sales and marketing plan
   E. Operations plan
   F. Organization plan
   G. Financial plan
   H. Supporting documents
   I. Summary

Exhibits:

Exhibit A　Executive Summary
   1. Written last, summarizes in global terms the entire plan;
      succinct expression of long- and short-term goals

Exhibit B　Description of the Business
   1. Long- and short-term goals
      Financial
      Nonfinancial

   2. Strategies
      Product line
      Sales and marketing
      Product development
      Operations
      Organizational
      Financial

   3. Location
      Reasons

Exhibit C　Product-Line Plan
   1. Product line and products
      Description

(Continued)

图 6.1　商业计划纲要（接上页）
Figure 6.1 (Continued)

      Price
      Costs
      Historical volume
      Future expectations

  2. Competition's product line and product position
     Pricing
     Advertising and promotion

Exhibit D Sales and Marketing Plan
  1. Person(s) responsible for generating product line and
     product sales
  2. Competition's approach to sales and marketing

Exhibit E Operations Plan
  1. Production and operations function
     Production scheduling
     Inventory (product line and product)
  2. Capital expenditures (if required)

Exhibit F Organization Plan
  1. Organization's structure
     Organization chart
     Résumés of key personnel
     Managerial style

Exhibit G Financial Plan
  1. Summary of operating and financial schedules
  2. Schedules*
     Capital equipment
     Balance sheet
     Cash flow (breakeven analysis)
     Income projections
     Pro forma cash flow
     Historical financial reports for existing business
     (Balance sheets for past three years; income statements
     for past three years; tax returns)

Exhibit H Supporting Documents
  1. Personal résumés
  2. Cost of living budget
  3. Letters of reference
  4. Copies of leases
  5. Anything else of relevance to the plan
Exhibit I Summary

*See Figures 6-2 to 6-5.

确定长期目标
Defining Long-Term Objectives

Start with the objectives of your import/export business. Think ahead. What do I want the business to be like in three years? Five years? Twenty years? How big a business do you want?

说明短期目标
Stating Short-Term Goals

根据销量和资金两个方面来确定你的进出口业务。你需要做到精确，即用可计算的时间和美元单位来表述。

Define your import/export business in terms of sales volume and assets. Be precise; state them in measurable units of time and dollars.

设计营销策略
Setting Marketing Strategies

如果你已经按照第 2 章的讲解完成了作业，并且运用了第 3 章所述的相关市场概念，那么商业计划书这一部分就变得非常简单了。

If you have done your homework as explained in Chapter 2 and applied the marketing concepts offered in Chapter 3, this part of the business plan should be simple.

如果没有销售，所有预测和其他计划都会落空。由于销售利润支持着业务运营，所以要把 75% 的时间花在市场营销策划上。

If not, go back and review the marketing section of Chapter 3, because nothing will happen with your business until you make a sale. If sales aren't made, projections and other plans fall apart. Profitable sales support the business, so be prepared to spend 75 percent of your planning time on marketing efforts. Ultimately, the best marketing information comes through your own industry, here or overseas. Talk to those with experience. Talk to manufacturers as well as other importers/exporters. Don't overlook the data that can be found in libraries and over the Internet.

Make your market plan precise. Describe your competitive advantage. Outline your geographical and product line priorities. Write down your sales goals. List your alternatives for market penetration. Will you sell direct or through agents? What is the advertising budget? Travel in an import/export business is a must. What is the travel budget? How much will it cost to expand your markets? What will be the cost of com-

低估实际花费的问题十分常见，应避免将成本预测最小化。通常的花费要比你预估的三倍还多。

munications? Don't minimize your cost projections. It is not unusual to underestimate expenses. They are often three times more than you think they will be.

可用资源分析
Analyzing Available Resources

Now for the pain. You must ask yourself whether you have the resources to make the plan work. Take a management inventory. Do you have the

---

projection 预测。fall apart 落空。penetration 渗透。

skills to market your products? Do you need administrative or account-ing skills? Will you need warehouse space? Will you need translators? How much cash will you need?

收集财务数据
Assembling Financial Data

After all the dreaming and reality testing of the first four steps, you must now express them in terms of cash flow, profit and loss projections, and balance sheets. Figure 6.2 shows a pro forma sales projection (three-year summary, detailed by month for the first year; detailed by quarter for the second and third years). Figure 6.3 is a pro forma income (profit and loss) statement (detailed by month for the first year; detailed by quarter for the second and third years), Figure 6.4 is a pro forma balance sheet, and Figure 6.5 is a pro forma cash flow statement (detailed by month for first year; detailed by quarter for the second and third years). This use of *pro forma* here means estimating information in advance in a prescribed form.

> 经过前四个步骤的试验之后，现在你必须以现金流、盈亏预测以及资产负债表的形式把它们表示出来。

The cash flow and the profit and loss projections serve double duty. They quantify the sales and operating goals, including use of person-nel and other resources expressed in dollars and time. As a guide to the future, they can be used as control documents and measure progress toward goals. The balance sheet shows what your business owns, what it owes, and how those assets and liabilities are distributed.

> 现金流和盈亏预测可以用来确认销售额以及经营目标，例如以金钱和时间的形式来表示人员和其他资源的使用情况。

回顾求实
Reviewing for Realism

Your plan must not set contradictory goals. A coherent plan fits together. You cannot be expanding the introduction of goose liver from China at the same time you are getting out of animal products and into irrigation machinery. Look at your plan as a whole and ask, "Does this make good business sense?"

重新编写
Rewrite

Now that the first draft is complete, let at least 10 experienced people look at it. Ask them to be critical and to tell you the truth. Let them know up

---

balance sheets 资产负债表。contradictory 矛盾的。irrigation 灌溉。

图 6.2 预计销售表

Figure 6.2 Pro Forma Sales Projections

Pro Forma Sales (Shipments) Projections
Fiscal Year 20xx

Product Line(s) Product(s)	Jan	Feb	March	April	May	June	July	Aug	Sept	Oct	Nov	Dec	Year
A. Product Line A													
1. Product 1													
Shipments (Units)													
× Avg. Price/Unit													
Gross Sales	$	$								$	$	$	$
2. Product 2													
3. Product 3													
— — —													
n. Product N													
Product Line A— Gross Sales	$	$								$	$	$	$

B. Product Line B

C. Product Line C

N. Product Line N

Total Gross Sales $ $ $ $ $ $ $ $ $ $ $

图 6.3　预计损益表（利润和亏损）

Figure 6.3 Pro Forma Income Statement (Profit and Loss)

Pro Forma Income Statement
Fiscal Year 20xx

	Jan	Feb	March	April	May	June	July	Aug	Sept	Oct	Nov	Dec	Year
Gross Sales													
less: Discounts, allowances, etc.	—	—	—	—	—	—	—	—	—	—	—	—	—
Net Sales	—	—	—	—	—	—	—	—	—	—	—	—	—
less: Variable costs													
Manufacturing:													
Material	—	—	—	—	—	—	—	—	—	—	—	—	—
Labor	—	—	—	—	—	—	—	—	—	—	—	—	—
Variable overhead	—	—	—	—	—	—	—	—	—	—	—	—	—
Other	—	—	—	—	—	—	—	—	—	—	—	—	—
Variable costs (manufacturing)	—	—	—	—	—	—	—	—	—	—	—	—	—
Operating:													
Commissions	—	—	—	—	—	—	—	—	—	—	—	—	—
Other	—	—	—	—	—	—	—	—	—	—	—	—	—
Variable costs (operating)	—	—	—	—	—	—	—	—	—	—	—	—	—
Variable costs (total)	—	—	—	—	—	—	—	—	—	—	—	—	—
Contribution													
Percent of net sales	(%)												

less: Fixed costs
Manufacturing
Engineering
Selling
General and
Administrative
Financial
Fixed costs (total)
Profit before taxes
less: Taxes
Net income

图 6.4 预计资产负债表

Figure 6.4 Pro Forma Balance Sheet

Pro Forma Balance Sheet Fiscal Year 20xx	Actual Dec	Jan	Feb	March	April	May	June	July	Aug	Sept	Oct	Nov	Dec
A. *Assets Employed*													
1. *Current Assets*													
Cash													
Accounts receivable (net)													
Inventory													
Prepaids													
Other													
Subtotal													
2. *Current Liabilities* (excluding debt)													
Accounts payable													
Accrued liabilities													
Taxes payable													
Other													
Subtotal													
Working capital (1 – 2)													
3. *Property, Plant, and Equipment*													
Land													
Building													

Equipment
Less: Accumulated
depreciation

Subtotal

4. *Other Assets*
Investments
Other

Subtotal

Assets Employed

B. *Capital Structure*
1. *Debt*

Short-term Notes
Long-term (current
portion)
Long-term Debt
Other

Subtotal

2. *Deferred Taxes*

3. *Shareholders Equity*
Paid-in Capital
Retained Earnings

Subtotal

Capital Structure

图 6.5 预计现金流量表

Figure 6.5 Pro Forma Cash Flow Statement

Pro Forma Cash Flow Statement (Operational)
Fiscal Year 20xx

	Jan	Feb	March	April	May	June	July	Aug	Sept	Oct	Nov	Dec	Year
Cash Receipts													
Collection of accounts receivable													
Sale of assets													
Borrowings													
Equity financing													
Other													
Cash receipts													
Cash Expenditures													
Material													
Freight													
Wages and salaries													
Commissions													
Fringe benefits													
Manufacturing expenses													
Selling expenses													
General and administrative expenses													
Financial expenses													
Subtotal													

Capital expenditures

Debt repayment

Dividends

Other

Cash expenditures

Cash flows

Cumulative cash flows

front that you have a lot of ego in this project, but that because you want to be a success, you want their criticism, no matter how much it hurts.

执 行
Implementation

商业计划只是提供了一张路线图，更严峻的考验在于计划是否可行。

Your business plan provides a road map, but the acid test is whether it will work. Like a map, you may have to detour to get where you are going, so don't put the map on the shelf and forget about it. Use it as an operating document. Review it and revise it as experience dictates.

Now you're ready to go. You've done your homework and written your business plan. If you've gotten this far, you have the style and determination to make it work.

By now, you have written your first letter and made your first contact. As an importer, you've asked for literature and samples; as an exporter you've sent them. You want early orders, and if you have done your homework, they should start rolling in, but be patient. Everything takes a little longer than you would expect or would like in international business.

正如在前五章中所学到的，大部分国际贸易的基本原则同样适用于进口和出口，差别主要体现在几个主要因素上。

As you have learned in the previous five chapters, most of the fundamentals of international trade are common to both importing and exporting, but some major elements are specific to one or the other. The next part of the book explains those things that are unique to exporting or to importing, such as government support systems, information systems, tax considerations, tariffs, and private sector support organizations.

---

criticism 批评。road map 路线图。

PART 2

THE DIFFERENCES

差异特性

CHAPTER 7

EXPORTING FROM THE UNITED STATES

从美国出口

The figure presented in the introduction to this book (Figure I.1) demonstrates that gross global merchandise trade has risen dramatically since the end of World War II. However Figure 1.1, in Chapter 1, shows that since about 1975, the United States has been in serious chronic trade deficit.

This chapter explores the processes that are unique to exporting from the United States and how you can take advantage of them to export your products and services, thus assisting in the reduction of the nation's deficits. Among other things, you will learn which public and private organizations support the export function and where to go for export information. The topics specific to export are:

- Government support
- Information sources
- Freight forwarding
- Export controls
- "Made in USA"
- Tax incentives for exporting
- How to gain relief from unfair import practices
- Export cities

本书中图 I.1 表明，自第二次世界大战结束以来，全球商品总贸易量显著增加。

本章研究从美国出口的特殊程序以及怎样利用它们出口商品和服务，以达到减轻国家赤字的目的。

与出口相关的特殊因素有：

- 政府支持；
- 信息资源；
- 货运代理；
- 出口控制；
- "美国制造"；
- 出口税收激励；
- 如何减轻进口业务中的不公平；
- 出口城市。

---

merchandise trade 商品贸易。take advantage of 利用。deficit 赤字。

政府支持
Government Support

由于出口能带来所需的外汇，并扩大就业市场，所有政府都鼓励出口。

All governments promote exporting because it brings needed foreign exchange and stimulates job expansion. Therefore, every nation and many states and provincial governments provide a wide range of export counseling and assistance programs.

国际贸易管理局
International Trade Administration (ITA)

大多数国家都有类似美国国际贸易管理局这样的机构，这种机构一般是商务部的分支。

Most countries have an organization similar to the U.S. International Trade Administration (ITA), which is a division of the Department of Commerce. Its importance to the nation is emphasized by the fact that it gets a dominant share of that department's budget. The ITA is organized basically into three arms: overseas, headquarters, and domestic covering the territorial boundaries of the United States. To make contact and find the office nearest you go to: www.export.gov or www.ita.doc.gov; phone: 800-USA-TRAD(E) (800-872-8723); e-mail: TIC@ITA.GOV

海外办事处
Overseas Offices

国际贸易管理局的海外职能被称为外国商贸服务。

国际贸易管理局提供出口方案，帮助小公司增加利润、降低风险。

商贸服务部官员鉴定并评估进口商、采购商、代理商、分销商以及合资伙伴。

The *overseas* function of the ITA is called the Foreign Commercial Service (FCS). It maintains offices in more than 108 domestic offices and 140 overseas posts in major foreign cities in the 80 countries that are the principal trading partners of the United States. ITA offers export solutions to help smaller firms increase profits and lower risk. To help U.S. firms compete, these offices provide a full range of business services, trade leads, and financial counseling services, which include political and credit risk analysis, advice on market entry strategy, sources of financing, and major project identification, tracking, and assistance. Commercial Service officers identify and evaluate importers, buyers, agents, distributors, and joint-venture partners. Through their local Commercial Service centers, they can introduce you to local business and government leaders and assist in trade disputes. These services are available to U.S. companies that either produce or have the export rights to a product or service that is composed of 51 percent or more U.S. content. All you have to do is call or write either your local Export

---

foreign exchange 外汇。international trade administration 国际贸易管理局。Department of Commerce 商务部。Foreign Commercial Service 外国商贸服务。joint-venture partner 合资伙伴

Assistance Center within the U.S. Commerce Department Office or check the list of offices found at www.ita.doc.gov

The senior Commercial Service officer in each country is a principal advisor to the U.S. Ambassador. Commercial Service staff members gather data on specific export opportunities, country trends affecting trade and investment, and prospects for specific industries. They also monitor and analyze local laws and practices that affect business conditions.

商贸服务部门的工作人员收集关于特殊出口机会、影响贸易和投资的国内趋势以及特殊产业前景的数据。他们还监控并分析影响商业条件的当地法律法规。

总部办事处
Headquarters Offices (Washington, DC)

The International Trade Administration of the U.S. Department of Commerce also has approximately 165 country and regional desk officers at its headquarters in Washington, DC. Their job is to be experts in assigned countries, from Afghanistan to Zimbabwe. These desk officers provide specific information about the laws and products of their assigned countries to U.S. business people. Desk officers are organized into two groups: (1) market access and commercial policy and (2) trade information/trade development.

美国商务部麾下的国际贸易管理局，总部位于华盛顿特区，在这里有来自约 165 个国家和地区的主管干事。

主管干事被分为两组：（1）市场准入和商业政策；（2）贸易信息 / 贸易发展。

The desk officers are specialists who assess the needs of an individual firm wishing to sell in a particular country in the full context of that country's economy, trade policies, and political situation. Trade development officers are industry specialists who work with manufacturing and service industry associations and firms to identify trade opportunities and obstacles by product or service, industry sector, and market.

主管干事是为想要进入特定国家市场的公司评估需求的专家，他们以特定国家的经济情况、贸易政策和政治形势为背景，为公司进行专业评估。贸易发展干事是行业专家，他们与制造业和服务业的组织以及公司协同工作，通过产品和服务、产业部门以及市场来识别商业机遇和障碍。

Exporters who are planning to visit Washington, DC and would like to schedule appointments with either desk officers or program specialists within the Commerce Department (and/or other agencies involved in international marketing) should contact the nearest Export Assistance Center; phone: 800-USA-TRAD(E); Web site: www.export.gov.

国内办事处
Domestic Offices

The United States offers a broad range of trade-related information, as well as one-on-one counseling from experienced trade specialists located in more than 50 Export Assistance Centers (EACs) in industrial and commercial centers throughout the United States. These are

美国不仅提供广泛的贸易相关信息，遍布美国商贸中心的 50 多家出口协助中心，也派出经验丰富的贸易专家提供一对一的咨询服务。

---

prospect 前景。desk officer 主管干事。market access 市场准入。specialist 专家。in the full context of 在全范围内。

customer-focused offices designed to streamline export marketing and trade finance assistance by integrating in a single location the counselors and services of the Commercial Service, Export-Import (EXIM) Bank, the Small Business Administration (SBA), and in some cities, the U.S. Agency for International Development. To contact call 800-USA-TRAD(E) or see the local Commercial Service office addresses listed at www.ita.doc.gov; or e-mail at tic@da.doc.gov.

The EACs can help exporters and other prospective businesses with:

出口协助中心能在以下方面帮助出口商和其他潜在商户：
- 市场调查；
- 海外贸易和投资机会；
- 美国产品和服务的外国市场；
- 潜在拨款机会；
- 外国信用保险协会的保险；
- 出口税收优惠；
- 国际贸易展会；
- 出口必要凭证；
- 外国经济常识；
- 出口授权制度；
- 产品服务升级；
- 定位出口前景。

- Market research
- Trade and investment opportunities abroad
- Foreign markets for U.S. products and services
- Possible grant opportunities
- Insurance from the FCIA
- Tax advantages of exporting
- International trade exhibitions
- Export documentation requirements
- Economic facts on foreign countries
- Export licensing requirements
- Promotion of products and services
- Locating export prospects

区域出口委员会
District Export Councils

区域出口委员会由地方商界领袖组成，他们由每届商务部部长指定。商务部部长根据其对国际商业的了解，为当地公司提供专业指导。

District Export Councils (DECs) are organizations of leaders from the local business community, appointed by successive Secretaries of Commerce, whose knowledge of international business provides a source of professional advice for local firms.

为了帮助小企业在世界经济中取得成功，区域出口委员会的成员不但要自愿利用时间赞助并参加大量贸易促进活动，而且还要提供专业知识并为有意出口的中小型企业进行培训。

In order to help small businesses succeed in the world economy, DECs volunteer their time to sponsor and participate in numerous trade promotion activities, as well as to supply specialized expertise and mentoring programs to small- and medium-sized businesses that are interested in exporting. They run seminars on export basics and trade finance, host international buyer delegations, design breakthrough guides to help firms export, and put exporters on the Internet to help build export assistance partnerships to strengthen the support given to local businesses in exporting.

---

market research 市场调查。grant 拨款。economic facts 经济常识。district export council 区域出口委员会。expertise 专业知识／技能。mentor 指导，培训。

The Commercial Service's Export Assistance Centers work closely with these experienced regional international business people through 56 District Export Councils. The 1,700 volunteer DEC members are available to counsel prospective exporters on:

- The how-tos of international trade
- Co-sponsoring seminars and workshops with the EACs
- Addressing business groups on international business opportunities
- Promote awareness of the trade-assistance programs of the Department of Commerce

小型企业发展中心
Small Business Development Centers (SBDCs)

SBDCs provide a full range of export assistance services to small businesses, particularly those new to export, and offer counseling, training, managerial, and trade finance assistance. To contact, phone: 800-UASK-SBA, 800-827-5722, or 202-606-4000; Web site: www.sba.gov; address: SBA Answer Desk, 6302 Fairview Road, Suite 300, Charlotte, North Carolina, 28210.

小型企业发展中心为小型企业，尤其是初涉出口业务的小型企业，提供全程出口援助。同时，它也提供咨询、培训、管理以及商业金融援助等服务。

退休执行官服务联合会
Service Corps of Retired Executives (SCORE)

The Service Corps of Retired Executives (SCORE), usually co-located with your local SBA office, provides one-on-one counseling and training seminars. For the office nearest you, phone: 800-634-0245; 202-205-6762; fax: 202-205-7636; Web site: www.score.org.

退休执行官服务联合会，通常位于当地小型企业管理局周边，提供一对一咨询，开办出口培训研讨班。

出口贸易公司事务管理局
Office of Export Trading Company Affairs (OETCA)

The Office of Export Trading Company Affairs (OETCA), a part of USITA Trade Development, is designed to promote the team concept of exporting through the formation and use of export trading companies (ETCs), export management companies (EMCs), and, in general, the intermediary industry. Office of Export Trading Company Affairs administers the Export Trade Certificate of Review program which permits an antitrust "insurance policy" under the Export Trading Company Act (ETCA). This law permits bankers' banks and holding

出口贸易公司事务管理局是美国国际贸易管理局贸易发展部的组成部分，它的职责是通过组建和使用出口贸易公司、出口管理公司等中间产业，提升出口业务中的团队理念。

---

co-locate 位于同一地方。SBA（美国）小企业管理局。export trading company 出口贸易公司。export management company 出口管理公司。intermediary 中间的。

companies to invest in ETCs, reduces the restrictions on export financing provided by financial institutions, and modifies the application of the antitrust laws to certain export trade.

出口合资企业可使公司缩小规模经济并分散风险。

Export joint ventures offer firms the opportunity to reduce economies of scale and spread the risks. Specific areas in which gains can be obtained are:

- Market research
- Market development
- Overseas bidding
- Non-tariff barriers
- Transportation and shipping
- Joint bidding and selling arrangements
- Pricing policies
- Service and promotional activities

For information, phone: 202-482-5131; fax: 202-482-1790; Web site: www.ita.doc.gov.

信息资源
Information Sources

出口所需的信息比国内市场销售所需的信息更容易获取。因为大多数政府会对收集和分析国际贸易数据进行补贴。

Information needed for exporting is easier to obtain than is information needed for domestic sales. Why? Because most governments subsidize the gathering and analysis of international trade data. A wealth of information, both on paper and electronic, exists to promote exporting. More information is available than one could digest in a lifetime, and the U.S. Department of Commerce has made it easy to acquire. For example, the Trade Opportunities Program (TOP) and the Export Contact List Service files are available in both printed form and up-to-the minute computer-resident databases.

Your nearest Export Assistance Center offers the following information services to U.S. exporters:

贸易信息中心拥有所有关于政府出口援助项目的数据资源。

- ***Trade Information Center (TIC).*** The TIC is the most comprehensive resource for information on all government export assistance programs. The center's staff advises exporters on how

---

spread the risk 分散风险。non-tariff barriers 非关税壁垒。comprehensive 全面的。

to locate and use government programs, guides exporters through the export process, supplies general market information, and provides basic export counseling. To contact, phone: 800-USA-TRAD(E) or 202-482-5131; e-mail: tic@ita.doc.gov; fax: 202-482-1790; Web site: tradeinfo.doc.gov. A special phone line is available for those who are hearing impaired using a TDD machine: 800-TDD-TRAD(E). Ask for a free copy of the excellent pamphlets *Export Programs: A Business Directory of U.S. Government Services*, *Export Programs Guide*, and *A Basic Guide to Exporting*.

- *National Trade Data Bank (NTDB).* The NTDB is a one stop source for export promotion and international trade data collected by 17 U.S. government agencies. Updated each month and released on two CD-ROMs, the NTDB enables IBM-compatible personal computers equipped with CD-ROM readers to access over 100,000 trade-related documents. To contact, phone: 800-STAT-USA; Web site: www.stat-usa.gov or tradeport.org. You may wish to visit www.buyusa.com, a site that matches U.S. suppliers with international buyers, the Yellow Pages of foreign countries, and www.globaledge.msu.edu.

  国家贸易数据库是出口推进和由 17 家美国政府机构所收集国际贸易数据的一站式资源。

- *Economic Bulletin Board (EBB).* The EBB, a personal computer–based electronic bulletin board, is your online source for trade leads as well as for the latest statistical releases from the Bureau of the Census, the Bureau of Economic Analysis, the Bureau of Labor Statistics, the Federal Reserve Board, and other federal agencies. To contact, phone: 800-STAT-USA, 800-782-8872, 202-482-3870, or 202-482-1986. You may use your fax machine to receive trade leads and the latest trade and economic information from the federal government. You can access this by dialing 900-RUN-A-FAX. Contact EBB/FAX help line, phone: 202-482-1986; fax: 202-482-2164.

  经济公告牌是一种以个人计算机为基础的电子布告牌，它既是商界精英的网络资源，也为人口普查局、经济调查局、劳动统计局、联邦储备金监察小组以及其他联邦机构提供了上传最新数据的平台。

- *Industry Sector Analysis (ISA).* This organization produces market research reports on location in leading overseas markets. The reports cover market size and outlook, characteristics, and competitive and end-user analysis for a selected industry sector in a particular country. Selected analyses are available on the National Trade Data Bank (NTDB).

  产业部门分析组织负责提供有关主要海外市场的市场调查报告。

---

one stop source 一站式资源。computer-based 以计算机为基础的。bulletin board 布告牌。the Federal Reserve Board 联邦储备金监察小组。leading overseas market 主要海外市场。

市场观察是在海外市场和多边发展储备银行中孕育的特定国外市场条件和机遇的简况。

- *International Market Insights (IMI).* Market insights are short profiles of specific foreign market conditions or opportunities prepared in overseas markets and at multilateral development banks. These non-formatted reports include information and updates on dynamic sectors of a particular country and could profile new major projects or trade events. These are also available on the NTDB.

出口前景
Export Prospects

多数政府都有促进出口商建立跨国交往的项目。

Most governments have programs to help exporters make cross-border contacts. The U.S. government is no exception. As a matter of fact, you should take advantage of its full range of programs. For basic information go to www.trade.gov/td/tic.

代理分销服务机构代表美国客户向感兴趣且符合标准的外国代表进行常规海外"调查"。

- *Agent Distributor Service (ADS).* ADS performs a custom overseas "search" for interested and qualified foreign representatives on behalf of a U.S. client. Commercial Services (CS) staff abroad conduct the search and prepare a report identifying up to six foreign prospects that have personally examined the U.S. firm's product literature and have expressed interest in representing the firm. ADS charges a fee per market or specific area. Contact your local EAC, phone: 800-USA-TRAD(E); Web site: www.ita.doc.gov.

世界各国的商界专家通过贸易展览中的对话和市场调查,搜寻商业机会项目的精英。

- *Trade Opportunities Program (TOP).* Commercial specialists around the world collect TOP leads at trade shows, through conversation, and through market research. Individual sales lead messages are then sent directly to subscribers and the EACs nationwide. They can be sent via computer or facsimile, or sent as a printed hard copy. Each message contains detailed information regarding a current foreign trade lead, typically including the specifications, quantities, end use, delivery and bid deadlines for the product or service desired by the foreign customer. A fee is required to set up the subscribers interest file and for each block of 50 leads up to five blocks. To contact, phone: 800-STAT-USA or 202-482-1986; e-mail: statmail@PSA.doc.gov.

---

market insight 市场观察。short profile 简况。multilateral 多边的。cross-border 跨国的。representative 代表。on behalf of 代表······

HOT TIP

The Trade Opportunities Program (TOP) matches product interests of foreign buyers with those of U.S. subscribers.

- ***International Company Profile (ICP).*** Information provided in an international company profile includes type of organization, year established, size, general reputation, territory covered, sales, product lines, principal owners, financial information, and trade references, with recommendations from on-site commercial officers as to the company's suitability as a trading partner.

国际企业概况组织提供的信息包括：组织的类型、成立年限、企业规模、企业信誉、营业范围、销售状况、生产线、主要所有者、企业金融信息、贸易参考，以及现场商务专员根据该公司作为合作伙伴的适合程度提出的建议。

- ***Commercial Service International Contacts (CSIC).*** CSIC provides the name and contact information for directories of importers, agents, trade association, government agencies, and the like on a country-by-country basis. Available on the NTDB.

商业服务国际交流中心为各企业董事会提供进口商、代理人、贸易伙伴、政府机构以及以国与国为基础的类似机构的名称和联络信息。

海外营销
Overseas Promotion

The ITA, U.S. Department of State offices within U.S. embassies, and consulates worldwide collaborate to assist in the promotion of products and services.

服务和项目
Services and Programs

- ***Agent/Distributor Services.*** Discussed earlier, these services are often used in conjunction with the Gold Key Service. They assist with issues of industrial property rights, territory covered (exclusive and nonexclusive contracts) the problems of terminating the contract, possibility of host country of switching from contract laws to labor laws according of the comparative size of the principal's company and distributor's company.

代理／分销服务负责有关产业产权问题，营业区内终止合同问题（排他性合同和非排他性合同），以及东道国根据负责公司和分销公司的相对规模，由合同法向劳动法转变的可能性。

- ***Gold Key Service.*** A custom-tailored service that combines orientation briefings, market research, appointments with potential

金钥匙服务是一项融合基础培训、市场调查、会晤潜在

---

territory covered 营业覆盖范围。on-site 现场。directory 董事会。property right 产权。nonexclusive 非排他性。terminate 终止。orientation briefing 基础培训。appointment 会晤。

合作伙伴、会议记录、协助
发展后续战略的定制服务。

贸易介绍代表团将美国公司
与国外潜在合作机构、分销
商、合资公司以及许可证发
放伙伴进行配对。

国际采购商项目组织负责直
接出口销售以及为有意愿的
美国展销商做国际代理。

在一定地理区域内蓬勃发展
的市场中，多国／系列展览
会展示美国公司产品的宣传
册。

贸易公平认证鼓励开办展览
的私人组织者培训初涉出口
业务的美国参展商，使其达
到商务部的标准并为美国参
展商提供从高级营销到现场
协助的一系列服务。

partners, interpreter service for meetings, and assistance in developing follow-up strategies. Gold Key Service is offered by the Commercial Service in export markets around the world. Prices and conditions vary by country.

- **Matchmaker Trade Delegations.** "Matches" U.S. firms with prospective agents, distributors, and joint-venture or licensing partners abroad. For each "matchmaker" the Commercial Service staff evaluates the marketing potential of U.S. firms' products and services, finds and screens contacts, and handles all event logistics. U.S. firms visit the designated countries with the delegation and, in each country, receive a schedule of business meetings and in-depth market and finance briefings.

- **International Buyer Program (IBP).** Supports selected leading U.S. trade shows in industries with high export potential. The Department of Commerce offices abroad recruit delegations of foreign buyers and distributors to attend the U.S. shows, while program staff members help exhibiting firms make contact with international visitors at the show. The International Buyer Program achieves direct export sales and international representation for interested U.S. exhibitors.

- **Multistate/Catalog Exhibitions.** The exhibitions showcase U.S. company product literature in fast-growing markets within a geographic region. During multi-state/catalog exhibitions, the U.S. Department of Commerce staff and representatives from state development agencies present product literature to hundreds of interested business prospects abroad and send the trade leads directly to participants.

- **Trade Fair Certification.** Supports major international industry trade shows, thereby providing high-profile promotion of U.S. products. Trade fair certification encourages private organizers to recruit new-to-market, new-to-export U.S. exhibitors to maintain Department of Commerce standards for events and to provide services ranging from advance promotion to on-site assistance for U.S. exhibitors.

---

matchmaker 介绍人。buyer 采购商。representation 代理。showcase 展示。fast-growing 蓬勃发展的。geographic region 地理区域。

Publications and Reports   刊物和报告

- *The Overseas Trade Promotions Calendar.* Revised quarterly, this calendar provides a 12-month schedule of U.S. Trade Center exhibitions and international trade fairs in which U.S. participation is planned. It also includes other overseas promotional activities that are planned and to be organized by the U.S. Department of Commerce.

《海外贸易营销日程》提供一年12个月中美国计划参加的美国贸易中心展览和国际贸易事项的日程表，每个季度进行一次修订。

- *How to Get the Most from Overseas Exhibitions.* Contains helpful planning tips and details the steps to be taken to participate in an overseas exhibition. Write to the Office of Export Development, International Trade Administration, U.S. Department of Commerce, Washington, DC 20230. No charge.

《如何充分利用海外展销报告》中包括有益的规划建议和参加海外展会的细节步骤。

- *Export Statistics Profile.* Provides a variety of export statistics by product and arrays the data in ways that make market analysis easy. It provides multiyear coverage, percentage of market shares, and top markets for products in rank order. The price ranges from $30 to $70 depending on the depth and specification. Go to www.trade.gov/td/tic.

《出口统计简报》提供一系列出口产品数据，并归纳数据，使数据信息更好地用于市场分析。

- *Customs Service Statistics.* This statistical service provides customs statistics in four export and/or import tables. Prices for these statistical reports range from $50 to $150 depending on complexity:

《海关服务统计》用4张出口和进口表来提供海关数据。

  1. For up to 10 selected products showing trade to 9 major world market areas.
  2. For up to 10 selected products showing trade to every country worldwide in rank order.
  3. For up to 10 selected countries showing trade in individually specified products in rank order.
  4. For the top 30 countries showing trade in up to 10 individually specified products in rank order.

- *Understanding U.S. Foreign Trade Data.* Explains the different foreign trade classifications and valuation systems and other factors that complicate the understanding of U.S. foreign trade data.

解释使了解美国外贸数据变复杂的因素，如不同的外国贸易分类和评估体系以及其他因素。

---

revise 修正。array 有序的安排，归纳。classification 分类。valuation 评估。complicate 使……变复杂。

Price: $7.50. Contact Superintendent of Documents at,
phone: 866-512-1800; fax: 202-512-2250; e-mail:
Orders@gpo.gov; Web site: www.gpoaccess.gov.

- *U.S. Government Information: Publications, Periodicals, and
Electronic Products.* Popular government publications are
organized into subject areas and can be ordered from the online
bookstore operated by the Government Printing Office (GPO)
Web site: www.gpoaccess.gov; e-mail orders@gpo.gov.
- *A Basic Guide to Exporting.* Published by the U.S. Department
of Commerce, it can be obtained by writing the Superintendent of
Documents, U.S. Government Printing Office, Washington, DC
20402; phone: 202-783-3238; or available online on NTDB's
"International Trade Library" at www.stat-usa.gov.

This booklet is designed to show step by step how to expand an existing
manufacturing business into the international marketplace. It is also an
excellent resource for the small importer/exporter. The cost is about $16.

- *The EMC—Your Export Department.* Describes the services
provided to exporters by export management companies as well as
how to go about selecting a suitable EMC. Write to the Office of
Export Development, International Trade Administration, U.S.
Department of Commerce, Washington, DC 20230.
- *Exporter Yellow Pages.* A public/private partnership that features
over 13,000 providers, trading companies, and manufacturers who
have registered their export interest with EACS. It can be found at
www.myexports.com; phone: 877-390-2629.
- *The U.S. Export Management Companies (EMCs) Directory.*
Emphasizes the marketing capability of EMCs. This is the
international trade import/export portal and is the source
for international trade business-to-business leads and news about
international trade. Visit the Web site at http://fita.org/emc.html.
- *Exporter's Encyclopedia (Annual).* A valuable publication for the
serious trader's library. It's chock full of fingertip information and
can be found in most libraries. Costs about $450. Order from
Dun & Bradstreet International, 103 JFK Parkway, Short Hills,

---

在主要地区发行的大众政府出版物，此类出版物可在政府印刷局开办的网上书店订购。

由美国商务部出版。

本书介绍出口管理公司为出口商提供的服务并介绍怎样选择合适的出口管理公司。

由向 EACS 注册过出口意向的 13 000 多家供应商、贸易公司和制造商组成的公共或私人合伙公司。

重点强调出口管理公司的营销能力。

资深贸易商的有价值出版物。

---

periodical 期刊。 order 订购。 EMC 出口管理公司。 yellow page 黄皮书。

NJ 07078. Phone: 800-234-3867 or 800-932-0025 (international); Web site: www.dnb.com/prods_svcs/allprods.htm.

- ***An Introduction to the Overseas Private Investment Corporation (OPIC).*** Reviews how OPIC can assist firms interested in investing in developing nations. Order from Overseas Private Investment Corporation, 1100 New York Avenue, NW, Washington, DC 20527. Phone: 202-336-8400; fax: 202-408-9859; e-mail: info@opic.gov.

评述海外私人投资公司如何帮助有意投资发展中国家的公司。

- ***Export–Import Bank of the United States.*** Explains U.S. export financing programs. No charge. Order from Export-Import Bank of the United States, 811 Vermont Avenue, NW, Washington, DC 20571. E-mail: www.exim.gov.

介绍美国出口融资项目。

- ***Carnet.*** Explains what a carnet is and how it can benefit exporters. Contains application forms for applying for a carnet. No charge. Order from U.S. Council for International Business, 1212 Avenue of the Americas, New York, NY 10036. Phone: 212-354-4480; fax: 212-575-0327; e-mail: info@uscib.org; Web site: www.uscib.org.

解释通关证的概念以及通关证对出口商的作用。

货运代理
Freight Forwarding

A *freight forwarder* is a private service company licensed to support shippers and the movement of their goods. These specialists in international physical distribution act as agents for the exporter (shipper) in moving cargo to an overseas destination. They are familiar with:

货运代理商是托运人授权私人服务公司对货物进行运输。

他们熟悉的领域有：

- The import rules and regulations of foreign countries
- Methods of shipping
- U.S. government export regulations
- The documents connected with foreign trade

- 外国进口法律法规；
- 货运条款；
- 美国政府出口法规；
- 外贸相关凭证。

From the beginning, freight forwarders can assist with an order by advising on such things as freight costs, consular fees, and insurance costs. They can recommend the degree of packing, arrange for an inland carrier, find the right airline, and even arrange for the containerization of the cargo. They quote shipping rates, provide information, and book

从一开始，货运代理会根据规程就运输费、签证费以及货物的保险费等向托运人提出相关建议。

---

financing program 融资项目。carnet 通关证。freight forwarder 货运代理商。be familiar with 对……熟悉。methods of shipping 货运条款。regulation 法规。consular fee 签证费。

cargo space. These firms are invaluable because they can handle everything from the factory to the final destination, including all documentation, storage, and shipping insurance, and they will route your cargo at the lowest customs charges.

托运人
Shipper

任何主营业务为销售商品的法人都可以未经授权为自己的货物装运或为其母公司、子公司、附属公司以及关联公司的装运或合并装运提供货运代理服务。

大型制造商大都拥有自己的运输部门以充当货运代理，而小型制造商以及小型进出口企业却没有人力、物力自己安排运输。货运代理负责帮助出口商整合对分销商的最终报价。

Any person whose primary business is the sale of merchandise may, without a license, dispatch and perform freight forwarding services on behalf of his or her own shipments, or on behalf of shipments or consolidated shipments of a parent, subsidiary, affiliate, or associated company. The shipper may not, however, receive compensation from the common carrier.

A large manufacturer usually has its own shipping department that serves as its own freight forwarder, but smaller manufacturing firms and small import/export businesses seldom have either the staff or the time to make their own arrangements. Often freight forwarders are called upon to help an exporter put together the final price quotation to a distributor. For example, when quoting CIF, in addition to the manufacturer's price and the commission, the forwarder can provide information on dock and cartage fees, forwarder's fees, marine insurance, ocean freight costs, duty charges, consular invoice fees, and packing charges. It's not unusual (and it may be quite prudent) to review a price quotation with the freight forwarder before sending it on the telex.

怎样成为货运代理
How to Become a Freight Forwarder

货运代理商分为两种类型——海洋货运代理和航空货运代理，而大多数货运代理公司均可代理上述两种业务。

海洋货运代理必须具有联邦海事委员会颁发的许可证。

Their are two types of freight forwarders—ocean and air—but most freight forwarding businesses can do both.

An *ocean freight forwarder* must be licensed by the Federal Maritime Commission (FMC). The criteria to become eligible for a freight forwarding license are:

• Three years' experience in ocean freight forwarding duties
• Necessary character to render forwarding services
• Possession of a valid surety bond

---

consolidated shipment 合并装运。subsidiary 子公司。affiliate 附属公司。associated company 关联公司。quotation 报价。Federal Maritime Commission 联邦海事委员会。

For more information on how to submit an application, contact the Office of Freight Forwarders, Bureau of Tariffs, Federal Maritime Commission, Washington, DC 20573.

Air cargo agents are administered by the International Air Transportation Association (IATA), headquartered in Montreal, Quebec, Canada. This organization through its subsidiary Cargo Network Services, Inc., administers the qualifications and certification of agents in the United States. Additional information can be obtained by writing CNS, 300 Garden City Plaza, Suite 400, Garden City, NY 11530.

航空货运代理隶属于国际航空运输协会，总部位于加拿大魁北克省的蒙特利尔市。

HOT TIP

You can become a licensed freight forwarder, but you do not have to be one to arrange movement of goods on behalf of your own shipments. Caution: Don't act as a forwarder for someone else before being issued a license.

当你成为合法的货运代理后，不仅可以安排自己的货物装运，也可以接受其他法人的货运委托。

出口管制
Export Controls

Another area in which exporting differs from importing is the licensing required to control exports. The history of export controls in the United States is based on the presumption that all exported goods and technical documentation are subject to regulation by the government. This presumption is fundamentally different from that of most nations, which often presume the freedom to export unless there is an explicit statement of a need to control.

出口与进口的另一点不同在于用于实现出口管制的授权要求。美国的出口管制基于所有出口商品和技术文献都归政府管辖的假设之上。

The exercise of controls by the United States varies from minimal (as is the case of Canada) to embargoes. Several departments have legal authority to control exports. Arms, ammunition, implements of war, technical data relating thereto, and certain classified information are licensed by the Department of State. Narcotics and dangerous drugs are licensed by the Department of Justics. Nuclear material is licensed by the Nuclear Regulatory Commission.

美国对于一些地区几乎不进行出口管制（如加拿大），而对另一些地区却颁布禁止贸易令。

IATA 国际航空运输协会。headquarter 总部。licensing 授权。minimal 微小的，最小的。embargo 禁止贸易令。

尽管有例外，但总体来说，产业安全局以及商务部的管制系统影响了大多数出口商。产业安全局通过隶属于它的出口服务部提供有关出口授权要求的援助。

There are other exceptions, but in general, the Bureau of Industry and Security (BIS)/Department of Commerce administers the control system that affects most exporters. The BIS provides assistance on exporting licensing requirements through its Office of Exporter Services (OEXS). OEXS interprets the Export Administration Regulations (EAR). Section 15 Federal Regulations 730–774 published in 1996, as amended, are designed to promote the foreign policy of the United States, protect national security, and protect the domestic economy from the excessive drain of scarce materials. Phone: 202-482-4811; fax: 202-482-2927; Web site: www.bis.doc.gov

出口许可证是政府允许特定出口商向特定目的地出口指定商品的一项权力。

An export license is a grant of authority from the government issued to a particular exporter to export a designated item to a specific destination. An export license is granted on a case-by-case basis for either a single transaction or for several transactions within a specified period of time. If an export license from BIS is required, the exporter must prepare a Form BIS-748P (Multipurpose Application Form) and submit it to the BIS. The applicant must be sure to follow the instructions on the form carefully. In some instances, technical manuals and support documentation must also be included. The BIS also gives the applicant the option of filing the license application electronically.

一旦申请被批准，申请人将获得出口许可证。许可证包含出口授权码、许可证到期日，这些均需在托运人出口报关单上注明。

If the application is approved, an export license is sent to the applicant. The license contains an export authorization number and expiration date that must be placed on the shipper's export declaration (SED). The SED is used to indicate to U.S. Customs the type of export authorization being used, and serves as an export control document for BIS. The SED is also used by the Department of Commerce's Bureau of Census to compile statistics on U.S. trade. Unlike some goods exported under NLR (no license required) or a license exception, all exports under an export license must be accompanied by an SED.

出口管制商品在商品管制清单中依国家或商品名称进行分类。

Export controls are organized on the Commodity Control List (CCL) by country or by item. Some, however, have a more general focus, such as those that advance the human rights cause or those prohibiting doing business with business entities that boycott for ethnic or political reasons.

With few exceptions, an exporter must complete a shipper's export declaration (Commerce Form 7525-V) and deposit it with the exporting carrier regardless of whether a shipment is exported under a validated license or a "license exception."

BIS 产业安全局。control system 管制系统。designate 标明，指明。authorization number 授权码。expiration date 到期日。SED 托运人出口报关单。CCL 商品管制清单。

The vast majority of all exports *do not* require a validated export license and require only the appropriate "license exception" notation on the SED. The symbol NLR is used in specific instances where (1) an item is subject to the EAR but is not listed on the CCL under a specific ECCN, or (2) is listed on the CCL but does not require a license to the destination in question. Virtually all shipments to Canada and the majority of exports to most other destinations are exported from the United States under NLR. Currently, less than 4 percent of U.S. manufactured exports require an export license.

大多数出口商品不需要有效出口许可证，只需在托运人出口报关单上盖有相应的"例外许可"字样。

迄今为止，美国只有不到4%的出口工业品需要出口许可证。

出口商的责任
Exporter Obligations

There are five questions that you need to ask to determine your obligations under the EAR:

1. *What is being exported?* The item's classification needs to be determined according to the CCL.
2. *Where is it going?* The country of ultimate destination is a factor in determining export licensing requirements using the country chart.
3. *Who will receive it?* There are restrictions on certain end users, such as persons denied export privileges.
4. *What will they do with it?* The ultimate end use of your item will affect the licensing requirements related to the proliferation of nuclear, chemical, or biological weapons and missile delivery systems.
5. *What else is involved in your transaction?* You may be restricted from engaging in a transaction based on conduct such as contracting, financing, and freight forwarding in support of a proliferation project.

1. 出口何种商品？出口商品的分类需要根据商品管制清单确定。
2. 向何处出口？出口目的国是使用国家图表确定出口授权制度的因素之一。
3. 收货人是谁？对某些最终收货人有许多限制，如否认出口优惠待遇的法人。
4. 收货人将用货物做什么？出口商品的最终用途会影响关乎核扩散、生化武器以及导弹发射系统的授权要求。
5. 贸易中还包含哪些其他因素？当你进行核扩散项目的签约、融资以及货运代理时，你将可能被禁止进行交易。

Once you determine that you require a validated license for a specific export, you should submit an application for a license to the Bureau of Industry and Security (BIS), PO Box 273, Washington, DC 20044. An application consists of a completed Form BIS-748P (Multipurpose Application Form) and required supporting information. Figure 7.1 is the application form for an export license.

---

validated 有效的。 notation 标记。 proliferation of nuclear 核扩散。 chemical or biological weapons 生化武器。 missile delivery system 导弹发射系统。

图 7.1 出口许可证申请表

Figure 7.1 Export License Application Form

B	U.S. DEPARTMENT OF COMMERCE Bureau of Export Administration	DATE RECEIVED (Leave Blank)	X

FORM BXA-748P
FORM APPROVED OMB NO. 0694-0088, 0694-0089

MULTIPURPOSE APPLICATION

Information furnished herewith is subject to the provisions of Section 12(c) of the Export Administration Act of 1979, as amended, 50 U.S.C. app. 2411(c), and its unauthorized disclosure is prohibited by law.

1. CONTACT PERSON

2. TELEPHONE

APPLICATION CONTROL NUMBER
This is NOT an export license number

3. FACSIMILE

Z181053

3. DATE OF APPLICATION

5. TYPE OF APPLICATION	6. DOCUMENTS SUBMITTED WITH APPLICATION		7. DOCUMENTS ON FILE WITH APPLICANT	8. SPECIAL COMPREHENSIVE LICENSE
☐ EXPORT	☐ BXA-748P-A	☐ LETTER OF EXPLANATION	☐ BXA-711	☐ BXA-752 OR BXA-752-A
☐ REEXPORT	☐ BXA-748P-B	☐ FOREIGN AVAILABILITY	☐ LETTER OF ASSURANCE	☐ INTERNAL CONTROL PROGRAM
☐ CLASSIFICATION REQUEST	☐ BXA-711	☐ OTHER	☐ IMPORT/END-USER CERTIFICATE	☐ COMPREHENSIVE NARRATIVE
☐ SPECIAL COMPREHENSIVE LICENSE	☐ IMPORT/END-USER CERTIFICATE		☐ NUCLEAR CERTIFICATION	☐ CERTIFICATIONS
☐ OTHER	☐ TECH. SPECS		☐ OTHER	☐ OTHER

9. SPECIAL PURPOSE

10. RESUBMISSION APPLICATION CONTROL NUMBER	11. REPLACEMENT LICENSE NUMBER	12. FOR ITEM(S) PREVIOUSLY EXPORTED, PROVIDE LICENSE EXCEPTION SYMBOL OR LICENSE NUMBER

13. IMPORT/END-USER CERTIFICATE COUNTRY   **NUMBER:**

14. APPLICANT	15. OTHER PARTY AUTHORIZED TO RECEIVE LICENSE
ADDRESS LINE 1	ADDRESS LINE 1
ADDRESS LINE 2	ADDRESS LINE 2

CITY	POSTAL CODE	CITY	POSTAL CODE
STATE/COUNTRY	EMPLOYER IDENTIFICATION NUMBER	STATE/COUNTRY	TELEPHONE OR FAX

17. PURCHASER	17. INTERMEDIATE CONSIGNEE
ADDRESS LINE 1	ADDRESS LINE 1
ADDRESS LINE 2	ADDRESS LINE 2

CITY	POSTAL CODE	CITY	POSTAL CODE
COUNTRY	TELEPHONE OR FAX	COUNTRY	TELEPHONE OR FAX

24. ADDITIONAL INFORMATION

For all applications: I certify that to the best of my knowledge, all the information on this form is true and correct, and that it conforms to the instructions accompanying this form and the Export Administration Regulations. For license applications: I certify or agree as appropriate that: (a) to the best of my knowledge all statements in this application, includin the description of the commodities, software or technology and their end-uses, and any documents submitted in support of this application are correct and complete and that they fully and accurately disclose all the terms of the order and other facts of the transaction: (b) I will retain records pertaining to this transaction and make them available as required by the Export Administration Regulations: (c) I will report promptly to the Bureau of Export Administration any material changes in the terms of the order or other facts or intentions of the transaction as reflected in this application and supporting documents, whether the application is still under consideration or a license has been granted: and (d) if the license is granted, I will be strictly accountable for its use in accordance with the Export Administration Regulations and all the terms and conditions of the license. A number of the parts of this form include certifications based on a person's knowledge. As defined in Part 772 of the Export Administration Regulations, "Knowledge" of a circumstance includes not only positive knowledge that the circumstance exists or is substantially certain to occur, but also an awareness of a high probability of its existance or future occurrence. Such awareness is inferred from evidence of the conscious disregard of facts known to a person and is also inferred from a persons willful avoidance of facts.

25. SIGNATURE (of person authorized to execute this application)	NAME OF SIGNER	TITLE OF SIGNER

This license application and any license issued pursuant thereto are expressly subject to all rules and regulations of the Bureau of Export Administration. Making any false statement or concealing any material fact in connection with this application or altering in any way the license issued is punishable by imprisonment or fine, or both, and by denial of export privileges under the Export Administration Act of 1979, as amended, and any other applicable Federal statutes. No license will be issued unless this form is completed and submitted in accordance with Export Administration Regulation.

X	X	B

USCOMM-DC 96-24024

Within 10 days after the date the OEXS receives the application, the office issues the license or denies it, sends the application to the next step in the license process, or, if the application is improperly completed or additional information is required, returns the application without action. Once the approved license is received, the exporter keeps the validated license on file. All the applicant must submit is the SED; however, all information on the SED must conform to that found in the validated license.

The Internet-based simplified network application process (SNAP) provides a secure environment for the electronic submission of license applications, commodity classification requests, and high-performance computer notices.

To avoid export control violations and shipping delays, applicants should contact their local ITA district office or the Exporter's Service staff, Office of Export Administration, International Trade Administration, for assistance.

出口服务部在收到申请表后的 10 天内，要做出签发或拒签的决定，然后将其送到办理流程中的下一部门。如果申请表填写不规范或不完整，则将原表退还给申请人。

互联网的发展简化了许可证的网申过程，精简的网申过程又为电子版的许可证申请的提交、商品分类要求的上传以及电子布告的高效传播提供了安全的网络环境。

HOT TIPS

How to Avoid Export Control Violations
- Determine whether a validated export license is required. When in doubt, contact the Export License Application and Information Network for assistance.
- Fully describe commodities or technical data on export shipping documents.
- Use the applicable destination control statement on commercial invoices, air waybills, and bills of lading, as required by Section 386.6 of the Export Administration Regulations.
- Avoid overshipments by maintaining an accurate account of the quantity and value of goods shipped against a validated export license.
- Be mindful of the expiration date on validated export licenses to avoid shipments after the applicable license has expired.
- Enter the applicable validated export license number or general license symbol on the shipper's export declaration (SED).
- Make certain that shipping documents clearly identify the exporter, intermediate consignee, and ultimate consignee.
- Mail the completed Form BIS-748P.

---

issue 签发。deny 拒签。SNAP 精简的网申过程。submission 提交。high-performance 高效。

何处求助
Where to Get Assistance

除了申请相关的出口许可证，美国出口商还要遵守特定法律法规以及美国其他的部门制定的国际贸易规则。

In addition to obtaining the applicable export license, U.S. exporters should be careful to meet all other international trade regulations established by specific legislation, regulation, or other authority of the U.S. government. The import laws and regulations of foreign countries must also be taken into account. The exporter should keep in mind that even if help is received with the license and documentation from others, such as banks, freight forwarders, or consultants, the exporter remains responsible for ensuring that all statements are true and accurate.

为了避免困惑，强烈建议出口商就如何确定严格意义上的出口资质向有关部门求助。

To avoid confusion, the exporter is strongly advised to seek assistance in determining the proper licensing requirements. The best source is the Bureau of Export Administration's Office of Exporter Services at 14th Street and Constitution Avenue, NW, U.S. Department of Commerce, Washington DC 20230. Telephone or write to the Exporter Counseling Division, Room 1099C, U.S. Department of Commerce, Washington, DC 20230; phone: 202-482-3825; fax: 202-482-0751. Exporters may also contact one of the western regional office locations at 3300 Irvine Avenue, Suite 345, Newport Beach, CA 92660; phone: 949-660-0144; fax: 949-660-9347; or the BIS Western Regional Office at 152 North Third Street, Suite 550, San Jose, CA 95112; phone: 408-998-7402.

你可以进入产业保险局的官方网站去查找大量出口相关信息，如研讨会、最新规章、热点政策，以及特殊控制政策所针对的国家、政府机构、公司和个体。

The BIS also has a Web site (www.BIS.doc.gov) from which you can access a variety of information related to exports, such as seminars, up-to-date regulations, policy issues, and lists of countries, government agencies, companies, and individuals for whom specific controls apply. Whenever there is any doubt about how to comply with the BIS's Export Administration Regulations, Department of Commerce officials should be contacted for guidance.

"美国制造"
"Made in USA"

采购商有权知晓他们所采购商品的原产地。通关证上"美国制造"的标志不能滥用。

Buyers have the right to know the true origin of the product they are purchasing. The coveted label "Made in USA" or "Made in America" cannot be randomly used. There are rules, and the rules are becoming more and more important in an international marketplace where U.S.

---

applicable 相关的。proper 严格意义上的。seminar 研讨会。origin 原产地。

manufacturers scour the globe for the right components at the best price, using input made in foreign countries.

The Federal Trade Commission (FTC) has a voluntary requirement that "all or virtually all" of a product be made in the United States, and it has issued a guide book, titled *Complying with the Made in the USA Standard*, that spells out the guidelines. The three essential rules are noted below:

联邦贸易委员会有一条任意条款，该条款要求产品"全部或几乎全部"为美国制造，委员会还发行了一本名为《遵守美国制造标准》的指导用书，此书阐述了美国制造的准则。3 项重要准则如下：

- Origin of the products significant parts
- Dominant value (must be U.S. dollars)
- Final assembly location (must be in the United States)

- 产品核心部件原产地；
- 主要价值（必须以美元为单位）；
- 最终装配地点（必须为美国）。

When in doubt, check the FTC guide book, which can be ordered by calling 877-FTC-HELP (382-4357) or by e-mailing via the Web site at www.ftc.gov. The mailing address is 600 Pennsylvania Avenue, NW, Washington, DC 20580.

出口税收减免
Tax Incentives for Exporting

A prominent tax attorney once said, "Business in America? It's all about taxes." International business is no exception.

一位著名的税务律师曾说：
"美国的贸易中处处是税收。"国际贸易也不例外。

Taxes on income derived from international trade are in accordance with current laws for other income except that tax incentives for exporting are substantial. There are no tax incentives for importing. See www.ncseonline.org and www.irs.gov/tax.

Tax incentives for exporters amount to approximately 15 percent exclusion of the combined taxable income earned on international sales. The tax law provides for a system of tax deferrals for domestic international sales corporations (DISCs) and foreign sales corporations (FSCs).

税收减免可以达到国际销售中复合应税收入额的 15%。税法为国内的国际销售公司和外国销售公司提供了税收延缓系统。

Prior to December 31, 1984, the DISC was the only medium for distributing export earnings. DISCs don't require a foreign presence and, in fact, are legal entities established only on paper. The DISC incentive was created by the Revenue Act of 1971 and provides for deferral of federal income tax on 50 percent of the export earnings allocated to the DISC with the balance treated as dividends to the parent

1971 年通过的《税收法案》对国内的国际销售公司是一种激励，法案规定出口收入的 50% 作为延缓上交的联邦收入税拨还给国内的国际销售公司，余额作为总公司的红利。

---

voluntary requirement 任意条款。virtually 事实上，实际上。comply with 遵守。spell out 阐述。significant part 核心部件。tax attorney 税务律师。DISC 国内的国际销售公司。FSC 外国销售公司

法案的通过使国内的国际销售公司成为美国和《关贸总协定》的其他签署国之间争论的焦点。

外国销售公司也必须是外国公司，必须在外国部门保有持续的账务汇总并且至少有一名非美国籍董事。

遵守新规定的要求对美国那些拥有海外子公司且丰富资源的大型跨国公司而言并不困难，但对于成千上万的涉及国际业务的小公司而言，管理成本和其他经费都将有所上升。

约有 23 个国家与美国达成了税收信息互换协定，美属维尔京群岛、关岛以及塞班岛都建立了办事处，可为建立外国销售公司提供直接的帮助。

年出口量超过 1 000 万美元的出口商还将通过国内的国际销售公司依照现行规则进行运作。

company. Since its enactment, the DISC had been the subject of an ongoing dispute between the United States and certain other signatories of the General Agreement on Tariffs and Trade (GATT). Other nations contended that the DISC amounted to an illegal export subsidy because it allowed indefinite deferral of direct taxes on income from exports earned in the United States.

Under new rules put into effect on January 1, 1985, to receive a tax benefit that is designed to equal the tax deferral provided by the DISC, exporters must establish an office abroad. The FSC must also be a foreign corporation, maintain a summary of its permanent books of account at the foreign office, and have at least one director resident outside the United States.

Meeting the requirement of the new regulations isn't difficult for big U.S.-based multinationals with overseas offices and ample resources, but thousands of small businesses involved in international commerce are concerned about administrative costs and other overhead. Actually small exporters have several options for their foreign sales operations. They may continue to export through a DISC, paying an interest charge on the deferred income, or they may join together with other exporters to own an FSC. Another alternative is that they may individually take advantage of relaxed, small FSC rules, under which they need not meet all the tests required of large FSCs. A small FSC, one with up to $5 million of gross receipts during the taxable year, is excused from the foreign management and foreign economic process requirements.

The mechanics of setting up a DISC or an FSC are somewhat complex but are within the capability of most accountants. Some 23 foreign countries that have an agreement to exchange tax information with the United States, and U.S. possessions such as the Virgin Islands, Guam, and Saipan have established offices that are capable of providing direct assistance in setting up an FSC.

Exporters with up to $10 million of annual exports may continue to operate through DISCs, generally under the present rules. But they must pay an annual interest charge on the amount of tax that would be due if the post-1984 accumulated DISC income were included in the shareholder's income. This interest is imposed on the shareholders and paid to the Treasury of the United States.

---

enactment 法律的制定（或通过）。signatory（合约）签署国。GATT 关贸总协定。deferral 延缓。books of account 账簿。

Multiple exporters, up to 25 of them, may jointly own an FSC, and through the use of several classes of common stock divide the profits of an FSC among the shareholders.

如何减少进口业务中的不公平
How to Gain Relief from Unfair Import Practices

Remaining competitive in world markets is an internal management problem. The underlying elements are quantity, quality, and price. Nevertheless, government intervention is sometimes necessary when you learn about foreign firms that are not competing on what has become known as a "level playing field."

如何在世界市场中保持竞争力是内部管理问题。保持竞争力的根本因素在于数量、质量和价格。

The Department of Commerce's Import Administration (IA) division participates with the U.S. trade representative in monitoring and negotiating fair and transparent international rules. The IA enforces laws and agreements to prevent unfairly traded imports and to safeguard jobs and the competitive strength of U.S. industry.

商务部的进口管理局与美国贸易代表，合作监督和商讨公平公开的国际规则。

Copies of the U.S. International Trade Committee's (ITC) *Rules of Practice and Procedure*, which set forth the procedures for the filing and conduct of investigations, are available from the Docket Section, U.S. International Trade Commission, 500 East Street SW, Washington, DC 20436; phone: 202-205-2000; Web site: www.USITC.gov.

The IA, ITC, Congress, and/or the U.S. trade representative can investigate the following allegations:

进口管理局、国际贸易委员会、国会以及美国贸易代表，可以调查以下指控：

- Countervailing duties imposed by a foreign country
- Antidumping
- General investigations of trade and tariff matters
- Investigations of costs of production
- Alleged unfair practices in import trade
- Investigations of injury from increased imports
- Workers adjustment assistance
- Firms adjustment assistance
- Enforcement of U.S. rights under trade agreements and response to certain foreign trade practices

- 外国实行的反倾销税；
- 反倾销政策；
- 贸易和关税普查；
- 生产成本调查；
- 被控的进口贸易不公平业务；
- 调查由于进口量增加所受到的损害；
- 工作人员调整协助；
- 公司调整协助；
- 贸易协定下，美国权利的执行以及对特定外国贸易业务的回应；

---

internal 内部的。IA 进口管理局。countervailing 抵消的。antidumping 反倾销的。general investigation 普查。enforcement 执行。

- 对外国限制或歧视美国贸易的回应；
- 调查从某些国家进口商品所造成的市场混乱。

- U.S. response to foreign trade practices which restrict or discriminate against U.S. commerce
- Investigations of market disruptions by imports from some countries

The point of contact for instituting investigations is Import Administration (IA), International Trade Administration, U.S. Department of Commerce, 1401 Constitution Avenue, NW, Washington, DC 20230; phone: 202-482-5497 or 1-800-USA-TRAD(E); Web site: www.ita.doc.gov; e-mail: TIC@ita.doc.gov.

出口城市
Export Cities

为了扭转美国巨额的贸易赤字，很多城市都蓄势待发。

To combat America's enormous imbalances, cities are rolling up their sleeves. Mayors are becoming more and more involved and are holding their city councils accountable for methods that contribute to international trade. Cities are calculating their contributions to gross national exports. International trade is too important not to seek solutions from the bottom up. One innovative American idea is the formation of export city clusters.

国际贸易很重要，我们必须从下至上寻求解决方案。美国人的创新解决方案之一是组建出口城市群。

何为出口城市
What Are Export Cities?

出口城市群通过年复一年地展示城市或地区的产品，参与到国际出口贸易中去。

Export cities organize clusters that are public–private partnerships to serve the unique products of their region. Export city clusters participate in international trade exporting by displaying the city or regional products year round. Some provide buildings, rooms, or space on the city's Web site.

出口城市群怎样运作
How Do Export City Clusters Work?

出口城市集群不仅提供了展

Most exporters travel to foreign buyers, but since the events of 9/11, such travel has been reduced. The export city cluster not only provides

---

combat 战斗。roll up one's sleeves 准备行动。from bottom up 从下至上。cluster 群。

a method for displaying products, but it also includes a travel company with an import/export marketing company, a bank, and hotels and restaurants, thus attracting buyers to the export city. Sister cities are being factored into the cluster equation.

The export cluster concept shows a city's involvement in trade and requires vision and creativity by leadership for the long term. You can become a part of this effort.

The next chapter explains those things that are unique to importing, such as customs, tariffs, and quotas.

示产品的方法，还出现了集进出口营销公司、银行、旅馆以及餐厅为一体的旅游公司以吸引采购商到出口城市旅游。

下一章将解释进口的特有因素，如海关、关税以及配额等。

---

custom 海关。tariff 关税。quotas 配额。

CHAPTER **8**

HOW TO IMPORT INTO THE UNITED STATES

怎样进口到美国

Importing is simply the flip side of exporting, but some aspects of exporting don't apply to importing. For example, the tariff schedule applies only to importing and the Customs Service is concerned only with goods coming into a country.

The following basics unique to importing are discussed in this chapter:

- World Customs Organization
- Homeland Security
- Government support
- Information sources
- Customs house brokers
- Getting through the customs maze
- How to use the tariff schedule
- Import quotas
- Special import regulations
- Free trade zones
- Customs bonded warehouses

进口就是出口的对应面,但出口的一些原则对进口并不适用。

本章将讨论影响进口的特有因素:

- 世界海关组织;
- 国土安全;
- 政府支持;
- 信息资源;
- 海关经纪人;
- 通关;
- 如何使用关税明细表;
- 进口配额;
- 特殊进口管制;
- 自由贸易区;
- 海关保税仓库。

---

flip side 对应面,对立面。homeland security 国土安全。maze 复杂的系统。
customs bonded warehouse 海关保税仓库

世界海关组织
World Customs Organization (WCO)

50 多年来，世界海关组织一直在为拓宽国际贸易渠道而不懈努力。组织的成功归功于长期坚持这一明确原则：世界海关程序越简单、和谐，国际贸易和世界经济就越繁荣。

世界海关组织创造和管理的主要国际协定包括：

- 《和谐系统协定》（美国进出口表的基础）；
- 《关贸总协定海关估价协议》；
- 《内罗毕和约翰内斯堡协定》（二者都与共享信息有关）；
- 关于海关程序的 1973 年《京都公约》；
- 1999 年修正《京都公约》（通常被称为简化和协调海关程序的国际惯例）。

For more than 50 years, the World Customs Organization (WCO) has provided leadership in expanding the avenues of international trade. The organization's success has been driven by a clear-minded adherence to a principle: the more simple and harmonized the world's customs procedures, the more prosperity for international trade and the world at large. The WCO has scored many triumphs across the entire spectrum of customs-based issues. For example, it created and administers several international agreements that facilitate world trade. The major international conventions created or administered by the WCO include:

- Harmonized System Convention (the basis for the U.S. import and export schedules)
- GATT Customs Valuation Agreement
- Nairobi and Johannesburg Conventions, both dealing with sharing of information
- 1973 Kyoto Convention on customs procedures
- 1999 Revised Kyoto Convention, formally known as the International Convention on the Harmonization and Simplification of Customs Procedures

In June 2002, the WCO council unanimously adopted a resolution on the security and facilitation of the international trade supply chain proposed by the United States that has resulted in the development of numerous guidelines, benchmarks, and best practices.

Together with the WCO, U.S. Customs and Border Protection (CBP) has been actively drafting and writing best practices, guidelines, and standards relating to the security of international supply chains. While much has been accomplished, the work continues both at the CBP and the WCO. To know more about the WCO go to www.cbp.gov/xp/cgov/border_security/international_activities/international_agreements/wco/ wco.xml.

国土安全
Homeland Security

The National Strategy for Homeland Security and the Homeland Security Act of 2002 served to mobilize and organize the United States to

---

expand the avenues 拓宽渠道。Nairobi 内罗毕。Johannesburg 约翰内斯堡。convention 协定，惯例。Kyoto 京都。national strategy 国家战略。mobilize 动员。

secure itself from terrorist attacks. The department's organization chart is shown in Figure 8.1. The vision and mission statements, strategic goals, and objectives provide the framework that guides the actions that make up the daily operations of the department.

Everything you wish to know—the department's mission, goals, operations, prevention measures, and means of protection—can be found on its Web site at www.dhs.gov.

为保卫国土安全而制定的国家战略以及 2002 年颁布的《国土安全法案》均用来动员和组织美国对抗恐怖袭击。

政府支持
Government Support
移民和海关总署
Immigration and Customs Enforcement (ICE)

When created in March 2003, Immigration and Customs Enforcement (ICE) became the largest investigative branch of the Department of Homeland Security (DHS). The agency was created after the events of 9/11 by combining the law enforcement arms of the former Immigration and Naturalization Service (INS) and the former U.S. Customs Service to more effectively enforce our immigration and customs laws and to protect the United States from terrorist attacks. ICE is a key component of the DHS "layered defense" approach to protecting the nation.

2003 年 3 月成立的移民和海关总署已经成为国土安全部最大的审查机构。此机构是在 9·11 事件后成立的, 合并了前移民局和海关部门的执法机构, 目的在于更高效地贯彻和执行移民和海关相关法律, 更好地对抗恐怖袭击。

To further understand ICE, its mission and processes, go to its Web site at www.ice.gov/about/index.htm or call 202-344-2370.

Before the events of 9/11, immigration and customs authorities were not widely recognized as an effective counterterrorism tool in the United States. ICE changed this by creating a host of new systems to better address national security threats and to detect potential terrorist activities in the United States. ICE:

在 9·11 事件前, 很多人认为移民和海关机构不是美国有效的反恐工具。移民和海关总署通过建立很多新系统改变了人们的看法, 建立这些系统的目的在于更好地处理威胁国家安全的事务以及侦查美国潜在的恐怖活动。

- Targets the people, money, and materials that support terrorist and criminal activity.
- Is the second largest federal law enforcement contributor to the Joint Terrorism Task Force.
- Dismantled gang organizations by targeting their members, seizing their financial assets, and disrupting their criminal operations through Operation Community Shield.

Immigration and Customs Enforcement 移民和海关总署。investigative 审查的。law enforcement 执法机构。
Immigration and Naturalization Service 移民局。Customs Service 海关总署。a host of 许多, 大量。address 处理（问题）。

图 8.1 美国国土安全系统图

Figure 8.1 Homeland Security Organization Chart

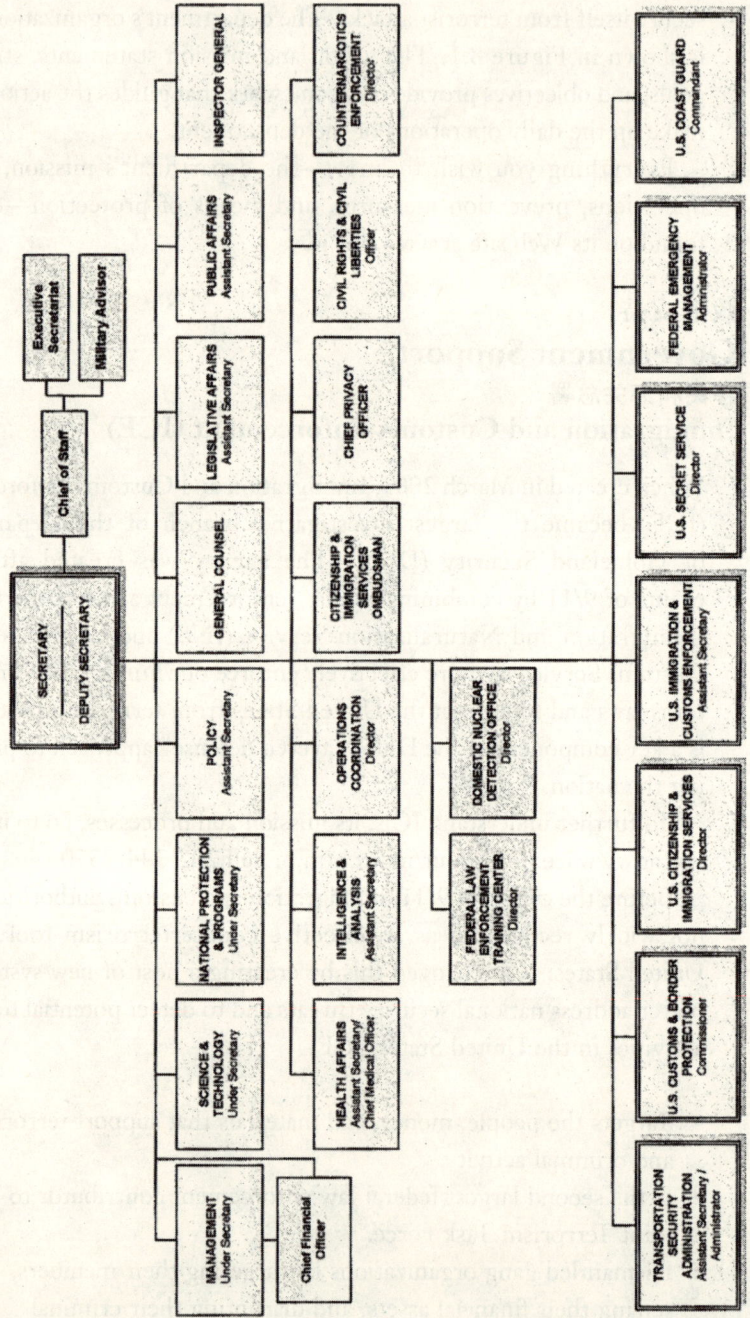

| | | | | SECRETARY | | | | |
| | | | | DEPUTY SECRETARY | | | | |

Executive Secretariat

Military Advisor

Chief of Staff

MANAGEMENT
Under Secretary

SCIENCE & TECHNOLOGY
Under Secretary

NATIONAL PROTECTION & PROGRAMS
Under Secretary

POLICY
Assistant Secretary

GENERAL COUNSEL

LEGISLATIVE AFFAIRS
Assistant Secretary

PUBLIC AFFAIRS
Assistant Secretary

INSPECTOR GENERAL

Chief Financial Officer

HEALTH AFFAIRS
Assistant Secretary/
Chief Medical Officer

INTELLIGENCE & ANALYSIS
Assistant Secretary

OPERATIONS COORDINATION
Director

CITIZENSHIP & IMMIGRATION SERVICES OMBUDSMAN

CHIEF PRIVACY OFFICER

CIVIL RIGHTS & CIVIL LIBERTIES
Officer

COUNTERNARCOTICS ENFORCEMENT
Director

FEDERAL LAW ENFORCEMENT TRAINING CENTER
Director

DOMESTIC NUCLEAR DETECTION OFFICE
Director

TRANSPORTATION SECURITY ADMINISTRATION
Assistant Secretary /
Administrator

U.S. CUSTOMS & BORDER PROTECTION
Commissioner

U.S. CITIZENSHIP & IMMIGRATION SERVICES
Director

U.S. IMMIGRATION & CUSTOMS ENFORCEMENT
Assistant Secretary

U.S. SECRET SERVICE
Director

FEDERAL EMERGENCY MANAGEMENT
Administrator

U.S. COAST GUARD
Commandant

- Investigates employers and targets illegal workers who have gained access to critical infrastructure worksites (like nuclear and chemical plants, military installations, seaports, and airports) through its Worksite Enforcement Initiative.

利用工地执法政策调查雇主和在关键基础设施岗位就职的非法员工（如核设备和化学设备、军事设备、海港、航空港等）。

- Helps to identify fraudulent immigration benefit applications and fraudulent illegal document manufacture, and targets violators through its Identity and Benefit Fraud Program.
- Investigates the illegal export of U.S. munitions and sensitive technology through its Project Shield America Initiative.

利用美国项目保护政策调查美国军需品和敏感技术的非法出口。

- Helps combat criminal organizations that smuggle and traffic in humans across U.S. borders through its Human Smuggling and Trafficking Initiative.
- Ensures that every alien who has been ordered removed departs the United States as quickly as possible. It works to reduce the number of fugitive aliens in the United States through its National Fugitive Operations Program.

保证被遣送的外国人能尽快离开美国，通过国家难民行动项目减少在美国的外国难民人数。

- Aggressively seeks to destroy the financial infrastructure that criminal organizations use to earn, move, and store illicit funds through its Cornerstone Initiative.
- Provides law enforcement and security services to more than 8,800 federal buildings that receive nearly 1 million visitors and tenants daily through its Federal Protective Service.

联邦保护服务局为每天接待近 100 万来宾和租户的 8 800 多幢联邦大楼，提供执法机构和安保服务。

- Plays a leading role in targeting criminal organizations responsible for producing, smuggling, and distributing counterfeit products through its National Intellectual Property Rights Coordination Center.
- Supports the law enforcement community through three units dedicated to sharing information and providing investigative support: the Law Enforcement Support Center, Forensic Document Laboratory, and the Cyber Crimes Center.

海关与边境保护局
Customs and Border Protection Service (CBP)

The U.S. Customs and Border Protection Service (CBP) cannot be thought of as supporting importing in the way the Department of

---

infrastructure 基础设施。installation 设备。Worksite Enforcement Initiative 工地执法政策。munitions 军需品。Project Shield America Initiative 美国项目保护政策。fugitive 难民。tenant 租户。

Commerce encourages exports. Nevertheless it is responsible for enforcement of relevant trade. To obtain more information about its functions, methods, and operations, see its Web site at www.cbp.gov or www.customs.gov.

在过去的 130 多年间，成立于 1789 年的海关部门的收入占联邦政府收入的绝大部分。

税收包括：（1）走私罚金；（2）美国 300 多个港口上缴的所有从量税费。

One of the nation's oldest public institutions, the Customs Service was probably the second thing the First Congress saw to after forming the new nation. Created in 1789, it provided most of the federal government's revenue for almost 130 years. After the income tax became the federal government's primary revenue source, the major responsibility of the Customs Service shifted to the administration of the Tariff Act of 1930, as amended. These duties include: (1) enforcing laws against smuggling and (2) collecting all duties, taxes, and fees due on the volumes of goods moved through the more than 300 ports of entry of the United States. A Customs Court, consisting of nine judges appointed by the U.S. President, reviews and settles disputes between importers and exporters and those who collect duties for the Bureau of Customs.

The CBP is organized with a domestic arm as well as an overseas arm. For additional information, call 202-344-2370.

国内办事处

Domestic Offices

海关与边境保护局国内办事处由 5 个战略贸易中心、20 个海关管理中心、317 个港口入境办事处组成。

The CBP's domestic offices are organized into five strategic trade centers (STC), 20 customs management centers (CMCs), and 317-plus ports of entry offices.

海关管理中心管理核心贸易过程的执行——贸易一致性、乘客操纵和离港操纵。

The 20 CMCs are responsible for oversight of operations within their area of jurisdiction and exercise line authority over the ports. They provide technical assistance and work with the ports in addressing operational problems. They oversee the execution of the core business processes—trade compliance, passenger operations, and outbound operations. They also coordinate with counterpart special agent-in-charge (SAIC) offices in executing anti-smuggling/K-9 and other enforcement strategies. CMCs are the point of contact for providing the answers to questions that concern the following issues:

- Release, classification, and valuation of imported merchandise
- Processing and entry of passengers into the United States
- Exported merchandise

---

smuggling 走私。collect duties on the volumes of goods 收取从量税。ports of entry 港口。compliance 一致。outbound 离港的。

- Fines, penalties, and forfeitures
- Seized properties
- Other activities engaging the trade and travel communities

Ports of entry are responsible for all daily operational aspects of the Customs Service. They are responsible for maintaining a focus on trade compliance (imports/cargo), passenger operations, outbound operations (exports), and antismuggling/K-9 strategies. Figure 8.2 illustrates the Customs Service organization.

港口办公室负责海关部门的日常事务，负责对贸易一致性（进口、货物）、乘客操纵、离港操纵（出口）以及对反走私/K-9战略的密切关注。

海外办事处
Overseas Offices

Although not as extensive as Commerce's Foreign Commercial Service (FCS), Customs attachés (Customs' *overseas arm*) are attached to the embassies or missions in the following countries:Belgium, Italy, Thailand,

图 8.2　美国海关部门系统
Figure 8.2 Organization of U.S. Customs Service

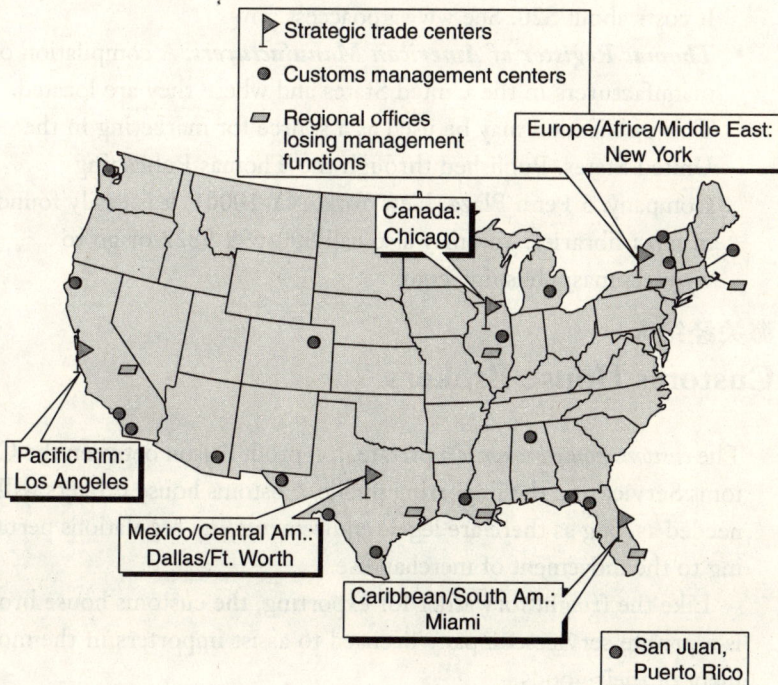

- ▶ Strategic trade centers
- ● Customs management centers
- ▱ Regional offices losing management functions

Europe/Africa/Middle East: New York

Canada: Chicago

Pacific Rim: Los Angeles

Mexico/Central Am.: Dallas/Ft. Worth

Caribbean/South Am.: Miami

San Juan, Puerto Rico

---

be responsible for 为……负责。cargo 货物。antismuggling 反走私。

Canada, Japan, West Germany, England, Republic of Korea, France, Mexico, China, and Pakistan.

进口信息资源
Import Information Sources

海关部门通过管理中心及政府印刷局，以宣传册、简报、研讨会等形式提供大量与进口活动相关的信息。

The Customs Service does provide considerable information related to the importing function in the form of booklets, newsletters, and seminars available through the management centers or the Government Printing Office (GPO). Most of this information amounts to extractions from and simplification of customs regulations. Information about how to make contacts and/or perform the import function must be obtained through private sector publishers and organizations such as chambers of commerce or trade associations. Two sources are helpful for learning more about importing:

下面这两种资源对了解进口相关知识很有帮助：《进口到美国》、《托马斯美国制造商名录》。

- *Importing into the United States.* This excellent booklet published by the Treasury Department through the GPO outlines the requirements that must be met by the importer to enter goods. It costs about $20. See www.gpoaccess.gov.
- *Thomas Register of American Manufacturers.* A compilation of manufacturers in the United States and where they are located. This publication may be used as a source for marketing in the United States. Published through the Thomas Publishing Company, 5 Penn Plaza, New York, NY 10001, it is easily found in most libraries. You may also call 800-699-9822 or go to www.thomaspublishing.com.

海关经纪人
Customs House Brokers

海关经纪人是海关部门与进口公众间的联络人，是以盈利为目的的私营组织。

The *customs house broker* is a private, for-profit liaison between the Customs Service and the importing public. Customs house brokers will be needed as long as there are legal requirements and regulations pertaining to the movement of merchandise.

像出口货运代理一样，海关经纪人是经批准用于帮助进口商运输货物的私人服务公司。

Like the freight forwarder for exporting, the customs house broker is a private service company licensed to assist importers in the movement of their goods.

---

considerable 大量的。booklet 小册子。newsletter 简报。seminar 研讨会。
Thomas Register of American Manufacturers 托马斯美国制造商名录。liaison 联络人。

Formal entries of foreign-made goods representing many billions of dollars in duty collections are filed each year with the Customs Service, and virtually all of them are prepared by customs house brokers on behalf of importers. Some brokers are sole proprietors with a single office at one port of entry, while others are large corporations with branches in many ports throughout the country, but all are licensed and regulated by the Treasury Department. Some even have offices throughout the world.

为关税贡献几十亿美元的制造外国商品的正规机构，每年都要在海关部门登记备案。实际上，所有过程都由海关经纪人代为准备。

Importers employ the customs broker as their agent, who is frequently their only point of contact with the Customs Service. It is not necessary for importers to employ a broker to enter goods on their behalf; however, a bond is required if they do not.

进口商聘请海关经纪人作为代理，仅负责代表他们与海关部门进行日常联系。

Most experienced importers will recommend the services of a broker because of the extras, such as the comfort in knowing that a professional is supporting their project and answering the many technical questions. Another good reason is that at some point, importers' time will become more valuable to them in managing their companies and marketing their product(s) than it might be in handling the paperwork of an entry.

很多有经验的进口商会因为其他原因推荐使用海关经纪人的服务，知道有专家在时刻支持他们的项目，解答技术疑问，进口商会有一种舒适感。

A broker advises on the technical requirements of importing, preparing, and filing entry documents; obtaining the necessary bonds; depositing U.S. import duties; securing release of the product(s); arranging delivery to the importer's premises or warehouse; and obtaining "drawback" refunds (see below). The broker often consults with customs to determine the proper rate of duty or bases of appraisement and, on many occasions, if dissatisfied with either rate or value, will pursue appropriate administrative remedies on behalf of the importer.

代理人对进口技术要求提出建议，准备并填写进口凭证；签订必要的合同；缴纳美国进口关税；保证安全卸货；安排货物运输至进口商所要求的地点或仓库；获取"退税"款项。

Consult the Yellow Pages of the local phone book for a listing of customs brokers in your area.

履约保证
Surety Bonds

Importers must post a *surety bond* with the customs service to ensure payment of the proper amounts of duties, taxes, and other charges associated with entry. Bonds can be for single entry or continuous (term). Based on the value of the shipment, customs determines the value of the required bond. Often a bond three times the value of the shipment is required. A surety company usually requires 100 percent collateral in

进口商必须与海关部门签署履约保证，用以保证其缴纳足额的关税、税金以及其他与进口相关的费用。

formal entity 正规机构。entry document 进口凭证。warehouse 仓库。drawback 退税。surety bond 履约保证。

保证费约为合同价值的 2%，最低溢价为 100 美元。

the form of an irrevocable letter of credit (L/C), trust deed, or cashiers check. Bond premiums are about 2 percent of the value with a minimum of about $100. The premium for a term bond is usually higher (5 percent). Collateral depends on the financial condition of the importer.

出口退税
Drawback

出口退税是对随后又出口的进口商品及其衍生产品所退还的税金。

出口退税的关键在于货物存货追踪和手续记录。

Drawback is the refunding of duties paid on imported goods and their derivatives if they are subsequently exported. Suppose, for example, that you simply re-export goods that were originally imported, or you export items that contain imported merchandise or that contain whole imported components. For each of these you might claim a drawback of tariffs paid when imported. The key to drawback is good inventory tracking and record-keeping procedures. Apply for drawback with your local customs port of entry office.

自动经纪人接口
Automated Brokerage Interface (ABI)

自动经纪人接口针对提供多笔简单分录并希望节省海关经纪人费用的大宗货物进口商。

The automated brokerage interface (ABI) is for those large-volume importers who file many simple entries and wish to avoid the cost of a broker. ABI permits importers (and brokers) to electronically file preliminary entry data in advance of the arrival of cargo.

怎样成为海关经纪人
How to Become a Customs Broker

海关经纪人是由海关和边境保护局批准、管理及授权的私营企业、合伙企业、组织或法人公司，用于帮助进出口商达到管理进出口的联邦标准。海关经纪人代表客户向海关及边境保护局提交必要信息，交纳必要款项，并向客户收取中介费。

法人公司、合伙企业和组织要进行海关商业贸易，必须持有经纪人许可证。

Customs brokers are private individuals, partnerships, associations, or corporations licensed, regulated, and empowered by U.S. Customs and Border Protection (CBP) to assist importers and exporters in meeting federal requirements governing imports and exports. Brokers submit necessary information and appropriate payments to CBP on behalf of their clients and charge the clients a fee for this service.

Corporations, partnerships, and associations must have a broker license to transact customs business. Each of these businesses must have at least one individually licensed officer, partner, or associate to qualify the company's license. Failure to have a qualifying officer or member

---

premium 溢价。derivative 衍生产品。subsequently 随后。automated brokerage interface 自动经纪人接口。simple entry 简单分录。empower 授权。

(of a partnership) for more than 120 days will result in the revocation of the broker license.

You can become a customs broker by (1) studying the Customs Service regulations and learning the application of the tariff schedules and then (2) passing an examination given several times a year. This license is not necessary for you to act on your own behalf, but it is needed if you act as an agent for others. Details about the examination and costs involved can be obtained from any Customs Service office. Figure 8.3 shows the application form required to obtain a license.

你可以通过以下方式成为海关经纪人：（1）学习海关部门规章和海关税则应用；（2）通过考试（一年内可多次报考）。

图 8.3　海关经纪人许可证申请表

Figure 8.3 Application for Customs Broker License

DEPARTMENT OF THE TREASURY
UNITED STATES CUSTOMS SERVICE

Form Approved: O.M.B. No. 1515-0076

APPLICATION
FOR
CUSTOMHOUSE BROKER'S LICENSE
19 U.S.C. 1641; 111.12 C.R.

Privacy Act Statement on Reverse of Form

1. APPLICANT'S NAME AND ADDRESS *(Principal Office OR Home Address)*

INSTRUCTIONS: Applicants must be United States citizens. Submit application in duplicate to the District Director of the District named in Block 3. All additional continuation sheets, if required, and attachments should also be in duplicate.

2. TYPE OF LICENSE APPLIED FOR
☐ Individual ☐ Corporation ☐ Partnership ☐ Association

3. CUSTOMS DISTRICT FOR WHICH LICENSE IS APPLIED

4. HAVE YOU EVER APPLIED FOR A CUSTOMHOUSE BROKER'S LICENSE? ☐ NO ☐ YES *(Explain in item 17)*

5. HAS THE APPLICANT (OR ANY OFFICER OR MEMBER THEREOF) EVER HAD A LICENSE SUSPENDED, REFUSED, REVOKED, OR CANCELED? ☐ NO ☐ YES *(Explain in item 17)*

6. IF APPLICANT HAS A CURRENT LICENSE, STATE WHEN AND FOR WHAT DISTRICT ISSUED.

7. IS THE APPLICANT (OR ANY OFFICER OR MEMBER THEREOF) AN OFFICER OR EMPLOYEE OF THE UNITED STATES? ☐ NO ☐ YES *(Explain in item 17)*

SECTION I — INDIVIDUALS ONLY

8. DATE OF BIRTH 9. BIRTHPLACE *(City & State)* 10. SOCIAL SECURITY NO. 11. HOME PHONE NO. 12. BUSINESS PHONE NO.

13. U.S. CITIZENSHIP
☐ NATURAL-BORN ☐ NATURALIZED- Give Date & Place →

14. HAVE YOU EVER BEEN A DEFENDANT IN A CRIMINAL PROSECUTION? *(You may exclude minor traffic violations where the fine was $50 or less.)* ☐ NO ☐ YES *(Explain in item 17)*

15. DO YOU PROPOSE TO ENGAGE IN THE BUSINESS OF A CUSTOMHOUSE BROKER:
(More than one may apply. Explain answer(s) in Item 17.)

(a) ☐ ON YOUR OWN INDIVIDUAL ACCOUNT? *(State name in which business is to be conducted; if trade name, state authority for use of the name and attach evidence of such authority.)*

(b) ☐ AS A MEMBER OF A PARTNERSHIP? *(State name of partnership and list names of all the partners.)*

(c) ☐ AS AN OFFICER OF AN ASSOCIATION? *(State name of the association, the title of the office you hold, and the general nature of your duties.)*

(d) ☐ AS AN OFFICER OF A CORPORATION? *(State name of the corporation, the title of the office you hold, and the general nature of your duties.)*

(e) ☐ AS AN EMPLOYEE? *(State name and address of your employer (if different than item 1)and the nature of your employment.)*

16. LIST THE NAMES AND ADDRESSES OF SIX REFERENCES.

SECTION III — CERTIFICATION *(ALL APPLICANTS)*

INDIVIDUAL

I, _____ certify that the statements contained in the foregoing application and supporting attachments thereto are true and correct to the best of my knowledge and belief. Written notice of any change in my mailing address, any business connection, or the name and style under which I conduct my business will be given to the Commissioner of Customs.

ASSOCIATION, CORPORATION, OR PARTNERSHIP

I, _____ certify that I am an officer or partner of the applicant; that I am a licensed customhouse broker; and that the statements contained in the foregoing application and supporting attachments thereto are true and correct to the best of my knowledge and belief. The officers or partners who are licensed customhouse brokers are aware of the requirements for the exercise by them of responsible supervision and control of the transaction of the customs business of the applicant. Written notice of any change in the applicant's mailing address, name, licensed officers or partners, or the charter, certificate, articles, or other instrument of organization of the applicant will be given to the Commissioner of Customs.

23. SIGNATURE

24. DATE

Customs Form 3124 (03-03-81)

---

customs service regulation 海关部门规章。tariff schedule 海关税则。

经纪人必须具备与进口货物相关的入境手续、可接受性条件、分类、价值评估、关税税率、适用税率和费用等方面的专业知识。

Brokers must have expertise in entry procedures, admissibility requirements, classification, valuation, and rates of duty and applicable taxes and fees for imported merchandise. Contact U.S. Customs and Border Protection, Trade Enforcement and Facilitation, Broker Management Branch, 1300 Pennsylvania Avenue, NW, Room 5.2C, Washington, DC 20229; phone: 202-344-2580.

Additional information on this profession may be obtained from local brokers or the National Customs Brokers and Forwarders Association of America (NCBFAA), which has its own Web site at www.NCBFAA.org.

通 关
Getting through the Customs Maze

关税表是关税税率的明细表。

A *tariff* is a schedule of duties. It is also the duty or tax imposed by a country and the duty or tax within the tariff schedule. As a tax, it is placed on goods as they cross the border between two countries.

关税曾一度是美国财政收入的主要渠道。

At one time, tariffs were the primary means by which the United States raised funds to support the federal government. However, in the early 1900s, when the income tax was introduced, tariffs for the purpose of raising revenue took on less importance. Since then, tariffs have been predominantly used to protect home industries.

HISTORICAL NOTE

The word *tariff* presumably comes from the Arabic term for inventory, which is *ta'rif*. The French word *tariff*, as well as the Spanish word *tarifa*, means price list or rate book. An alternate version has it that the word originated sometime after 700 AD. At that time, near Gibraltar, there was a village called Tarifa, where a small band of thieves lived. The thieves stopped every merchant ship and forced the captain to pay a handsome sum of money before the vessel could proceed through the strait. Seamen began calling the money they were forced to pay a tariff.

---

entry procedure 入境手续。admissibility 可接受性。applicable taxes 适用税率。raise funds 筹备资金。

四步入境手续
The Four-Step Entry Process

When a shipment of goods intended for commercial use reaches the United States, it may not be legally entered until after (1) it enters the port of entry, (2) estimated duties have been paid, and (3) customs authorizes delivery of the merchandise. During this process only the owner (or the owner's agent) is responsible for the entry—the Customs Service simply checks each step to ensure correctness. Table 8.1 compares the steps of the commercial entry process.

当商用货物抵达美国后，必须完成下列手续才能合法入境：（1）进入进口港；（2）货物完税；（3）海关授权货物运输。

表 8.1 商业入境手续
Table 8.1 Commercial Entry Process

Who Is Responsible?	What Does Customs Do?
Owner; agent; purchaser	
Step	Step
1. Entry: Shipment arrives within port	1. Check and verify. Store in general warehouse?
a. Decide consumption or bonded warehouse/FTZ	
b. If consumption, file entry documents	
c. Documents required	Check
1. Entry manifest	
2. Right to make entry	
3. Invoices	
4. Packing lists	
5. Entry summary	
6. Evidence of bond	Verify
2. Valuation	
3. Classify/appraise	
4. Estimate and pay tariff (check or cash)	2. Examine
	3. Validate
	a. Classification
	b. Appraisement
	4. Authorize entry
	5. Liquidate transaction

- If pay more than required tariff: refund (90 days)
- If pay less: billed to pay or protest (90 days)
- Protest: U.S. Court of International Trade (180 days)
- If re-export: Drawback

---

intend for 为……而准备。commercial use 商业用途。port of entry（货物的）进口港。authorize 授权。

入境手续最简单最基本的 4 个步骤，即入境、价值评估、分类和支付。

The process, in its simplest form has four basic steps: entry, valuation, classification, and payment.

步骤 1：入境
Step One: Entry

在货物到达美国进口港的 24 小时内，货主或代理人必须决定是为商用货物办理入境手续，还是将其存放于保税仓库或自由贸易区。

Within twenty-four hours of arrival of a shipment at a U.S. port of entry, the owner/agent must decide whether to *enter* the goods for consumption or place them into a bonded warehouse or free (foreign) trade zone (explained in detail later in this chapter). This can be done electronically. If the decision is made to enter for consumption, the following entry documents must be filed:

- Entry manifest, customs form 7533, or application and special permit for immediate delivery, customs form 3461
- Evidence of right to make entry
- Commercial invoice or pro forma invoice
- Packing list(s) if appropriate
- Entry summary, form 7501, and other documents necessary to determine merchandise admissibility
- Evidence of bond

表 3461 是立即放行的特殊许可，提供立即放行运输的替代手续。

Form 3461 is a special permit for immediate delivery and is an alternative procedure that provides for the immediate release of a shipment. Figure 8.4 shows the form used for land shipments, and Figure 8.5 the form used for ocean and air shipments. Application should be made before the arrival of the goods, and if approved, the goods won't have to sit on the dock or in a warehouse. They are released on arrival. You are allowed 10 working days to file a proper entry summary (form 7501) and to deposit estimated duties. Release under this provision is limited to:

- Merchandise arriving from Canada or Mexico
- Fresh fruits and vegetables for human consumption arriving from Canada or Mexico
- Articles for a trade fair
- Tariff-rate quota merchandise and, under certain circumstances, merchandise subject to an absolute quota

---

free trade zone 自由贸易区。immediate delivery 立即放行。alternative procedure 替代手续。

图 8.4　立即放行特殊许可（陆路）
Figure 8.4 Special Immediate Entry Permit (Land)

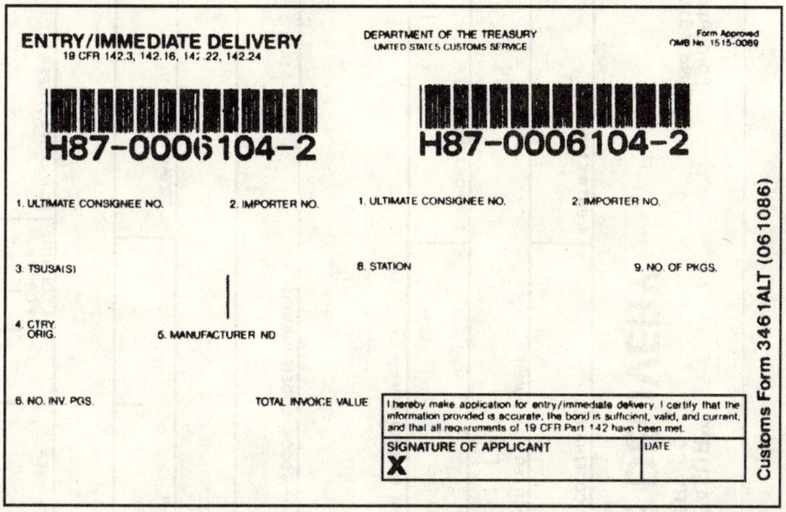

- Merchandise specifically authorized by customs because of perishability or inconvenience to the importer, carrier, or agent

步骤 2：价值评估
Step Two: Valuation

This step determines the *value* of the goods for purposes of applying any tariffs or duties. Generally, the customs value will be the transaction value or the price actually paid or payable for the merchandise when sold for exportation to the United States, plus amounts for the following items if they are not included in the price:

- The packing costs incurred by the buyer
- Any selling commission paid by the buyer
- The value of any assist (Note: An example of an assist would be tools, dies, molds, engineering, artwork, etc.)
- Any royalty or license fee that is required from the buyer as a condition of the sale
- The proceeds from the sale of the imported goods that accrue to the seller

这个步骤是为了确定货物的价值，目的在于对货物使用适当的关税税率。通常情况下，海关价值是交易价格或向美国出口的同类货物的市场公允价值加上下列不包含在价格中的各种费用：

- 采购商所支付的包装成本；
- 采购商支付的销售佣金；
- 救援费用（注：救援可以是工具、颜料、铸模、设计、工艺品等）；
- 销售时需要向采购商购买的特许使用费和许可证费用；
- 进口货物的销售增值收益。

---

customs value 海关价值。transaction value 交易价格。selling commission 销售佣金。royalty 特许使用费。license fee 许可证费

208

图 8.5 立即放行特殊许可（海运、空运）

Figure 8.5 Special Immediate Entry Permit (Ocean and Air)

Form Approved
OMB No. 1515-0069

DEPARTMENT OF THE TREASURY
UNITED STATES CUSTOMS SERVICE

ENTRY/IMMEDIATE DELIVERY

19 CFR 142.3, 142.16, 142.22, 142.24

1. ARRIVAL DATE	2. ELECTED ENTRY DATE	3. ENTRY TYPE CODE/NAME	4. ENTRY NUMBER
5. PORT	6. SINGLE TRANS. BOND	7. BROKER/IMPORTER FILE NUMBER	
	8. CONSIGNEE NUMBER		9. IMPORTER NUMBER
10. ULTIMATE CONSIGNEE NAME		11. IMPORTER OF RECORD NAME	
12. CARRIER CODE	13. VOYAGE/FLIGHT/TRIP	14. LOCATION OF GOODS—CODE(S)/NAME(S)	
15. VESSEL CODE/NAME			
16. U.S. PORT OF UNLADING	17. MANIFEST NUMBER	18. G O NUMBER	19. TOTAL VALUE
20. DESCRIPTION OF MERCHANDISE			
21. IT/BL/AWB CODE	22. IT/BL/AWB NO.	23. MANIFEST QUANTITY	24. TSUSA NUMBER	25. COUNTRY OF ORIGIN	26. MANUFACTURER NO.

27. CERTIFICATION

I hereby make application for entry/immediate delivery. I certify that the above information is accurate, the bond is sufficient, valid, and current, and that all requirements of 19 CFR Part 142 have been met.

SIGNATURE OF APPLICANT

X

PHONE NO.

DATE

29. BROKER OR OTHER GOVT. AGENCY USE

28. CUSTOMS USE ONLY

☐ OTHER AGENCY ACTION REQUIRED, NAMELY:

☐ CUSTOMS EXAMINATION REQUIRED.

☐ ENTRY REJECTED, BECAUSE:

DELIVERY AUTHORIZED: SIGNATURE   DATE

Paperwork Reduction Act Notice: This information is needed to determine the admissibility of imports into the United States and to provide the necessary information for the examination of the cargo and to establish the liability for payment of duties and taxes. Your response is necessary.

Customs Form 3461 (112085)

如果无法使用货物的交易价格，则按下列优先次序对货物价值进行评估：

- 同类商品交易价格；
- 类似商品交易价格；
- 扣减价格；
- 计算价格。

If the transaction value for the goods cannot be used, then secondary bases are used in the following order of precedence:

- Transaction value of identical merchandise
- Transaction value of similar merchandise
- Deductive value
- Computed value

步骤 3：分类

Step Three: Classification

分类的重要性无论怎样强调都不为过，因为它决定了应用于货物评估的从价关税税率。

The responsibility for *classification* rests with the importer, customs house broker, or other person preparing the entry papers. The importance of this step cannot be overemphasized because it determines the ad valorem (percentage) tariff rate that should be applied to the valuation of the goods. Familiarity with the Tariff Schedule of the United States of America (TSUSA) and the Harmonized Tariff Schedule of the United States facilitates the process.

HOT TIP

The first rule of importing is this: *always* get advance ruling from customs.

步骤 4：支付

Step Four: Payment

Payment of duties is made by check or cash to the Treasurer of the United States.

海关部门职责

Customs Service Responsibilities

海关部门在货物入境过程中要完成 5 个步骤：检查与核实、审查、批准、授权入境和清理。

The Customs Service involvement in the entry process can be characterized by five steps: check and verify, examine, validate, authorize entry, and liquidate.

步骤 1：检查与核实

Step One: Check and Verify

For this step, customs officers *check* the entry documents and *verify* evidence of a bond. Of course, on arrival of the goods at the port of entry,

---

deductive value 扣减价格。overemphasize 过分强调。ad valorem tariff 从价关税。validate 批准。liquidate 清理。

the owner or agent is responsible to immediately make arrangements for the shipment and storage of the goods. Those goods that are not claimed are stored in a general warehouse. Storage is billed to the owner when the goods are retrieved, or they are sold at auction.

步骤2：审查
Step Two: Examine

This step, which is the customs officer's *examination* to determine the value of the goods and their suitability for entering, has five substeps:

在本步骤中，用于确定货物价值和货物进口适宜性的海关官方审查共有5个分步骤：

- Valuation of the goods for customs purposes and their dutiable status
- Checking the proper markings of the goods with the country of origin
- Determining whether the shipment contains prohibited items
- Determining whether the goods are correctly invoiced
- Taking inventory to determine whether there are excesses or shortages of the invoiced quantities

- 以计算关税为目的的货物评估及其应纳税情况；
- 检查带有货物原产地的标识是否正确；
- 确定是否装有禁运物品；
- 确定货物发票是否正确；
- 根据存货清单，确定装运数量是否与发票数量相符。

步骤3：批准
Step Three: Validate

The *validation* step consists of checking the classification of the goods and appraising them to ensure correct valuation.

步骤4：授权入境
Step Four: Authorize Entry

After the classification and valuation, and after other required import information has been reviewed for correctness, proper appraisement, and agreement of the submitted data, the merchandise may be *authorized* for actual import.

经过分类和价值评估，其他进口信息核对无误，评估合理，提交数据一致，则可授权货物入境。

步骤5：清理
Step Five: Liquidation

If the goods are accepted without changes, they are *liquidated* "as entered." This step is finalized in the traditional way of posting a notice on the public bulletin board at the customs house. The bulletin board is now a computer printout. After the liquidation, an importer may pursue claims for adjustment or refund by filing, within 90 days, a protest

若原封不动地接受货物，它们就被清理为"入境货物"。

---

dutiable 应纳税的。prohibited item 禁运物品。invoice 发票。excesses or shortages of the quantities 溢短装。appraisement 评价，评估。

on customs form 19. Time limits do not begin to run until the date of posting. If, after further review, the importer is still not satisfied, a summons may be filed with the U.S. Customs Court of International Trade.

调和关税制度
The Harmonized System

调和关税制度是设计用于促进进出口数据收集和服务关税目的的国际化多用途的分类系统。

The Harmonized System (HS) is an international multipurpose, classification system designed to improve the collection of import and export statistics as well as to serve customs purposes. Intended as a core for national systems, it promotes a high degree of international uniformity in the presentation of customs tariffs and foreign trade statistics.

The U.S. Harmonized Tariff Schedule (often referred to as HTSUS) is about the size of a major city's telephone book and is available through the GPO in three-hole, loose-leaf form for about $99 or as a CD from www.Boskage.com for about $89.00. It can also be downloaded from the International Trade Commission's Web site at www.usitc.gov. It can also be ordered from the government bookstore.

调和关税制度是在编号系统框架下形成的一套完整的产品分类系统。

The HS is a complete product classification system, which is organized in a framework that employs a numbering system. To assist the user, a section in the front of the book gives instructions known as General Notes and General Rules of Interpretation (GRI), which explain the use and interpretation of the schedule.

以国际视野来看，将近5 000种货物品名被分成21篇、97章。

At the international level, about 5,000 article descriptions are grouped into 21 sections and arranged into 97 chapters. The U.S. version has 22 sections and 99 chapters. Chapter 98 includes information from the "old" TSUSA Schedule 8 (articles 806.20, 806.30, and 807) related to offshore assembly. Chapter 99 contains information transformed from the TSUSA Schedule 9. The 22 sections and their chapter headings are listed in a table of contents in the front of the book.

HISTORICAL NOTE

For decades, the international trading community was confronted with problems caused by the number of differing classification systems covering the movement of goods in international trade. In 1970, representatives of

---

harmonized system 调和关税制度。multipurpose 多种用途的。numbering system 编号系统。article descriptions 货物品名。

the Customs Cooperation Council (CCC), formerly known as the Brussels Tariff Nomenclature (BTN), undertook a study of commodity description and coding with a view to developing a system capable of meeting the principal requirements of customs authorities, statisticians, carriers, and producers. The result of the study was that the development of such a system was not only feasible but imperative. Some 13 years later the "Harmonized Commodity Description and Coding System" and a convention for its implementation were completed. Forty-eight countries and more than a dozen private and public organizations participated in its development.

HOT TIP

Reading the Harmonized Tariff Schedule
CHAPTER: FIRST TWO DIGITS, Example: 44
HEADING: FIRST FOUR DIGITS, Example: 4409
SUBHEADING: FIRST SIX DIGITS, Example: 4409.10
ITEM: FIRST EIGHT DIGITS, Example: 4409.10.10

案例分析：吉他
Case Study: Guitars

Let's hypothesize that you are an importer of "guitars valued at less than $100." Your order from Germany arrives. Assuming that you wish to enter the guitars immediately into commerce, within five working days you must present the documents listed in step one of the entry process to customs.

Note: If the guitars were perishable or if you had a special scheduling problem, you could have applied (in advance) for their immediate delivery using special entry permit form 3461.

In this case, let us assume there was no need for immediate entry, so we proceed as a normal, formal entry. Let's further assume that you used an L/C to make payment, so you can pick up your entry documents only after you square your account with your banker. The invoice shows 1,000 guitars at $89 each, for a total of $8,900. This is the transaction value for purposes of valuation. Because the value is over $1,250,

假设你是"进价低于100美元的吉他"的进货商，你从德国订的货物已经到达。假设你希望吉他能够立刻进入市场，在5个工作日内，你必须提交海关入境手续第一步中的所有文件。

在本案例中，假设货物不需要立即入境，我们就办理正常且正式的入境手续。我们进一步假设你使用信用证进行支付，因此你只有在与银行结清账款才能拿到入境凭证。每把吉他进货价格为89美元，共计1 000把，发票总额为8 900美元。这是可

---

entry process 入境手续。immediate entry 即刻入境。square account with 与⋯⋯结清账款。

以用于评估的交易价格。由于价格超过了 1 250 美元，你必须填写正式入境手续。如果货物价值低于 1 250 美元，就可以办理更简单的非正式入境手续，你只需要简要地做好自己的文书工作，并不需要签订履约保证。

如果你的出境时间超过 48 小时且物品是私人用途的，那么低于 400 美元的部分是免税的；高于 400 美元且低于 1 400 美元的部分收取 10% 的关税；高于 1 400 美元的部分按照美国关税税率明细表的从价率收取。

新手有时会问："如果我以私人用途的名义进口少量产品然后再出售，结果会怎样呢？"一位海关代理人回应："第一次你可能侥幸逃脱，但我们（电脑）有记录，早晚会抓住你。一旦被抓，会被处以至少 5 000 美元的罚款。"

在本案例中，由于吉他的价值大于 1 250 美元，所以需要办理正式入境手续。要办理正式入境手续，你就必须将物品进行分类。

you must make a formal entry. Had the value been under $1,250, the informal entry process would have been much simpler; you could very easily do your own paperwork, and a bond would not have been required. Figure 8.6 shows an entry summary, the basic form used for both formal and informal entry. Table 8.2 shows the difference between a formal and an informal entry.

Had the goods been for your personal use and you had been out of the country for more than 48 hours, the first $400 ($800 when returning from a U.S. insular possession) would have been exempt, the next $1,000 dutied at 10 percent, and the remainder at the ad valorem rate from the TSUSA.

Beginners sometimes ask, "What if I entered the goods for personal use in small quantities and then sold them?" One customs agent responded, "You may get away with it the first time, but we (the computers) remember, and sooner or later, we'll catch you. The penalty is at least a $5,000 fine."

Full, complete, and honest disclosure is the responsibility of the importer. The penalties are severe and not worth the gamble. Make your money and pay your duties.

In the guitar example, because the value is $1,250 or greater ($8,900), a formal entry is required. For the formal or informal entry process, you need to classify the product. Begin by scanning the table

表 8.2　正式 VS 非正式入境

Table 8.2 Formal versus Informal Entry

	Informal	Formal
Value	Less than $2,000*	$1,250 or greater
Bond	No	Yes
Duties	Pay on entry	Pay within 10 days†
Liquidation	On the spot	Liquidation notice
Forms required	7501, invoice, B/L, check ($$$ duties), packing list	7501, entry invoice, B/L, packing list, check ($$$ duties), other agency, documents, bond

*For some articles, formal entry is specified regardless of value (check your local Customs Service office or customs house broker).
†An example of a good that might require immediate payment is an item under quota.

---

paperwork 文书工作。exempt 使免除。sooner or later 迟早。

图 8.6　入境总表样图

Figure 8.6 Sample Entry Summary

DEPARTMENT OF THE TREASURY
UNITED STATES CUSTOMS SERVICE

ENTRY SUMMARY

1. Entry No.	2. Entry Type Code	3. Entry Summary Date
4. Entry Date	5. Port Code	
6. Bond No.	7. Bond Type Code	8. Broker/Importer File No.
10. Consignee No.	11. Importer of Record Name and Address	12. Importer No.

9. Ultimate Consignee Name and Address

	13. Exporting Country	14. Export Date
State	15. Country of Origin	16. Missing Documents
20. Mode of Transportation	17. I.T. No.	18. I.T. Date
24. Foreign Port of Lading	21. Manufacturer I.D.	22. Reference No.
27. Import Date	25. Location of Goods/G.O. No.	

19. B L or AWB No.

23. Importing Carrier

26. U.S. Port of Unlading

(Continued)

215

图 8.6 入境总表样图（接上页）

Figure 8.6 Sample Entry Summary (Continued)

(28) Line No.	(29) Description of Merchandise 30. (A) T.S.U.S.A. No. B. ADA CVD Case No.	31. (A) Gross Weight B. Manifest Qty.	(32) Net Quantity in T.S.U.S.A. Units	33. (A) Entered Value B. CHGS C. Relationship	34. (A) T.S.U.S.A. Rate B. ADA/CVD Rate (C) I.R.C. Rate D. Visa No.	(35) Duty and I.R. Tax Dollars	Cents

(36) Declaration of Importer of Record (Owner or Purchaser) or Authorized Agent

I declare that I am the

☐ importer of record and that the actual owner, purchaser, or consignee for customs purposes is as shown above. OR ☐ owner or purchaser or agent thereof.

I further declare that the merchandise

☐ was obtained pursuant to a purchase or agreement to purchase and that the prices set forth in the invoice are true. OR ☐ was not obtained pursuant to a purchase or agreement to purchase and the statements in the invoice as to value or price are true to the best of my knowledge and belief.

I also declare that the statements in the documents herein filed fully disclose to the best of my knowledge and belief the true prices, values, quantities, rebates, drawbacks, fees, commissions, and royalties and are true and correct, and that all goods or services provided to the seller of the merchandise either free or at reduced cost are fully disclosed. I will immediately furnish to the appropriate customs officer any information showing a different state of facts.

Notice required by Paperwork Reduction Act of 1980. This information is needed to ensure that importers/exporters are complying with U.S. Customs laws, to allow us to compute and collect the right amount of money, to enforce other agency requirements, and to collect accurate statistical information on imports. Your response is mandatory.

↓ U.S. CUSTOMS USE ↓		TOTALS	
A. Liq. Code	B. Ascertained Duty	(37) Duty	
	C. Ascertained Tax	(38) Tax	
	D. Ascertained Other	(39) Other	
	E. Ascertained Total	(40) Total	

(41) Signature of Declarant, Title, and Date

Customs Form 7501 (030984)

of contents for the general category within which your product fits. In this case "Musical instruments" is in Section XVIII, Chapter 92.

If you have a copy of the HS available, turn to page 92-2. If not, refer to Figure 8.7, which is a replication of page 92-2 from the Harmonized Tariff Schedule related to our case study about guitars.

Run your finger down the page until you find "Guitars: Valued not over $100." In this case, the classification of guitars is straightforward, but keep in mind that classifying a product is usually the most difficult part of using any tariff schedule. The correct classification can save you money and heartache. Consult the Customs Service or your customs house broker if you have any doubts.

在本案例中，吉他的分类是很简单的，但要记住，任何使用关税税率明细表对产品进行分类都是最难的部分。正确的分类可以节省成本和减少麻烦。

The heading for this product is 9202.90.20. The first two digits refer to the chapter number, in this case Chapter 92. The next two refer to the heading, the next two to the international subdivision or subhead, then the U.S. subdivision or item, and finally the U.S. statistical subdivision or item.

Now, draw your finger across the page. Note that there are three columns with an ad valorem duty rate. In column 1 "general," the rate is 6.8 percent. This is the rate for most favored nations (MFNs) such as England, France, or Germany. Thus, because your guitars came from Germany, you will pay 6.8 percent of $8,900, or $605.20 ad valorem duty.

Note that the duty rate shown in column 1, "special," is *free* (pay no tariff) for country groups A, E, IL, and J and only 3.4 percent for CA. The countries in these groups are listed in the "special" category programs in the front of the Harmonized Tariff Schedule under head notes. Table 8.3 shows these special programs.

注意第一列中显示关税税率，"特殊"是对 A、E、IL、J 国家组免税，对加拿大只收取 3.4% 的关税。

The column labeled "2" shows a rate of 40 percent for guitars valued under $100. This column shows the ad valorem duty rate for countries under "Communist domination or control," such as Cuba, and the like. If the guitars had come from Cuba instead of Germany, the ad valorem duty paid to the U.S. Treasury would be 40 percent of $8,900 or $3,560.

标有"2"的一列显示低于 100 美元的吉他应按 40% 的税率交税。这一列标明的是应用于"共产主义主导式控制"的国家的从价税率，如古巴等。如果吉他来自古巴而非德国，交给美国财政部的从价税应为 8 900 美元的 40%，即 3 560 美元。

Having estimated your duties as $605.20, the next step is to fill out the required entry documents and post surety in the form of cash or evidence of having a bond (minimum of $10,000). If a customs broker

---

straightforward 简单的。communist 共产主义的。U.S. Treasury 美国财政部。

图 8.7 调和关税系统明细表样本页

Figure 8.7 Sample Page from Harmonized Tariff Schedule

HARMONIZED TARIFF SCHEDULE of the United States (1993)

Annotated for Statistical Reporting Purposes

XVIII
92-2

Heading/ Subheading	Stat. Suf-fix	Article Description	Units of Quantity	Rates of Duty 1 General	Rates of Duty 1 Special	Rates of Duty 2
9201		Pianos, including player pianos; harpsichords and other keyboard stringed instruments:				
9201.10.00	00	Upright pianos	No.	5.3%	Free (A, E, IL, J) 2.6% (CA)	40%
9201.20.00	00	Grand pianos	No.	5.3%	Free (A, E, IL, J) 2.6% (CA)	40%
9201.90.00	00	Other	No.	5.3%	Free (A, E, IL, J) 2.6% (CA)	40%
9202		Other string musical instruments (for example, guitars, violins, harps):				
9202.10.00 37.5%	00	Played with a bow	No.	4.9%	Free (A, E, IL, J) 2.4% (CA)	
9202.90		Other:				
		Guitars:				
9202.90.20	00	Valued not over $100 each, excluding the value of the case	No.	6.8%	Free (A, E, IL, J) 3.4% (CA)	40%
9202.90.40	00	Other	No.	13%	Free (A, E, IL, J) 6.5% (CA)	40%
9202.90.60	00	Other	No.	7%	Free (A, E, IL, J) 3.5% (CA)	40%
9203.00		Keyboard pipe organs; harmoniums and similar keyboard instruments with free metal reeds:				
9203.00.40	00	Keyboard pipe organs	No.	Free		35%
9203.00.80	00	Other	No.	5.3%	Free (A, CA, E, IL, J)	40%

Heading/ Subheading	Stat. Suffix	Article Description	Unit of Quantity	Rates of Duty 1 General	1 Special	2
9204		Accordions and similar instruments; mouth organs;				
9204.10		Accordions and similar instruments:				
9204.10.40	00	Piano accordions	No.	4.7%	Free (A, CA, E, IL, J)	40%
9204.10.80	00	Other accordions	No.	5.1%	Free (A, CA, E, IL, J)	40%
9240.20.00	00	Mouth organs	Doz.	4.7%	Free (A, E, IL, J) 2.3% (CA)	40%
9205		Other wind musical instruments (for example, clarinets, trumpets, bagpipes):				
9205.10.00		Brass-wind instruments		5.8%	Free (A, E, IL, J) 2.9% (CA)	40%
	40	Valued not over $10 each	No.			
	80	Valued over $10 each	No.			
9205.90		Other:				
		Woodwind instruments:				
9205.90.20	00	Bagpipes	No	Free	Free (A, E, IL, J)	40%
9205.90.40		Other		4.9%	Free (A, E, IL, J) 2.4% (CA) 1/	40%
	20	Clarinets	No.			
	40	Saxophones	No.			
	60	Flutes and piccolos (except bamboo)	No.			
9205.90.60	80	Other	No.	3.4%	Free (A, E, IL, J) 1.7% (CA)	40%
9206.00		Percussion musical instruments (for example, drums, xylophones, cymbals, castanets, maracas):				
9206.00.20	00	Drums	No.	4.8%	Free (A, CA, E, IL, J)	40%
9206.00.40	00	Cymbals	No.	Free	Free (A, CA, E, IL, J)	40%
9206.00.60	00	Sets of tuned bells known as chimes, peals or carillons	No.	2.5%	Free (A, CA, E, IL, J)	50%
9206.00.80	00	Other	No.	5.3%	Free (A, CA, E, IL, J)	40%

1/ See subheading 9905.92.10.

表 8.3 特殊关税待遇
Table 8.3 Special Tariff Treatment Programs

General System of Preferences	A or A*
Automotive Products Tade Act	B
Agreement on Trade in Civil Aircraft	C
North American Free Trade Agreement:	
Goods of Canada, under the terms of general note 12 of this schedule.	CA
Goods of Mexico, under the terms of general note 12 of this schedule.	MX
Caribbean Basin Economic Recovery Act	E or E*
United States–Israel Free Trade Area	IL
Andean Trade Preference Act	J or J*

*Extracted from the Harmonized Tariff Schedule of the United States.

通常情况下，经纪人会帮助你获取保证金。保证金有 3 种：
- 只可用于一个进口港的定期保证金；
- 可用于美国所有港口的通用保证金；
- 可代替上述两种保证金的连续保证金。

makes the entry for you, the broker may use its own bond. This is not automatic. In many cases brokers will assist you to obtain your own bond. There are three types of bonds:

- Term bonds cover only one port of entry
- General bonds cover all U.S. ports
- Continuous bonds can substitute for both

After filling out the commercial customs invoice, the special (consular) customs invoice, the bill of lading, and the entry form, the goods may now be picked up from the carrier.

海关部门对本项交易的最终清理可能要花费几个月时间，但必须要在一年内（有例外）完成。

Remember that you or your agent (customs broker) originally classified and estimated the duties owed. Final liquidation of this transaction by the Customs Service could take as much as several months but must be finalized (with exceptions) within one year. You will receive notice of the date of liquidation and what amounts are due, if any.

Generalized systems of preference (GSP). GSP countries are those designated by the United Nations as "developing." To assist in their economic growth, they receive special preference and therefore pay no tariff.

term bond 定期保证金。general bond 通用保证金。continuous bond 连续保证金。

进口配额
Import Quotas

The importation of certain products is controlled by quantity. *Quotas* for this control are established by specific legislation, usually to protect infant industries or established industries under marketing pressure from foreign countries. Most textiles and apparel are subject to these quotas country by country and product by product. Most of the quotas have fixed ceilings for the amount that can be imported in a calendar year. The status of quotas is maintained by a central Customs Service computer in Washington, DC. Access to current quota status country by country can be obtained by calling 202-927-5850, the "Quota Watch" column in the *Journal of Commerce*, or accessing www.customs.gov.

特定商品的进口受到数量控制。特定法律为实施控制规定了配额，通常用于保护幼稚产业和处于外国营销压力之下的已有产业。

大多数配额规定了一年内可进口的数量上限。

United States import quotas are divided into two types: absolute and tariff rate.

绝对配额
Absolute Quotas

Absolute quotas are *quantitative quotas*, that is, no more than the amount specified may be permitted during the quota period. Some are global, while others apply only to certain countries. When an absolute quota is filled, further entries are prohibited during the remainder of the quota period.

绝对配额是数量配额，即在配额期限内，超额物品不允许入境。

当绝对数额已满，在配额期限的剩余天数内，不允许更多的物品入境。

关税配额
Tariff-Rate Quotas

Tariff-rate quotas provide for the entry of a specified quantity at a reduced rate of duty during a given period. Quantities entered in excess of the quota for the period are subject to higher duty rates.

关税配额在给定期间内对给定数量的入境货物减免关税税率。

特殊进口制度
Special Import Regulations

Many countries require a license to import, but the United States does not. Thousands of products are imported freely with no restrictions. Although the importation of goods does not require a license from the Customs Service, certain classes of merchandise might be prohibited or restricted by other agencies (1) to protect the economy and the security

虽然货物进口不需要海关部门的许可证，但某些类型的货物可能由于以下原因会被其他机构禁止或限制：(1)

---

calendar 日历，历法。license 许可。

维护经济和国家安全；（2）保障国民健康；（3）保护国内动植物。

of the country, (2) to safeguard health, or (3) to preserve domestic plant and animal life. The importer is wise to inquire (complete with samples and specifications) with the regulatory body involved well before entering into any business arrangements. There are cases in which the importer ended up with a warehouse full of products unfit or prohibited from entering the United States. For more information go to www.customs.gov/impoexpo/impoexpo.htm.

农产品
Agricultural Commodities

美国食品与药物管理局和农业部对大多数动物、动物食品、昆虫、植物以及禽类产品进行管制。

The U.S. Food and Drug Administration and the Department of Agriculture control or regulate the importation of most animals, animal foods, insects, plants, and poultry products.

军火、弹药以及放射性材料
Arms, Ammunition, and Radioactive Materials

烟酒管理局以及财政部旗下的枪械部门严令禁止进口任何与战争相关的物品，除非获得批准。

The Bureau of Alcohol, Tobacco, and Firearms of the Department of the Treasury, Washington, DC 20226, prohibits the importation of implements of war except when it issues a license. Even temporary importation, movement, and exportation are prohibited unless licensed by the Office of Munitions Control, Department of State, Washington, DC 20520. Of course, the Nuclear Regulatory Commission controls all forms of radioactive materials and nuclear reactors. To contact the bureau, e-mail ATFMail@atf.gov. Their Web address is www.atf.treas.gov.

消费品——安全与节能
Consumer Products—Safety and Energy Conservation

能源部旗下的消费品效率部门管制如冰箱、冷冻机、洗碗机、热水器、电视机、熔炉以及其他耗能产品等消费品的进口。

Consumer products such as refrigerators, freezers, dishwashers, water heaters, television sets, and furnaces, as well as other energy-using products, are regulated by the Consumer Products Efficiency Branch of the Department of Energy. The Consumer Product Safety Commission (CPSC) overseas safety issues.

电子产品
Electronic Products

包括声辐射，如电子射线管，以及类似的放射性产品，都被美国食品和药物管理局管制。

Radiation-producing products, including sonic radiation such as cathode ray tubes and the like, are regulated by the FDA, Center for

---

Food and Drug Administration 食品与药物管理局。poultry 家禽。firearm 枪械。
Consumer Product Safety Commission 消费品安全委员会。

Devices and Radiological Health, Rockville, MD 20850 and the FCC, Washington, DC 20554.

食品、药物、化妆品和医疗器械
Food, Drugs, Cosmetics, and Medical Devices

The Federal Food, Drug, and Cosmetic Act governs the importation of food, beverages, drugs, medical devices, and cosmetics. This act is administered by the Food and Drug Administration of the Department of Health and Human Services, Rockville, MD 20857.

联邦食品药物化妆品法案规定了食品、饮料、药物、医疗器械以及化妆品的进口事宜。

金、银、货币和邮票
Gold, Silver, Currency, and Stamps

Provisions of the National Stamping Act, enforced by the Department of Justice, Washington, DC 20530, regulate some aspects of importing silver and gold.

美国司法部颁布的银保证认定法案中的条款对进口金银的某些方面进行了规定。

杀虫剂、毒药和危险品
Pesticides and Toxic and Hazardous Substances

Three acts control the importation of these substances: the Insecticide, Fungicide, and Rodenticide Act of 1947; the Toxic Substances Control Act of 1977; and the Hazardous Substances Act. Further information can be obtained from the Environmental Protection Agency, Washington, DC 20460.

3套法案控制上述物品的进口：1947年颁布的杀虫剂、杀真菌剂和灭鼠剂法案，1977年颁布的有毒物品控制法案和危险品法案。

纺织品、毛纺品和皮制品
Textile, Wool, and Fur Products

Textile fiber products must be stamped, tagged, and labeled as required by the Textile Fiber Products Identification Act. Similarly, wool products must be clearly marked in accordance with the Wool Products Labeling Act of 1939. Fur, not to be left out, must be labeled as required by the Fur Products Labeling Act. Regulations and pamphlets containing the text of these labeling acts may be obtained from the Federal Trade Commission, Washington, DC 20580.

纺织品必须按照纺织品鉴定法案的要求贴上标签。与其相类似，毛纺品必须按照1939年颁布的毛纺品标志法案进行标记。

商标、商号和版权
Trademarks, Trade Names, and Copyrights

The Customs Reform and Simplification Act of 1979 strengthened the protection afforded trademark owners against the importation of

---

provision 条款。National Stamping Act 银保证认定法案。fungicide 杀真菌剂。rodenticide 灭鼠剂。in accordance with 按照。

通常情况下，带有复制或模仿已有美国或外国公司商标的产品，一律禁止进口。

articles bearing counterfeit marks. In general, articles bearing trade-marks or marks that copy or simulate a registered trademark of a United States or foreign corporation are prohibited importation. Similarly, the Copyright Revision Act of 1976 provides that the importation into the United States of copies of a work acquired outside the United States without authorization of the copyright owner is an infringement of the copyright.

野生动物与宠物
Wildlife and Pets

美国内务部下属的渔业和野生动物部门控制以下物品的进口：（1）野生动物、被猎动物、鸟类，或与其相关的产品（2）野生或被猎鸟类的蛋。

The U.S. Fish and Wildlife Service, Department of Interior, Washington, DC 20240, controls the importation of (1) wild or game animals, birds, and other wildlife, or any part or product made therefrom and (2) the eggs of wild or game birds. The importation of birds, cats, dogs, monkeys, and turtles is subject to the requirements of the U.S. Public Health Service, Centers for Disease Control, Quarantine Division, Atlanta, GA 30333.

海关货柜安全倡议计划
Customs Container Security Initiative

世界上 90% 的货物要用集装箱运输。通过海运集装箱到达美国的贸易额占到了总贸易额的一半左右。

货柜安全倡议计划的主要目的在于保护全球贸易系统，以及货柜安全倡议计划港和美国之间的贸易航线。

About 90 percent of all world cargo moves by container. Almost half of incoming trade (by value) arrives in the United States by sea containers.

The primary purpose of the Container Security Initiative (CSI) is to protect the global trading system and the trade lanes between CSI ports and the United States. First announced in 2002, the CSI deploys a team of officers with host nation counterparts to target all containers that pose a potential threat. Phone: 202-344-2990; Web site: www.cbp.gov.

自由贸易区
Free Trade Zones

自由贸易区，又被称做保税仓库地区，直到 19 世纪才有了显著发展。

Special zones for free trade, sometimes called *in-bond regions*, did not develop in any significant way until the nineteenth century. Some of the more notable zones worldwide are the port regions of Hamburg, Hong Kong SAR, Koushieng in Taiwan area, and Jurong Port in Singapore.

---

simulate 模仿。game 猎物。therefrom 从那里。Container Security Initiative 货柜安全倡议计划。lane 航线。in-bond 保税的。

Inland free trade zones also exist, most notable of which are the in-bond, free zones surrounding the Mexican Maquiladoras. Even Russia is establishing free zones to promote interchange of business with market economies.

内陆自由贸易区也是存在的，最著名的是在墨西哥返销型外资企业周边的保税自由区。

Free trade zones, under legislation of the sovereign nation where they are located, are considered outside the customs territory of that country. The concept is an ancient one, dating back to Egyptian times. Goods entering the zone pay no tariff or other taxes, under a guarantee (bond) that they will not be entered into the domestic market. Should they enter the domestic market, all duties must be routinely paid. While in these free zones, typically goods can be altered, assembled, manufactured, and manipulated. Thus the zones become areas where barriers to free trade are circumvented.

自由贸易区要遵守所在国的法律，但并不被认为属于该国的海关辖区。

美国对外贸易区
U.S. Foreign Trade Zones

Every where else in the world they are called free zones, but in the United States they are called foreign trade zones (FTZs). In the United States like elsewhere, they are restricted areas considered outside the territory under the supervision of the Customs Service.

世界其他地方都被称为自由区，但在美国它们叫做对外贸易区。

Typically an FTZ is a large warehouse, fenced and alarmed for security reasons, which tenants lease in order to bring in merchandise, foreign or domestic, to be stored, exhibited, assembled, manufactured, or processed in some way. They are usually located in or near customs ports of entry, usually in industrial parks or in terminal warehouse facilities. The usual customs entry procedures and payment of duties are not required on foreign merchandise in the zone unless it enters the customs territory for domestic consumption. The importer has a choice of paying duties either on the original foreign material or the finished product. Quota restrictions do not normally apply to foreign merchandise in a zone.

典型的对外贸易区是一个大仓库，出于安全考虑受到防护和警戒，租客为了储存、展示、调集、制造或加工国内外商品而租用对外贸易区的仓库。

配额限制一般情况下不能应用于处于本区域内的外国商品。

From the point of view of the local governments in the United States that build them, the purpose of FTZs is to stimulate international trade and thus contribute to the economic growth of a region by creating jobs and income. But from the point of view of an import/exporter, it's all about *profits*.

建造对外贸易区的美国当地政府，其目的在于促进国际贸易，从而创造就业机会、提高收入以及促进地区经济发展。而对于进出口商而言，关于贸易区的一切都与利益息息相关。

Maquiladora（外资公司在墨西哥开办的、产品回销本国的）返销型外资企业。
FTZ 外国贸易区。fence 防护。alarm 警戒。

HISTORICAL NOTE

The success of free zones like the "free port of Hamburg" stimulated American interest that culminated in the passage of the Foreign Trade Zones Act of 1934 and its amendment in 1950. The early history of American foreign trade zones is not glamorous. Growth was slow and profits modest. Until the early 1970s there were fewer than 25 authorized foreign trade zones in operation in the United States; that number had not changed appreciably from the time the enabling legislation was passed in 1934. However, since 1975 the number of FTZs has grown to more than 110 with 56 special subzones. See www.cbp.gov/xp/cgov/home.xml.

实际上，我们能清楚地意识到对外贸易区的优势是数不胜数的，然而有些建立在对外贸易区的企业却亏了本。

下面是一系列对外贸易区的管理优势：

- 只需要极少的海关手续；
- 货物可以在此区域无限期停留，无需考虑是否受到关税限制；
- 海关安全标准能够提供防盗保护；
- 海关税和内地的关税收入，只有在货物从对外贸易区运入境内销售时，才需交纳；
- 当货物位于此区域时，无需交纳任何美国关税和特许权税；
- 从贸易区出口的商品不需交任何税；
- 当货物从此区域进入海关辖区时，进口商可选择按不同的方式交税，因此进口商可以交最低的进口关税。

使用对外贸易区的优势
Advantages of Using an FTZ

Actually, perceived advantages of FTZs are limitless; unfortunately, there are many cases of firms that have begun operations in FTZs and lost money. Each operation in the zone must make business and profit sense and must be individually analyzed. Here is a list of the regulatory advantages:

- Customs procedural requirements are minimal.
- Merchandise may remain in a zone indefinitely, regardless of whether it is subject to duty.
- Customs security requirements provide protection against theft.
- Customs duty and internal revenue tax, if applicable, are paid when merchandise is transferred from a foreign trade zone to the customs territory for consumption.
- While in a zone, merchandise is not subject to U.S. duty or excise tax. Tangible personal property is generally exempt from state and local ad valorem taxes.
- Goods may be exported from a zone free of duty and tax.
- The zone user who plans to enter merchandise for consumption in the customs territory may elect to pay the duty and taxes

---

limitless 无限制的。revenue tax 关税收入。excise tax 特许关税。elect 选择。

on the foreign material placed in the zone or on the article transferred from the zone. The rate of duty and tax and the value of the merchandise may change as a result of manipulation or manufacture in the zone. Therefore, the importer may pay the lowest duty possible on the imported merchandise.

- Merchandise under bond may be transferred to a foreign trade zone from the customs territory for the purpose of satisfying a legal requirement to export or destroy the merchandise. For instance, merchandise may be taken into a zone in order to satisfy any exportation requirement of the Tariff Act of 1930 or an exportation requirement of any other federal law insofar as the agency charged with its enforcement deems it advisable. Exportation or destruction may also fulfill requirements of certain state laws.

海关部门职责
The Role of the Customs Service

The director of the Customs Service district office is responsible for controlling the admission of merchandise into the FTZ, the handling and disposition of merchandise within the FTZ, and the removal of merchandise from it.

海关部门地区办公处处长负责控制进入对外贸易区的商品许可、贸易区内商品处置以及贸易区内商品移除。

有资质在对外贸易区成立的机构
Operations that May Be Performed in an FTZ

All businesses may not benefit from FTZ operations, and those contemplating leasing a zone must analyze their market potential and economic potential. Some businesses that might benefit are:

不是所有的贸易都能在对外贸易区中获益，那些经过深思熟虑后租用外国贸易区的企业必须分析它们的市场潜力和经济潜力。

- Automotive parts—repack, remark, and distribute
- Clothing—cut and sew imported fabric for import and export
- Food stuffs—label, sample, and repack for shipment
- Liquor—affix stamps, destroy broken bottles, defer duty
- Machinery—inspect, repair, clean, and paint
- Office equipment—inspect and distribute
- Sporting goods—sort and repackage for shipment
- Televisions and other electronics—repackage for shipment

---

admission 准许进入。handle 处理。disposition 安排，处置。removal 移走。contemplate 深思。

使用外贸区节省花销的原因
Money-Saving Reasons to Use an FTZ

The uses of an FTZ for money-saving reasons are only limited by the creativity of the user and the trade-off of the costs of leasing space in an FTZ versus storing goods in a commercial warehouse. Here are several standard reasons:

出口退税会退还已交纳的关税，是一种费时费力的过程。财政部的退税过程十分漫长，即使过程全部完成，也只退还原数额的 99%，收取 1% 的管理费用。

- *Cost of money.* The drawback is the recovery of duty already paid and is a costly and time-consuming process. The Treasury Department does not expedite the repayment of duties already paid, and if it finally does, it pays only 99 percent of the original amount, keeping 1 percent to cover administrative costs. If the duty had not been paid in the first place, that sum of money could have been earning interest. The interest and administrative costs result in a cost of money that for companies with high inventories could have been avoided by using an FTZ.

按照关税明细表交纳给海关部门的费用并不能再用于其他用途，即使以后这笔钱通过出口退税退还到你手中也不行。

在外贸区进行回收利用能够节省成本；实际上，这种节省成本的机会只受到使用者想象力和法律的约束。

- *Cash flow.* The money paid to the Customs Service under the tariff schedule is money no longer available for other uses, even if that money is later recovered under drawback procedures. Using an FTZ to defer duty or taxes improves a cash flow position.
- *Reclamation.* There are many examples of reclamation within an FTZ that can provide a cost savings; in fact, the possibilities are limited only by the imagination of the user and the legality of the operation. Consider this example: A computer manufacturer imports chips from offshore (Asia or Mexico). Before importing them into the United States, the manufacturer conducts the quality assurance (QA) check within the FTZ. The firm reclaims the gold and other materials from the failed boards, sends the recovered material back to the offshore plant, and imports only the chips that pass QA, thus avoiding duty on the failed units.

在美国法律约束下，只有在外贸区的进口商才能够选择是交纳原材料税还是成品税。

- *Inverted tariff.* An FTZ is the only method under U.S. law whereby an importer can choose between paying the duty rate of material parts or the rate of a finished product. The importer would of course make the choice that provided the greatest cost savings.

外贸区被规定为安全区域。它常常受到防护、警戒和守卫。

- *Lower insurance costs.* An FTZ is required to be a secure area. It is fenced and alarmed and often guarded. For that reason, and

---

expedite 加快进展。reclamation 回收利用。finished product 成品。

because the value of an inventory is not increased by the value added in the FTZ, the inventory stored within a zone is often charged at lower insurance rates.

- *Transportation time savings.* Goods destined for an FTZ are not delayed on the dock for customs, but rather, because they are considered in-bond, are usually given priority for pierside movement. Therefore, those items that have some manipulations or reclamation or that need to be broken into smaller shipping amounts can be expedited by using the FTZ.

指定到达贸易区的货物不会因为海关检查而在码头积压，因为它们是保税货物，所以会被码头优先运输。

- *Reduced pierside pilferage and/or damage.* Because there are no dockside delays, there is less risk of theft, pilferage, and damage to the incoming goods.

由于货物不在码头积压，被盗、被扒、被损害的风险都相应降低。

- *Fine avoidance.* Goods imported into the United States with improper or incorrect labels are subject to fines. By checking the labels within an FTZ, the fines can be avoided.

带有不合格或不正确标签的产品进入美国，会被处以罚金。在外贸区检查标签，就能避免此类罚款。

- *Advantage over a bonded warehouse.* Users of FTZs can avoid the cost of a bond; the zone operator buys the bond.

使用外贸区的用户可以避免交纳保证金，保证金由区域运营者交纳。

- *Environmental protection.* Reclamation activities within an FTZ are centered within an enclosed area, using special machines, and can be carefully controlled.

外贸区的回收利用活动一般在圈定区域，使用特定机器进行，能够得到严密监控。

- *General system of preferences (GSP).* The duty-free advantage of this multilateral trade agreement can be combined with the benefits of FTZs.

多边贸易协定的免税优势可与外贸区的优势相辅相成。

- *Customs item 9802.00.8050.* Duty reduction can be obtained through the use of this method of incorporating this item of customs law (relates to labor content) in offshore assembly.

- *Customs item 9801.00.10108.* This item offers duty-free treatment of goods of U.S. origin that are improved or advanced in condition or value while abroad. (Relates to packaging material content.)

- *State and local taxes.* Under federal law, tangible personal property imported into an FTZ, and tangible personal property produced in the United States and held in an FTZ for export, is exempt from state and local ad valorem taxes.

根据联邦法律规定，进口到外贸区的有形个人财产，以及美国制造并放置在外贸区准备出口的有形个人资产，都免收州际和地方从价税。

- *Quota allocations.* Duty and charges against quota allocations can be avoided if shipments are rejected.

---

destine 指定。dock 码头。pier side 码头。enclosed 被圈定的。multilateral trade agreement 多边贸易协定。tangible 有形的。

外国货物关税交纳时间可被
延迟到他们离开外贸区时。

货物可以无限期储存在贸易
区，等待可接受的市场或有
利的销售条件。

- *Duty elimination.* Duty on merchandise that is re-exported or destroyed in the zone is eliminated.
- *Duty deferral.* Duty on foreign goods will be deferred until they leave the zone.
- *Indefinite storage.* Goods may be stored indefinitely while awaiting a receptive market or favorable sales conditions.

海关保税仓库
Customs Bonded Warehouse

保税仓库是在海关辖区内的
一栋楼或其他安全区域，应
税的外国货物可以在此免税
保存长达 5 年之久。

A *bonded warehouse* is a building or other secure area within the customs territory where dutiable foreign merchandise may be placed for a period of up to five years without payment of duty. Only cleaning, repacking, and sorting may take place. The owner of the bonded warehouse incurs liability and must post a bond with the U.S. Customs Service and abide by those regulations that pertain to control and declaration of tariffs for goods on departure. The liability is canceled when the goods are removed.

保税仓库的类型
Types of Bonded Warehouses

美国海关规定授权的 8 种保
税仓库：

1. 国有储存区域，存放经海
关检查或扣押的物品，通
常也用于无人认领的物
品；

2. 私有保税仓库，只储存由
所有人联名保证的商品；

3. 储存进口产品的公共保税
仓库；

4. 存放大型和重型进口商品
的保税院或保税库；

5. 储存谷物的料仓；

U.S. customs regulations authorize eight different types of bonded warehouses:

1. Storage areas owned or leased by the government to store merchandise undergoing customs inspection or that is under seizure; these areas may also be used for unclaimed goods.
2. Privately owned warehouses used exclusively for the storage of merchandise belonging or consigned to the proprietor.
3. Publicly bonded warehouses used exclusively to store imported goods.
4. Bonded yards or sheds for the storage of heavy and bulky imported merchandise such as pens for animals—stables and corrals—and tanks for the storage of imported fluids.
5. Bonded grain storage bins or elevators.

---

receptive 善于接受的。inspection 检查。seizure 扣押。unclaimed 无人认领的。consign 把……交付给。proprietor 业主。
bin 大储藏箱。elevator 谷物仓库。

6. Warehouses used for the manufacture in bond, solely for exportation, of imported articles.

7. Warehouses bonded for smelting and refining imported metal-bearing materials.

8. Bonded warehouses created for sorting, cleaning, repacking, or otherwise changing the condition of imported merchandise, but not for manufacturing.

6. 用于储存制造业保税品的仓库；

7. 用于储存熔炼提纯后的进口保税金属材料；

8. 用于提供分类、清洗、再包装以及其他非加工性质但能改变进口商品状态服务的保税仓库。

如何建立保税仓库
How to Establish a Bonded Warehouse

Your local Customs Service district office has all the needed information on how to get started, but in general, the following five requirements must be fulfilled:

你可以在当地海关部门所在地办事处找到建立保税仓库所需的所有信息，但通常来说，至少要完成以下5个步骤：

1. Submit an application to the district office giving the location and stating the class of warehouse to be established. Such application should describe the general character of the merchandise, the estimated maximum duties and taxes that could become due at any one time, and whether the warehouse will be used for private storage or treatment or as a public warehouse.

2. A fee of about $80.

3. A certificate that the building is acceptable for fire insurance purposes.

4. A blueprint of the building or space to be bonded.

5. A bond of $5,000 or greater on each building, depending on the class of the bonded area.

1. 向所在地区办事处提交申请表，说明建立仓库的地点和等级；

2. 交纳80美元的手续费；

3. 用于火灾保险目的的建筑物的合格认证；

4. 保税空间及建筑物蓝图；

5. 依据保税地区的等级为每栋建筑物交纳5 000美元或更多的保证金。

保税仓库还是外贸区
Bonded Warehouse or FTZ?

Table 8.4 shows a comparison of an FTZ and a bonded warehouse.

Awareness of all the possibilities is a vital part of competing and winning the trade game. Not every importer/exporter will need countertrade or make use of an FTZ or a customs bonded warehouse, but proper and advance planning is essential in order to take advantage

关注每一种可能性是竞争和赢得贸易博弈的重要部分。

---

certificate 证明书。fire insurance 火灾保险。blueprint 蓝图。

表 8.4 外贸区与保税仓库的对比

Table 8.4 Comparison of an FTZ and Bonded Warehouse

Function	Bonded Warehouse	Zone
Customs entry	A bonded warehouse is within U.S. customs territory; therefore a customs entry must be filed to enter goods into the warehouse.	A zone is not considered within customs territory. Customs entry is, therefore, not required until merchandise is removed from a zone.
Permissible cargo	Only foreign merchandise may be placed in a bonded warehouse.	All merchandise, whether domestic or foreign, may be placed in a zone.
Customs bonds	Each entry must be covered by either a single-entry term bond or a general term bond.	No bond is required for merchandise in a zone.
Payment of duty	Duties are due prior to release from bonded warehouses.	Duties are due only upon entry into U.S. territory.
Manufacture of goods	Manufacturing is prohibited.	Manufacturing is permitted with duty payable at the time the goods leave the zone for U.S. consumption. Duty is payable on either the imported components or the finished product, whichever carries a lower rate.
Appraisal and classification	Immediately.	Tariff rate and value may be determined either at the time goods are admitted into a zone or when goods leave a zone, at the importer's discretion.
Storage periods	Not to exceed 5 years.	Unlimited.
Operations on merchandise destined for domestic consumption	Only cleaning, repackaging, and sorting may take place and under customs supervision.	Zone operations include sort, destroy, clean, grade, mix with foreign or domestic goods, label, assemble, manufacture, exhibit, sell, and repack.
Customs entry regulations	Apply fully.	Applicable only to goods actually removed from a zone for U.S. consumption.

of the subtleties of the trade laws. An appreciation of the capabilities of each of the business tools presented in this chapter could lead to the recognition of a winning opportunity.

The next part of the book is dedicated to understanding the basics of doing business in the globalized world and covers such things as world trade centers, integrated economies like NAFTA, the European Union, and specific nations.

本书的下一部分将帮助理解全球贸易中的基本要素，包括世界贸易中心、经济一体化（如北美自由贸易区，欧盟以及特定国家）等。

CHAPTER 9

20 KEYS TO IMPORT/EXPORT SUCCESS

进出口业务成功的20条基本原则

Success in the international market place is measured in profits and market share. It is also measured in the satisfaction you feel in reaching new horizons and visiting places that previously were only dreams. You and your firm can be successful if you act on these 20 critical keys.

市场收益和市场份额是在国际市场中衡量成功与否的准则，这种成功也可以是打开新视野或踏上梦想之地带来的满足感。

郑重承诺，挺进全球

1. The most important key to success is commitment by you, the decision maker, to enter the global market.

You'll reap tax advantages, sales volume advantages, the excitement of the international experience, and lots of profit.

你会获得优惠的税率、激增的销量、精彩的国际体验和巨额的利润。

Change your game and get into the global competition. Get to work and earn a share of the more than $7 trillion that's out there waiting for enthusiastic entrepreneurial Americans.

理解文化，跨越藩篱

2. Get beyond cultural obstacles.

Accept the fact that the rest of the world isn't like the United States. People in other countries like their way of doing things. Get used

---

critical keys 重要原则。obstacles 障碍。trillion 万亿。

至少，要能够尊重和理解文化差异。

to the idea that cultural differences exist, but be assured that the differences can be understood and learned. At a minimum, the differences can be appreciated and respected. Remember that there are more similarities among peoples of the world than there are differences.

问题在于美国的汽车制造商不了解如何迎合日本消费者，这些消费者已经习惯了另外一种不同的风格，特别是另一套服务体系。

For example, the Japanese like cars, and they don't dislike American cars. The problem is that American car manufacturers haven't figured out how to satisfy the Japanese car consumer who is used to a different style and, above all, different service considerations. The world is becoming more and more internationalized.

运筹策划，通盘考虑
3. Plan, plan, plan, but do not treat international trade as a stand-alone process.

假如前期调研反映了市场对你的产品有需求，无论是否需要对产品设计做修改，都要先拟定战略规划。一开始就要写出计划。

Plan for success. Assuming that your initial market research effort reveals some demand for your product, either as it is or with minor redesign, develop a strategic plan for your business. From the beginning, *write* the plan. What is your competitive advantage? What are your geographical and product line priorities? How are you going to penetrate the market?

把握市场，调查为先
4. The market, the market, the market.

不要试图一开始就能立即销遍全美、全球甚至仅仅是一个国家的市场，要记住，卖出才是硬道理。

An early investigation of the market is the key that leads to success. Get an estimate of the demand for the products that you already manufacture. The best information will come from your own industry—here and overseas. Talk to those who have experience. Don't overlook available statistics and library resources. Lay out a map of the world and apply some logic. If you plan to export, divide the world into export regions and prioritize the regions based on broad assumptions of their need for your product and their ability to pay. Based on your common understanding of the various countries, regions, languages, environments, and cultures, select one or more target countries for start-up. Be sure to consider the political and financial stability of the country. Use the same logic for imports. Examine a map of the United States or your region and divide the map into target segments. Do not try to sell to all of the United States, the entire world, or even one entire foreign country immediately, but remember that nothing happens until you sell something.

---

consideration 考虑的方面。product line 产品系列。prioritize 优先排序。

信息分类，举足轻重
5. Information is critical.

Research is critical to the success of your market plan. Begin with a list
of the kinds of information you will need to support your analysis.
What do you need to know about the regions of the United States
(imports) or the foreign country (exports) you have selected? What level
of detail will you require? Next, organize a list of the potential sources
of your research. Classify your sources and begin the process of doing
a logical sort of the material. You can gain the most accurate and mean-
ingful information by traveling to the potential market.

最精确的实用信息来自于对
潜在市场的实地考察。

分析确定，市场目标
6. What are your market goals?

Develop a well-researched, solidly reasoned market plan; it should
include a background review, an analysis of the market environment,
and a description of your goals in terms of your company.

要制定一个调查充分、论证
翔实的市场计划、这个计划
必须包含背景调查、市场环
境分析以及公司的市场目标
概述。

有竞争的地方才有市场
7. Where there are competitors, there is a market.

Take a close look at the competition. It will be to your benefit to
discover that there is competition. Why? Because where there is competition, there is a market.

坚持到底，永不言弃
8. Be persistent—don't give up.

Don't become discouraged if you find that your product is ahead of its
time in the international marketplace. Don't give up on exporting. WD-
40 and Coca-Cola created a global market for their products. Search
for products that have an overseas market and are similar to yours.

如果你发现自己的产品在国
际市场尚属超前、时机尚未
成熟，不要沮丧，不要就此
放弃出口。

产品调整，贴近市场
9. Adapt the product to the market.

Learn what products your customers like and how they like the products, whether you are importing an article for American tastes or
exporting a product for a foreign market. Be ready to adapt your product to the market. Redesign your product and compete.

精打细算，步步为赢
10. Budget for success.

Include international goals in your financial plan. Treat import/export
start-up as you would any other entrepreneurial venture. Budget from

将进出口的启动视为一项新
创事业。

---

level of detail 细化程度。WD-40 防锈润滑剂。an article 一款产品。entrepreneurial venture 新创事业。

the beginning and keep good books. Watch your costs and cash flow. Like any new business, expect short-term losses, but plan for long-term gains.

全面规划，管理成功

11. Manage for success.

实施总体战略规划时，要制定战术策略，如人事计划、广告宣传策略、进入市场途径以及销售方式等。

Develop the tactical plans that implement your overall strategic plan, such as a personnel plan, an advertising policy, a market entry, and a sales approach. Motivate your personnel by emphasizing teamwork.

开展国际贸易要具备足够耐心

12. Be patient in developing international trade.

国际融资业务和银行业务发达先进，总体很好，但是跨国业务中的谈判和交易往往比国内业务耗时更长。

International trade takes a little longer than domestic trade. After all, there are oceans in between, and the transportation systems are slower. Every transaction will require financing. International financing and banking methods are sophisticated and generally excellent, but negotiations and transactions across borders take more time than does domestic business.

长期投资，精心考察

13. The best long-term investment is a well-planned trip.

老板勤于督察，事情才能做好。

再没有什么方式能比这样更好地获取第一手资料了。

Things go right when the boss checks everything. And, in international business that means international travel. After you have developed your strategic plan, visit the overseas sources or markets you have chosen. There is nothing like getting first-hand information. You will find it interesting, rewarding, and essential to meet the people with whom you will be doing business. Even after you have established a successful sales and distribution network, it is necessary that you or representatives of your company visit at least twice a year.

脚踏实地，扎实前行

14. Walk on two legs.

建立起良好合作关系，并加以维护。

Carefully choose a good international banker, freight forwarder, and customs house broker. Talk with them to learn the language of international business—pricing, quotations, shipping, and getting paid. Establish a good relationship, and then stick with it. Deal with a bank that has personnel who are experienced in the international marketplace.

---

cash flow 现金流。overseas sources 海外货源。walk on two legs 脚踏实地。

沟通得当，交易成功

15. Proper communication gets sales results.

Provide customer service the international way by communicating often, clearly, and simply. Keep your overseas business partners on the team by being particularly sensitive to communications, letters, faxes, and phone calls. Above all, develop a Web site and use the Internet.

> 与国际合作伙伴保持良好的关系有赖于对沟通、信件、传真及电话的正确处理。

专业咨询，少走弯路

16. Expert counsel saves money.

Minimize your inevitable mistakes by asking for help. Banks, customs house brokers, freight forwarders, and the U.S. Department of Commerce are sources of free information. And most private consultants ask reasonable fees.

> 寻求专业人士帮助可以避免生意中的不必要失误。

销售途径，至关重要

17. Selection of distributors is critical.

Your objective is to get your product in front of your buyer—the decision-making unit (DMU). The wrong distributor can stifle your market efforts and tie you up legally.

营销策略，贵在坚持

18. Stick to a marketing strategy.

Don't chase orders. Of course, fill the over-the-counter orders, but be proactive rather than reactive. Establish an effective marketing effort according to your market plan.

> 不要一味追求订单。

国内国外，一视同仁

19. International partners and customers should be treated the same as domestic counterparts.

It may surprise some people that foreigner's debt ratios are often less than half of the U.S. bad debt ratios. The reason is that in the United States credit is a way of life. In overseas markets, credit is still something to be earned as a result of having a record of prompt payment. Use common sense in extending credit to overseas customers, but don't use tougher standards than you use for your U.S. clients.

> 在授信时，要依常理对待海外顾客，而不要用比对待本土客户更加苛刻的标准。

商海沉浮，泰然处之

20. Don't fret about the international business cycle.

Don't worry about booms or busts; just do it. International trade is exciting and profitable because there are so many side benefits. Think of

> 是生意就有起有伏，不要惧怕，放胆去做吧。

---

ask 收取（费用）。the decision-making unit 决策群体。stifle efforts 使努力付之东流。over-the-counter orders 场外订单。•
debt ratio 负债率。side benefits 额外好处。

traveling to such exotic places as Vienna and writing off the trip as an expense to the company.

既然找到了货源，开拓了市场，拟好了商业计划，再加上创业精神，你就可以带领自己的进出口公司直奔成功了。

Okay, you've found the sources, developed the markets, written the business plan, and have the entrepreneurial spirit to make your own import/export business a success. The time to get into the import/export market—and make lots of money—is now! Good luck.

＊   write off 冲销（账）。

HOMELAND SECURITY
国土安全

See the Homeland Security organization chart on the following page.

国土安全系统图见下页

图 A.1 国土安全系统图

Figure A.1 Homeland Security Organization Chart

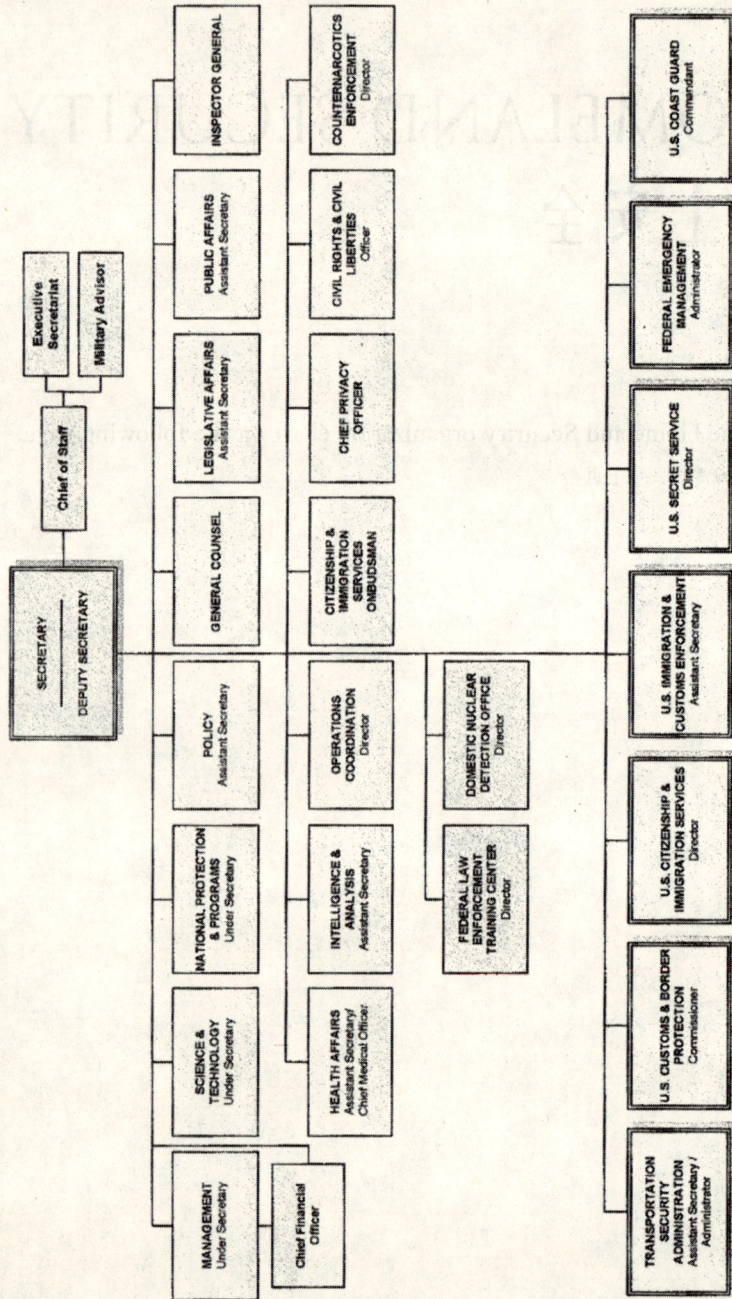

ATA CARNET COUNTRIES AND THEIR CUSTOMS TERRITORIES (2008)

实施暂准通关单证册制度的国家和地区（统计截至2008年）

For updates and additional information on the countries listed, please go to www.atacarnet.com/CountriesandTerritoriesAccepting ATACarnets.aspx.

Algeria (DZ)
Andorra (AD)
Australia (AU)
Austria (AT)

Balearic Isles
Belarus (BY)
Belgium (BE)
Botswana (BW)
Bulgaria (BG)

Canada (CA)
Canary Islands
Ceuta
Chile (CL)
China (CN)
Corsica
Côte d'Ivoire (CI)

Croatia (HR)
Cyprus (CY)
Czech Republic (CZ)

Denmark (DK)

Estonia (EE)
European Union (EU)

Finland (FI)
France (FR)
French Guiana (GF)

Guam
Germany (DE)
Gibraltar (GI)
Greece (GR)
Guadeloupe (GP)
(Bailiwick of) Guernsey

Hong Kong SAR (HK)
Hungary (HU)

Iceland (IS)
India (IN)
Iran (IR)*
Ireland (IE)
Isle of Man
Israel (IL)
Italy (IT)

Japan (JP)
Jersey

Korea (Republic of Korea) (KR)

Latvia (LV)
Lebanon (LB)
Lesotho (LS)
Liechtenstein
Lithuania (LT)
Luxembourg (LU)

Macao SAR
Macedonia (MK)
Malaysia (MY)
Malta (MT)
Martinique (MQ)
Mauritius (MU)
Mayotte
Melilla
Miquelon
Monaco (MC)
Mongolia (MN)
Morocco (MA)

Namibia (NA)
Netherlands (NL)
New Caledonia (NC)

New Zealand (NZ)
Norway (NO)

Pakistan (PK)
Poland (PL)
Portugal (PT)
Puerto Rico
Reunion Island (RE)
Romania (RO)
Russia (RU)

Saipan
Senegal (SN)
Serbia (CS)
Singapore (SG)
Slovakia (SK)
Slovenia (SI)
South Africa (ZAR)
Spain (ES)
Sri Lanka (LK)
St. Barthelemy
St. Martin, French part
St. Pierre
Swaziland (SZ)
Sweden (SE)
Switzerland (CH)

Tahiti (French Polynesia – PF)
Taiwan area (TW)
Tasmania
Thailand (TH)
Tunisia (TN)
Turkey (TR)

Ukraine (UA)
United Kingdom (GB)
United States of America (US)

Wallis and Futuna Islands

*Iran is accepting carnets. However, U.S. restrictions do not allow a U.S.-issued carnet for Iran.
†Taiwan area requires a separate carnet called a TECRO.

常用贸易术语

International trade, like other specialized fields, has developed its own distinctive vocabulary that can mystify lay people. Many businesspeople stumble over the commonly used terms and acronyms that guide, regulate, and facilitate trade. Lack of precision in the language impedes communication, causes misunderstandings, and delays transactions. Undoubtedly, it loses sales for global companies.

This glossary of terms frequently used in global trade was sourced from the U.S. Information Agency; U.S. Departments of Commerce, State, and Treasury; the U.S. International Trade Commission; the Office of the U.S. Trade Representative; the World Trade Organization; and the UNCTAD Secretariats in Geneva. It also includes other terms researched by the author that are particularly applicable to the scope of this book.

承 兑
acceptance A bill of exchange accepted by the drawee, as evidenced by the drawee's signature on the face of the bill. The drawee commits to pay the bill at maturity. (The payee of the bill must be sure that the drawee has the means and the will to do this.)

承兑汇票
acceptance draft A sight draft document against acceptance. See *sight draft* and *documents against acceptance*.

承兑信用证
acceptance letter of credit A letter of credit (L/C) available by acceptance calling for a *time draft* (or *usance draft* in international parlance). Drawn on an intermediate accepting bank, acceptance L/Cs are popular where both buyer and seller need interim finance to facilitate cash flow.

从 价
ad valorem According-to-value. See *duty*.

预付款

advance payment   The buyer delivers cash to the seller before the seller releases the goods. Some sellers ask for such partial payment to show good faith on the part of the buyer and also to enhance their cash flow related to the sale of a particular custom-made item. May not mean exactly the same thing as *payment in advance*.

通知行

advising bank   The bank, usually in the country of the exporter, that notifies the exporter of the availability of the *letter of credit*. The advising bank is responsible for authenticating and forwarding the L/C but makes no commitment to pay unless it agrees to act as confirming bank. See also *negotiating bank*.

顾问资格

advisory capacity   A term indicating that a shipper's agent or representative is not empowered to make definitive decisions or adjustments without approval of the group or individual represented. Compare *without reserve*.

包运租船（合同）

affreightment (contract of)   An agreement between a steamship line (or similar carrier) and an importer or exporter in which cargo space is reserved on a vessel for a specified time and at a specified price. The importer/exporter is obligated to make payment whether or not the shipment is made.

出票后（若干天）付款

after date   A phrase indicating that payment on a draft or other negotiable instrument is due a specified number of days after presentation of the draft to the drawee or payee. Compare *after date* and *at sight*.

见票后（若干天）付款（事先确定票据到期日）

after sight   A phrase indicating that the date of maturity of a draft or other negotiable instrument is fixed by the date on which it was drawn a specified number of days after presentation of the draft to the drawee or payee. Compare with *at sight* and *after date*.

代理（商）

agent   See *representative*.

航空运单

air waybill   The carrying agreement between shipper and air carrier which is obtained from the airline used to ship the goods. Technically, it is a nonnegotiable instrument of air transportation which serves as a receipt for the shipper, indicating that the carrier has accepted the goods listed and obligates itself to carry the consignment to the airport of destination according to specified conditions. Compare *inland bill of lading*, *ocean bill of lading*, and *through bill of lading*.

一切险条款
all-risks clause   An insurance provision which provides additional coverage to an open cargo policy usually for an additional premium. Contrary to its name, the clause does not protect against all risks. The more common perils it does cover are theft, pilferage, nondelivery, fresh water damage, contact with other cargo breakage, and leakage. Loss of market and losses caused by delay are not covered.

船 边
alongside   A phrase referring to the side of a ship. Goods to be delivered alongside are to be placed on the dock or lighter within reach of the transport ship's tackle so that they can be loaded aboard the ship.

改 证
amendment—letter of credit   A change in the terms, amount, or expiration date of a letter of credit usually in the interest of the beneficiary. (Exporters should check Art. 9.d.iii of UCP 500 very carefully, especially regarding adverse amendments.)

开证申请人
applicant   Party (usually an importer) applying to the issuing bank to issue the letter of credit.

套 利
arbitrage   The process of buying foreign exchange, stocks, bonds, and other commodities in one market and immediately selling them in another market at higher prices.

款项让渡
assignment of proceeds   Document signed by the beneficiary under a letter of credit assigning the rights to proceeds from an L/C drawing to a third party. From the perspective of the assignee, an assignment differs radically from a transferable letter of credit. The latter conveys a right to the transferee to present documents under an L/C; the former does not.

［法语缩写］暂时准入
ATA   A French abbreviation signifying temporary admission.

货物暂准通关证
ATA carnet   A customs document that enables the holder to carry or send goods temporarily into certain foreign countries without paying duties or posting bonds.

见票即付
at sight   A phrase indicating that payment on a draft or other negotiable instrument is due upon presentation or demand. Compare *after sight* and *after date*.

委托付款

authority to pay   A document comparable to a revocable letter of credit but under whose terms the authority to pay the seller stems from the buyer rather than from a bank.

副证，子证

baby letter of credit   Second of two letters of credit in a back-to-back L/C arrangement.

背对背信用证

back-to-back letter of credit   A baby letter of credit in which the issuing bank is secured by a master L/C. The applicant of the baby L/C will be the beneficiary of the master, and the terms of the two L/Cs will be such that documents presented under the baby can obtain payment under the master. Back-to-backs are popular among intermediaries wanting to protect their position between the buyer and manufacturer.

贸易平衡

balance of trade   The balance between a country's exports and imports.

银行附属贸易协会

bank affiliate trade association   A trade association partially or wholly owned by a banking institution.

银行承兑汇票

banker's acceptance   A draft bearing the acceptance of a drawee bank thus qualifying for financing in the liquid U.S. dollar banker's acceptance market. (A useful vehicle for fixed-term, fixed-rate financing, especially for banks without access to low-cost U.S. dollar funds.)

银行的银行

banker's bank   A bank that is established by mutual consent by independent and unaffiliated banks to provide a clearinghouse for financial transactions.

银行控股公司

bank holding company (BHC)   Any company that directly or indirectly owns or controls, with power to vote, more than 5 percent of voting shares of each of one or more other banks.

（船长或船员）不当行为

barratry   Negligence or fraud on the part of a ship's officers or crew resulting in loss to the owners. See *open cargo policy*.

易货贸易

barter   Trade in which merchandise is exchanged directly for other merchandise without use of money. Barter is an important means of trade with countries using currency that is not readily convertible.

受益人
beneficiary   The person in whose favor a letter of credit is issued or a draft is drawn, usually an exporter.

汇　票
bill of exchange   A written, unconditional demand, signed by the drawer and addressed to the drawee, to pay a sum of money at sight or at some future date (*x* days after sight or *x* days after bill of lading date) to the order of the payee or to the bearer. Frequently known as a draft or as a bill. See *draft*.

海运提单
bill of lading   A document that provides the terms of the contract between the shipper and the transportation company to move freight between stated points at a specified charge. A receipt for goods delivered to a carrier for shipment, a contract of carriage, and a document of title issued by a carrier to the shipper. This transport document is the primary evidence of shipment of goods and the exporter's key to prompt payment. See also *charter party bill of lading*.

总括保单，总括保险单, 统保单
blanket policy   See *open cargo policy*.

冻结货币
blocked currency   Exchange that cannot be freely converted into other currencies. Cash deposit that cannot be transferred to another country because of local regulations or a shortage of foreign exchange.

保税仓库
bonded warehouse   A building authorized by customs authorities under bond or guarantee of compliance with revenue laws for the storage of goods without payment of duties until removal.

订　舱
booking   An arrangement with a steamship company for the acceptance and carriage of freight.

经纪人
broker   See *export broker*.

布鲁塞尔税则目录
Brussels Tariff Nomenclature   See *Customs Cooperation Council Nomenclature*.

购货代理
buying agent   An agent who buys in a country for foreign importers, especially for such large foreign users as mines, railroads, governments, and public utilities. Synonymous with *purchasing agent*.

成本加运费
C&F Cost and freight. See *CFR*.

成本加保险费
C&I Cost and insurance. A pricing term indicating that certain costs are included in the quoted price.

免税通关证
carnet A customs document allowing special categories of goods to cross international borders without payment of duties.

承运人
carrier A transportation line that hauls cargo.

付现交单
cash against documents (CAD) Payment for goods in which a commission house or other intermediary transfers title documents to the buyer upon payment in cash.

交货前付现款
cash in advance (CIA) Payment for goods in which the price is paid in full before shipment is made. This method is usually used only for small purchases or when the goods are built.

订货付现
cash with order (CWO) Payment for goods in which the buyer pays when ordering and in which the transaction is binding on both parties.

自由销售证书
certificate of free sale A certificate, required by some foreign governments, stating that the goods for export, if products under the jurisdiction of the U.S. Federal Food and Drug Administration, are acceptable for sale in the United States; that is, that the products are sold freely without restriction. The FDA will issue shippers a letter of comment to satisfy foreign requests or regulations.

检验证书
certificate of inspection A document in which certification is made as to the good condition of the merchandise immediately prior to shipment. The buyer usually designates the inspecting organization, usually an independent inspection firm or government body.

制造证书
certificate of manufacture A statement by a producer, sometimes notarized, which certifies that manufacture has been completed and that the goods are at the disposal of the buyer.

原产地证明
certificate of origin   Certificate stating origin of goods, usually signed by the embassy in the country of the exporter which represents the country of the importer.

成本加运费
CFR   Cost and freight. Incoterm indicating that the sale price includes all costs of shipment and freight up to the port of destination. The buyer must insure the cargo from the port of loading because if the cargo is lost, the buyer will bear the consequence. See also *Incoterms 2000*.

商　会
chamber of commerce   An association of businesspeople whose purpose is to promote commercial and industrial interests in the community.

租船合同
charter party   A written contract, usually on a special form, between the owner of a vessel and a charterer who rents use of the vessel or a part of its freight space. The contract generally includes the freight rates and the ports involved in the transportation.

租船提单
charter party bill of lading   A bill of lading subject to a charter party arrangement. Note also that charter party bills of lading are not acceptable under letters of credit unless allowed explicitly (see UCP 500 Art. 25.a.).

成本加保险费、运费
CIF   Cost, insurance, and freight. Incoterm indicating that costs are included in the quoted sale price. Includes all costs of shipment and insurance and freight up to the port of destination. The seller must insure the cargo as far as the port of delivery, because if the cargo is lost, the seller will bear the consequence. See *Incoterms 2000*.

成本加保险费、运费和佣金
CIF&C   Cost, insurance, freight, and commission. A pricing term indicating that commission costs are included in the price.

成本加保险费、运费和汇费
CIF&E   Cost, insurance, freight, and exchange (currency). A pricing term indicating that currency exchange costs are included in the price.

清洁提单
clean bill of lading   A bill of lading signed by the transportation company indicating that the shipment has been received in good condition with no irregularities in the packing or general condition of all or any part of the shipment. See *foul bill of lading*.

光　票
clean draft   A draft to which no documents have been attached.

代收行

collecting bank   Bank in the importer's country involved in processing a collection.

托　收

collection   The procedure involved in a bank's collecting money for a seller against a draft drawn on a buyer abroad, usually through a correspondent bank.

托收单据

collection papers   All documents (invoices, bills of lading, etc.) submitted to a buyer for the purpose of receiving payment for a shipment. Also the documents submitted, usually with a draft or against a letter of credit, for payment of an export shipment.

多式联运提单

combined transport bill of lading   A bill of lading used when more than one carrier is involved in a shipment, for example when a consignment travels by rail and by sea. Sometimes referred to as a *multimodal bill of lading*.

商务专员

commercial attaché   The commercial expert on the diplomatic staff of a country's embassy or large consulate in a foreign country.

商业发票

commercial invoice   Seller's itemized list of goods shipped with descriptions, details, prices, and costs addressed to the buyer. The invoice should represent a complete record of the business transaction between the exporter and the foreign importer with regard to the goods sold. It is also a document of content and, therefore, must fully identify the overseas shipment as well as serve as the basis for the preparation of all other documents covering the shipment. In addition, some countries may require further documentation such as quality certificates, certificates of origin, certificates of free sale, and customs invoices.

跟单信用证

commercial letter of credit   Common parlance in the United States for a documentary letter of credit, or DC, as it is known elsewhere. See *letter of credit*.

佣金代理

commission agent   See *purchasing agent* and *foreign sales representative*.

佣金代理

commission representative   See *foreign sales representative*.

商品信贷公司

commodity credit corporation   A government corporation controlled by a country's department or ministry of agriculture to provide financing and stability to the marketing and exporting of agricultural commodities.

公共承运人

common carrier   An individual, partnership, or corporation that transports persons or goods for compensation.

补偿贸易

compensation   A form of countertrade in which the seller agrees to take full or partial payment in goods or services generated from the sale.

班轮公会

conference line. A member of a steamship conference. See *steamship conference*.

保　兑

confirmation   The act of a bank to add its commitment to that of the issuing bank to pay the beneficiary for compliant documents. Under Art. 9.b. of UCP 500, confirming banks must be requested or authorized by the issuing bank to "add their confirmation" to the letter of credit. Note that the act of confirmation does not relieve the issuing bank of its obligation to the beneficiary.

保兑信用证

confirmed letter of credit   Issued by a bank abroad whose validity and terms are confirmed to the beneficiary in the home bank. A letter of credit bearing the confirmation, or commitment to pay, of a second bank, most often in the country of the exporter. Confirmations are the exporter's insurance against nonpayment by the issuing bank for most reasons other than a discrepancy.

保兑行

confirming bank   Bank adding its commitment to pay for compliant documents to that of the issuing bank, usually at the request of same. Confirming banks are very often correspondents of issuing banks. L/C beneficiaries should understand clearly how soon the confirming bank will pay after presentation of conforming export documents.

收货人

consignee   The person, firm, or representative to whom a seller or shipper sends merchandise and who, upon presentation of the necessary documents, is recognized as the owner of the merchandise for the purpose of the payment of customs duties. This term is also applied to one to whom goods are shipped, usually at the shipper's risk, when an outright sale has not been made. See *consignment*.

唛　头

consignee marks   See *marks*.

寄售，寄售货物

consignment Payment method in which the buyer pays for goods after selling them. The exporter retains title to the goods until they are sold (as well as 100 percent risk of nonpayment by the buyer). Also a term pertaining to merchandise shipped to a consignee abroad when an actual purchase has not been made, under an agreement by which the consignee is obligated to sell the goods for the account of the consignor, and to remit proceeds as goods are gold.

集拼提单

consolidator's bill of lading Bill of lading issued by consolidator (forwarder) to a shipper as a receipt for goods to be consolidated with other cargoes prior to shipment.

领　事

consul A government official residing in a foreign country who is charged with the representation of the interests of his or her country and its nationals.

领事声明

consular declaration A formal statement, made to the consul of a foreign country, describing goods to be shipped.

领事发票

consular invoice A detailed statement regarding the character of goods shipped, duly certified by the consul of the importing country at the port of shipment.

领事馆

consulate The official premises of a foreign government representative.

卖方利益险

contingency insurance Insurance taken out by the exporter complementary to insurance bought by the consignee abroad.

货物控制权

control of goods Of vital interest to all parties involved in trade, control of goods is exercised through the transport document. It determines whether the buyer will be able to clear an inbound shipment without the transport document (and thus without paying for the documents held at the bank).

往来行，代理行

correspondent bank A bank overseas with which a local bank has a relationship. Relationships between banks are just one factor that determine appetite for confirmation and thus have relevance to importers and exporters.

互　购
counterpurchase   One of the most common forms of countertrade in which the seller receives cash but contractually agrees to buy local products or services as a percentage of cash received and over an agreed period of time.

对销贸易
countertrade   International trade in which the seller is required to accept goods or other instruments of trade in partial or whole payment for its products.

反补贴税
countervailing duty   An extra duty imposed by importing country to offset export grants, bounties, or subsidies paid to foreign suppliers in certain countries by the government of those countries as an incentive to export.

原产国
country of origin   The country where a product is made, as determined by the amount of work done on the product in the country and attested by a certificate of origin.

信用风险保险
credit risk insurance   A form of insurance that covers the seller against loss resulting from nonpayment of the buyer.

海　关
customs   The duties levied by a country on imports and exports. The term also applies to the procedures and organization involved in such collection.

报关行
customs broker   A firm representing the importer in dealings with customs, responsible for obtaining and submitting documents for clearing merchandise through customs, arranging inland transport, and paying related charges.

海关合作理事会税则目录
Customs Cooperation Council Nomenclature (CCCN)   The customs tariff used by many countries worldwide, including most European nations. It is also known as the Brussels Tariff Nomenclature. Compare *Standard Industrial Classification, Standard International Trade Classification*, and *tariff schedule*.

承兑交单
D/A   See *documents against acceptance*.

付款交单
D/P   See *documents against payment*.

定期汇票
date draft   A draft drawn to mature in a specified number of days after the date it is issued, with or without regard to the date of acceptance.

跟单信用证
DC   Popular abbreviation outside the Americas for documentary letter of credit. The equivalent in the United States is L/C, or more properly the commercial L/C.

延期付款信用证
deferred payment L/C   A letter of credit available by deferred payment calling for a time draft (or usance draft in international parlance) drawn on the issuing bank. Popular in cases of supplier credit.

交货地点
delivery point   See *specific delivery point.*

滞期费
demurrage   Storage fee for inbound merchandise held beyond the free time allowed by the shipping company. Excess time taken for loading or unloading a vessel as a result of a shipper. Charges are assessed by the shipping company.

商务部
department of commerce   An agency of government whose purpose it is to promote commercial industrial interests in the country.

贬　值
devaluation   The official lowering of the value of one country's currency in terms of one or more foreign currencies. Thus, if the U.S. dollar is devaluated in relation to the French franc, one dollar will buy fewer francs than before.

贴现（融资）
discount (financial)   A deduction from the face value of commercial paper in consideration of cash by the seller before a specified date.

（票据）不符
discrepancy   An instance in which documents presented do not conform to the L/C. Article 13.a. of UCP 500 state that "banks must examine all documents stipulated in the credit with reasonable care." In fact banks exercise extreme care, and international standard banking practice dictates that exporters must exercise detailed vigilance in preparing documents under letters of credit if they are not to be frustrated by delays in obtaining payment.

信用证不符，信用证与单据不符
discrepancy—letter of credit   When documents presented do not conform to the terms of the letter of credit, it is referred to as a "discrepancy."

拒　付
dishonor   Refusal on the part of the drawee to accept a draft or pay upon maturity.

速遣费
dispatch   An amount paid by a vessel's operator to a charterer if loading or unloading is completed in less time than stipulated in the charter party.

经销商
distributor   A firm that sells directly for a manufacturer, usually on an exclusive contract for a specified territory, and who maintains an inventory on hand.

场站收据
dock receipt   A receipt issued by an ocean carrier or its agent acknowledging that the shipment has been delivered or received at the dock or warehouse of the carrier.

跟单托收
documentary collection   An order written by the seller to the bank to deliver documents against payment, or *documents against acceptance*, to the buyer. The seller's bank will act on the instruction of the seller in a principal agent relationship and remit the documents to a branch, or a correspondent, in the country of the buyer, with instructions for collection. A key factor in the effectiveness of such collections is the control of goods exercised through the transport document.

跟单信用(证)
documentary credit   See *commercial letter of credit*.

跟单汇票
documentary draft   A draft to which documents are attached.

单　证
documentation documents   See *shipper's documents*.

承兑交单
documents against acceptance (D/A)   A type of payment for goods in which the documents transferring title to the goods are withheld until the buyer has accepted the draft issued against him or her.

付款交单
documents against payment (D/P)   A type of payment for goods in which the documents transferring title to the goods are withheld until the buyer has paid the value of a draft issued against him or her.

国内国际销售公司（DISC）

Domestic International Sales Corporation (DISC)   The DISC incentive was created by the Revenue Act of 1971 and provides for deferral of federal income tax on 50 percent of the export earnings allocated to the DISC with the balance treated as dividends to the parent company. Since its enactment, the DISC had been the subject of an ongoing dispute between the United States and certain other signatories of the General Agreement on Tariffs and Trade (GATT). Other nations contended that the DISC amounted to an illegal export subsidy because it allows indefinite deferral of direct taxes on income from exports earned in the United States. Under new rules put into effect on January 1, 1985, to receive a tax benefit that is designed to equal the tax deferral provided by the DISC, exporters must establish an office abroad.

期票支付场所

domicile   The place where a draft or an acceptance is made payable.

汇　票

draft   The same as a bill of exchange. A written order for a certain sum of money to be transferred on a certain date from the person who owes the money or agrees to make the payment (the drawee) to the creditor to whom the money is owed (the drawer of the draft). See *date draft, documentary draft, sight draft,* and *time draft.* Also colloquial American terminology for a documentary collection. Internationally this may refer to the bill of exchange.

（进口产品）退税

drawback (import)   The repayment, up to 99 percent of customs duties paid on merchandise which later is exported as part of a finished product, is known as a drawback. It refers also to a refund of a domestic tax which has been paid upon exportation of imported merchandise.

受票人

drawee   One on whom a draft is drawn and who owes the stated amount. See *draft.*

开票人

drawer   One who draws a draft and receives payment. See *draft.*

倾　销

dumping   Exporting merchandise into a country (e.g., the United States) at prices below the prices in the domestic market.

关　税

duty   The tax imposed by a government on merchandise imported from another country.

电子数据交换

EDI   Electronic data interchange. The exchange between computers of trade documentation. EDI can take two forms, financial and documentary, and suffers from a curse common in the world of computers, at least two message format standards. They are ANSI (popular in the United States) and EDIFACT (popular elsewhere).

出口管理公司

EMC   See *export management company*.

出口贸易公司

ETC   See *export trading company*.

欧洲美元

eurodollars   U.S. dollars on deposit in any branch of any bank located outside the United States. Likewise, euroyen are Japanese yen on deposit in banks outside Japan and may be outside of Europe too. Any eurocurrency is a foreign currency deposit and should be treated with care if offered as a form of payment. For example, a U.S. exporter offering U.S. dollars to be delivered in some countries may face a challenge to convert these eurodollars to U.S. dollars.

常青条款，自动展期条款

evergreen clause   A provision in the letter of credit for the expiration date to extend without requiring an amendment.

（原产地）交货

EX (point of origin)   A pricing term (EXF-⊠-ex factory; EXW-⊠-ex warehouse, etc.) under which the seller agrees to place the goods at the buyer's disposal at the agreed place, with costs from that point being paid by the buyer.

汇　兑

exchange   A pricing term indicating that costs are included in the price.

调汇许可

exchange permit   A governmental permit sometimes required of an importer to convert its own country's currency into foreign currency with which to pay a seller in another country.

汇　率

exchange rate   The price of one currency expressed in terms of another. Exchange rates may be quoted spot, for delivery within two working days, or forward, for delivery at some future time. Exchange rates are apt to fluctuate. Any international trader with an eye for profit will be aware of the currency circumstances affecting a partner.

外汇管制

exchange regulations/restrictions   Restrictions imposed by an importing country to protect its foreign exchange reserves. See *exchange permit.*

消费税/国内消费税/国产税/货物税

excise tax   A domestic tax assessed on the manufacture, sale, or use of a commodity within a country. Usually refundable if the product is exported.

进出口银行(ex–im bank)

EXIMBank   Export-Import Bank of the United States.

到期日

expiration date   The final date upon which the presentation of documents and drawing of drafts under a letter of credit may be made.

出　口

export   To send goods to a foreign country or overseas territory.

外销经纪人，代理出口

export broker   One who brings together the exporter and importer for a fee and then withdraws from the transaction.

出口申报

export declaration   A formal statement made to the collector of customs at a port of exit declaring full particulars about goods being exported.

出口许可证

export license   A governmental permit required to export certain products to certain destinations.

出口管理/代理公司

export management company (EMC)   A firm that acts as a local export sales agent for several noncompeting manufacturers.

出口商

export merchant   A producer or merchant who sells directly to a foreign purchaser without going through an intermediate such as an export broker.

出口贸易公司

export trading company (ETC)   Firm formed under the Export Trading Company Act of 1982 that buys domestic products for sale overseas taking title to the goods (which an export-management company usually does not do).

保理商

factor   A finance company willing to purchase a receivable at a discount, either with recourse to the seller or without. In exchange for immediate payment, the seller will transfer title to the receivable to the factor. This is a convenient but expensive alternative to other methods of converting receivables to cash.

保　理

factoring   A method used by businesses including trading companies to obtain cash for discounted accounts receivables or other assets.

（装运港）船边交货

FAS   Free alongside ship. Incoterm indicating that the sale price includes cost of transport to the port of embarkation, but not the costs of loading, export clearance, ocean freight, or insurance. The buyer must insure the cargo as far as the port of delivery, because if the cargo is lost, the buyer will bear the consequence. See *Incoterms 2000*.

外国信用保险协会

FCIA   See *Foreign Credit Insurance Association*.

（船方）管卸不管装

FI   Free in. A pricing term indicating that the charterer of a vessel is responsible for the cost of loading goods into the vessel.

（船方）装和卸均不管

FIO   Free in and out. A pricing term indicating that the charterer of a vessel is responsible for the cost of loading and unloading goods from the vessel.

流动保险单，浮动保险单，统保单

floating policy   See *open cargo policy.*

（船方）管装不管卸

FO   Free out. A pricing term indicating that the charterer of a vessel is responsible for the cost of loading goods from the vessel.

（装运港）船上交货，离岸价

FOB   Free on board. Incoterm indicating that the sale price includes the cost of transport to and loading at the port of embarkation, but not the costs of export clearance, ocean freight, or insurance. The buyer must insure the cargo as far as the port of delivery, because if the cargo is lost, the buyer will bear the consequence. See *Incoterms 2000*.

不可抗力
force majeure   The title of a standard clause in marine contracts exempting the parties for nonfulfillment of their obligations as a result of conditions beyond their control, such as earthquakes, floods, or war.

外国信用保险协会
Foreign Credit Insurance Association (FCIA)   An association of about 50 insurance companies that operate in conjunction with the EXIMBank to provide comprehensive insurance for exporters against nonpayment. The FCIA underwrites the commercial credit risks. EXIMBank covers the political risk and any excessive commercial risks.

外汇账户
foreign currency account   An account maintained by a bank in foreign currency and payable in that currency.

海外销售
foreign distribution   See *distributor*.

外　汇
foreign exchange   A currency or credit instruments of a foreign country. Also, transactions involving purchase and/or sale of currencies.

运输行
foreign freight forwarder   See *freight forwarder*.

海外销售代理
foreign sales agent   An individual or firm that serves as the foreign representative of a domestic supplier and seeks sales abroad for the supplier.

海外销售公司
foreign sales corporation (FSC)   An American territorial tax scheme whereby a corporation within a U.S. possession, such as the Virgin Islands, or within a qualifying jurisdiction, such as Barbados, may exempt 15 to 30 percent of export profits from U.S. corporate tax. To qualify for special tax treatment, an FSC must be a foreign corporation, maintain a summary of its permanent books of account at the foreign office, and have at least one director resident outside of the United States. A portion of the foreign sales corporation's income (generally corresponding to the tax-deferred income of the DISC) would be exempt from U.S. tax at both the FSC and the U.S. corporate parent levels. This exemption is achieved by allowing a domestic corporation that is an FSC shareholder a 100 percent deduction for a portion of dividends received from an FSC attributable to economic activity actually conducted outside the U.S. customs territory. Interest, dividends, royalties, or other investment income of an FSC would be subject to U.S. tax.

海外销售代表，海外销售代理

foreign sales representative   A representative or agent residing in a foreign country who acts as a salesperson for a U.S. manufacturer, usually for a commission. Sometimes referred to as a sales agent or commission agent. See also *representative*.

对外贸易区（外贸区）

foreign trade zone (FTZ)   U.S. term for a site sanctioned by the authorities in which imported goods are exempted from duties until withdrawn for domestic sale or use. Can be used for commercial warehousing, assembly plants, and reexport.

福费廷，买断

forfeit   The sale of a term debt against a discounted cash payment in which the seller forfeits the right to future payments by the debtor. A popular method for exporters of capital equipment to dispose of long-term overseas debt.

货运代理人提单

forwarder's bill of lading   Bill of lading issued by a forwarder to a shipper; a receipt for merchandise to be shipped.

不清洁提单

foul bill of lading   A receipt for goods issued by a carrier bearing a notation that the outward containers or goods have been damaged. See also *clean bill of lading*.

平安险

FPA   Free of particular average. The title of a clause used in marine insurance indicating that partial loss or damage to a foreign shipment is not covered. (Note: Loss resulting from certain conditions, such as the sinking or burning of a ship, may be specifically exempted from the effect of the clause.)

欺 诈

fraud   The misrepresentation of information. All too common in international trade, especially transactional deals relating to commodities and a perfect reason why any sensible importer, exporter, or middleman will develop a relationship with a competent trade bank.

自由港

free port   An area generally encompassing a port and its surrounding locality into which goods may enter duty-free or are subject to only minimal revenue tariffs.

自由销售

free sale   See *certificate of free sale*.

自由贸易区
free trade zone   A term used by all countries (except the United States) for a site sanctioned by the authorities in which imported goods are exempted from duties until they are withdrawn for domestic sale or use. Can be used for commercial warehousing, assembly plants, and reexport. See *foreign trade zone*.

运输行，货运代理
freight forwarder   A company that books shipment of goods, often as an agent for an airline. Usually, many small shipments are combined to take advantage of bulk discounts. Forwarders also may provide other services, such as trucking, warehousing, and document preparation.

关税与贸易总协定（关贸总协定）
General Agreement on Tariffs and Trade (GATT)   A Geneva-based organization that governed world trade until the formation of the World Trade Organization (WTO) in 1995. Formed by 23 countries at a conference in Geneva in 1947 to increase trade by lowering duties and quotas. GATT is a multilateral trade treaty among governments, embodying rights and obligations. The detailed rules set out in the agreement constitute a code that the parties to the agreement have agreed upon to govern their trading relationships.

一般许可证（出口）
general license (export)   Government authorization to export without specific documentary approval.

毛　重
gross weight   Total weight of goods, packing, and container, ready for shipment.

保　函
guarantee letter   Commitment popular outside the United States guaranteeing payment in the event of nonperformance by the applicant. See also *standby letter of credit*.

装卸作业费
handling charges   The forwarder's fee to a shipper client.

商品编码，标准代码；《商品名称及编码协调制度》
harmonized code   Harmonized Commodity Description and Coding System. An international classification system that assigns identification numbers to specific products. The code ensures that all parties use a consistent classification for purposes of documentation, statistical control, and duty assessment.

横向贸易行业/协会，水平贸易行业/协会

horizontal trade association   A trade association that exports a range of similar or identical products supplied by number of manufacturers or other producers. An association of agricultural cooperatives is a prime example.

国际商会

ICC   See *International Chamber of Commerce.*

进　口

import   To bring merchandise into a country from another country or overseas territory.

进口许可证

import license   A governmental document that permits the importation of a product or material into a country where such licenses are necessary.

尚未完税

in bond   A term applied to the status of merchandise admitted provisionally into a country without payment of duties. See *bonded warehouse.*

不可兑换

inconvertibility   The inability to exchange the currency of one country for the currency of another.

2000年国际贸易术语解释通则

Incoterms 2000   Terms of sale indicating costs and responsibilities included in the price under a sales contract (i.e., EXW FOB, CFR, CIF, DDP). Defined under ICC Publication No. 460, these are worldwide standardized terms that transcend borders and should be clearly understood by all parties negotiating an international sales contract.

内在缺陷

inherent vice   An insurance term indicating defects or characteristics of a product that could lead to deterioration without outside influence. See *all-risks clause.*

内陆提单

inland bill of lading   A bill of lading used in transporting goods overland to the exporter's international carrier. Although a through bill of lading can sometimes be used, it is usually necessary to prepare both an inland bill of lading and an ocean bill of lading for export shipments. See also *air waybill, ocean bill of lading,* and *through bill of lading.*

内陆承运人

inland carrier   A transportation line that handles export or import cargo between the port and inland points.

保险凭证

insurance certificate   A certificate furnished, usually in duplicate, whenever the seller provides ocean marine insurance. The certificates are negotiable documents and must be endorsed before being submitted to the bank. The seller can arrange to obtain an open cargo policy that the freight forwarder maintains.

国际商会

International Chamber of Commerce (ICC)   A nongovernmental organization serving worldwide business. Members in 123 countries represent tens of thousands of business organizations and companies and promote world trade and investment based on free and fair competition. ICC Publishing SA, based in Paris, produces many publications, some of which are de facto standards in global commerce, such as Uniforms Customs and Practices for Documentary Credits (UCP 500), Uniform Rules for Collections (URC 522), and Incoterms 2000 (ICC 460).

国际货运代理

international freight forwarder   See *freight forwarder*.

发　票

invoice   See *commercial invoice*.

不可撤销的

irrevocable   An adjective attached to an L/C to denote an instrument that cannot be amended or canceled without the agreement of all parties (including the beneficiary). The adjective is popular and redundant: Under Article 6 of UCP 500, credits shall be deemed to be irrevocable unless otherwise indicated. In most circumstances, revocable L/Cs are worthless and, as a consequence, are very rare.

合资企业

joint venture   A commercial or industrial arrangement in which principals of one company share control and ownership principals of other.

最迟装运日期

latest shipment date   Last day on which goods may be shipped (as evidenced by "on board" date on a bill of lading or the flight date on air waybill).

法定重量

legal weight   The weight of the goods plus immediate wrappings which go along with the goods such as the contents of a tin can together with its can. See also *net weight*.

信用证

letter of credit (L/C)   An undertaking written by the issuing bank to pay the beneficiary a stated sum of money, within a certain time, against the presentation of conforming documents. Other parties to a letter of credit may be the advising bank, the confirming bank, the negotiating bank, the paying bank and the reimbursing bank, but the main contract of payment is between the issuing bank and the beneficiary. Since the issuing bank is very often located in a separate country from the beneficiary, the beneficiary relies on the advising bank, locally, for notification of the arrival of the L/C and to authenticate it. Conforming documents may consist of various export documents, as in a documentary letter of credit, or a simple statement by the beneficiary, as in a standby letter of credit.

许可证

license   See *export license, import license,* and *validated license.*

授　权

licensing   The grant or technical assistance service and or the use of product rights, such as a trademark in return for royalty payments.

驳　船

lighter   An open or covered barge towed by a tugboat and used mainly in harbors and inland waterways.

驳船费

lighterage   The loading or unloading of a ship by means of a barge, or lighter, that because of shallow water, prevents the ship from coming to shore.

海运提单

marine bill of lading   B/L for shipment by sea.

海运保险

marine insurance   An insurance that will compensate the owner of goods transported on the seas in the event of loss which cannot be legally recovered from the carrier. Also covers air shipments.

唛　头

marks   A set of letters, numbers, and/or geometric symbols, generally followed by the name of the port of destination, placed on packages for export for identification purposes.

原信用证（Master Credit），（进口人开具的）信用证

master letter of credit   First of two *letters of credit* in a *back-to-back L/C* arrangement.

到期日
maturity date   The date upon which a draft or acceptance becomes due for payment.

制造商出口代理（商）
MEA   Manufacturer's export agent. See *export management company*.

最惠国待遇
most-favored-nation status   Designation of a country's status in relation to a trading partner. All countries having this designation receive equal treatment with respect to customs and tariffs.

多式联运提单
multimodal bill of lading   A bill of lading used when more than one mode of transport is involved in a shipment; for example, when a consignment travels by rail and by sea. Sometimes referred to as a combined transport bill of lading.

指定的交货地点
named point   See *specific delivery point*.

可转让提单
negotiable bill of lading   Bill of lading consigned to the order of, and endorsed in blank by, the shipper. Whoever carries a negotiable bill of lading in their hand carries the document of title to the goods. That is why banks often call for a "hill set" of bills of lading under their L/Cs. See also *straight bill of lading*.

议付行
negotiating bank   The bank that checks the exporter's documents under the letter of credit and advances cash to the exporter, at a small discount, in the expectation of reimbursement by the issuing bank.

净　重
net weight   Weight of the goods alone without any immediate wrapping; for example, the weight of the contents of a tin can without the weight of the can. See *legal weight*.

海关合作理事会税则目录
nomenclature of the Customs Cooperation Council   See *Customs Cooperation Council Nomenclature*.

海运提单
ocean bill of lading   A bill of lading indicating that the exporter consigns a shipment to an international carrier for transportation to a specified foreign market. Unlike an inland bill of lading, the ocean bill of lading also serves as a collection document. If it is a "straight B/L," the foreign buyer can obtain the shipment from the carrier by simply showing proof of identity. If a "negotiable B/L" is used, the buyer must first pay for the goods, post a bond, or meet other conditions agreeable to the seller. See also *air waybill*, *inland bill of lading*, and *through bill of lading*.

抵消贸易

offset   A variation of countertrade in which the seller is required to assist in or arrange for the marketing of locally produced goods.

已装船提单

onboard bill of lading   A bill of lading in which a carrier acknowledges that goods have been placed onboard a certain vessel.

记账赊销

open account   A trade arrangement in which goods are shipped to a foreign buyer without guarantee of payment. The obvious risk this method poses to the supplier makes it essential that the buyer's integrity be unquestionable.

流动保单；"预约"货物保险单

open cargo policy   Synonymous with "floating policy." An insurance policy that binds the insurer automatically to protect with insurance all shipments made by the insured from the moment the shipment leaves the initial shipping point until delivered at the destination. The insuring conditions include clauses naming such risks insured against as perils of the sea, fire, jettison, forcible theft, and barratry. See *all-risks clause, barratry*, and *perils of the sea*.

开证行

opening bank   Common terminology among bankers for issuing bank in the letter of credit process.

预约保险单

open insurance policy   A marine insurance policy that applies to all shipments made by an exporter over a period of time rather than to one shipment only.

（美国）海外私人投资公司

OPIC   Overseas Private Investment Corporation. A wholly owned government corporation designed to promote private investment in developing countries by promoting political risk investment and some financing assistance.

指示提单

"order" bill of lading   A negotiable bill of lading made out to the order of the shipper.

打包放款

packing credit   Common international parlance, especially in Asia, for pre-export finance provided against a letter of credit.

装箱单

packing list   A list prepared by the seller itemizing goods shipped, quantities, sizes, weights and packing marks. Very common in trade finance, the packing list should be prepared so as to be consistent with other documents especially tinder a letter of credit.

邮政收据
parcel post receipt   The postal authorities' signed acknowledgment of delivery to them of a shipment made by parcel post.

付款行
paying bank   The bank nominated in the letter of credit to pay out against conforming documents, without recourse. Exporters interested in their cash flow should understand whether the paying bank is in their own country or the country of their customer, the importer.

预付货款
payment in advance   The buyer delivers cash to the seller before the seller releases the goods. Can be referred to as cash in advance or CAD and may not mean exactly the same as advance payment.

海上风险
perils of the sea   A marine insurance term used to designate heavy weather, straining, lightning, collision, and sea water damage.

植物检验证书，植物检疫证书
phytosanitary inspection certificate   A certificate, issued to satisfy import regulations of foreign countries, indicating that a shipment has been inspected and is free from harmful pests and plant diseases.

搭载，借道，捎带销售
piggybacking   The assigning of export marketing and distribution functions by one manufacturer to another.

港口唛头
port marks   See *marks*.

出口前融资
pre-export finance   Terminology of U.S. bankers for a loan to an exporter to finance the accumulation of materials, the manufacture, assembly, production, packaging, and transport of physical goods to fulfill an export order. Commonly guaranteed by EXIMBank or SBA Working Capital Guarantee programs.

提示有效期
presentation period   Time allowed after issue of transport document to present documents under an L/C.

提示行
presenting bank   Bank in a documentary collection process presenting export documents to the drawee for payment. The exporter and the presenting bank behave in a principal/agent relationship, and it is therefore wise for the uncertain exporter to ensure that the collection is presented by some bank other than the importer's bank.

采购代理
procuring agent   See *purchasing agent*.

形式发票
pro forma invoice   A provisional invoice written by the seller which serves as a quotation to the buyer. Following negotiations, the exporter issues this document which confirms product details, prices, shipping, and payment terms. This is the starting point for further documentation.

采购代理
purchasing agent   An agent who purchases goods in his or her own country on behalf of large foreign buyers such as government agencies and large private concerns.

配　额
quota   The total quantity of a product or commodity that may be imported into a country. Usually quotas protect a domestic market. In the United States, sugar, wheat, cotton, tobacco, textiles, and apparel are governed by quotas.

标　价
quotation   An offer to sell goods at a stated price and under stated terms.

汇　率
rate of exchange   The basis upon which money of one country will be exchanged for that of another. Rates of exchange are established and quoted for foreign currencies on the basis of the demand, supply, and stability of the individual currencies. See *exchange*.

备运（海运）提单，收货待运提单
received for shipment bill of lading   Bill of lading indicating goods received for shipment (but not "onboard"). Unacceptable B/L unless specifically allowed by the letter of credit or unless it is marked "onboard" with a date and signature.

追　索
recourse   Payment with recourse means that the paying party retains the right to the funds in the event that reimbursement (from another party) is not forthcoming. An important concept in trade finance.

红条款信用证，红（色）条款信用证
red clause letter of credit   An L/C allowing the beneficiary to draw down an advance payment prior to shipment, usually against presentation of a simple receipt. So called because traditionally it was written in red ink, the purpose of this clause is to finance the seller during the preparation of the export order. The applicant will be liable for any drawings even if goods are never shipped. This is one reason why importers should expect red clause L/Cs to be collateralized differently from plain import L/Cs.

偿付行
reimbursing bank   The bank empowered by the issuing bank (i.e., with a bank balance) to charge the account of the issuing bank and to pay to the bank collecting funds under a letter of credit.

托收行
remitting bank   Exporter's bank in a documentary collection process taking export documents and sending them to a correspondent in the country of the importer (the drawee in the collection process).

代 理
representative   An individual or firm that acts on behalf of aa supplier. The word "representative" is preferred to the word "agent" in writing since agent, in an exact legal sense, connotes more binding powers and responsibilities than representative. See also *foreign sales representative*.

可撤销的
revocable   An adjective attached to an L/C indicating that it can be altered or canceled after the buyer has opened the L/C through his or her bank. Compare to *irrevocable*.

循环信用证
revolving letter of credit   L/C that reinstates automatically. It may revolve in relation to time or value, the latter being cumulative or noncumulative.

收取权利金，版税
royalty payment   The share of the product or profit paid by a licensee to a licensor. See *licensing*.

［法语缩写］公司
SA   societé anonyme. French expression for a corporation.

即期汇票
S/D   See *sight draft*.

销售代理
sales agent   See *foreign sales representative*.

销售代表
sales representative   See *foreign sales representative*.

卫生证书
sanitary certificate   A certificate that attests to the purity or absence of disease or pests in a shipment of food products, plants, seeds, and live animals.

承运收据

shipper's documents   Commercial invoices, bills of lading, insurance certificates, consular invoices, and related documents.

承运信用证

shipper's letter of credit   An L/C issued by the exporter to the freight forwarder. It covers key details of the transaction, shipping terms, and other applicable instructions that the freight forwarder must follow.

载货清单

ship's manifest   A true list in writing of the individual shipments comprising the cargo of a vessel, signed by the captain.

标准产业分类

SIC   See *Standard Industrial Classification*.

即期汇票

sight draft (S/D)   A draft drawn so as to be payable upon presentation to the drawee or at a fixed or determinable date thereafter. See *documents against acceptance* and *documents against payment*.

国际贸易标准分类

SITC   See *Standard International Trade Classification*.

特定交货地点

specific delivery point   A point in sales quotations which designates specifically where and within what geographical locale the goods will be delivered at the expense and responsibility of the seller; for example, FAS (named vessel) at (named port of export).

即期外汇

spot exchange   The purchase or sale of foreign currency, usually against an equivalent amount of local currency, for immediate delivery (e.g., within two working days after the agreement).

标准产业分类

Standard Industrial Classification (SIC)   A numeric system developed by the U.S. government for the classification of commercial services and industrial products. SIC also classifies establishments by type of activity.

国际贸易标准分类，国际贸易分类标准

Standard International Trade Classification (SITC)   A numeric system developed by the United Nations to classify commodities used in international trade and in reporting trade statistics.

备用信用证

standby letter of credit   An L/C popular in the United States that guarantees payment in the event of nonperformance by the applicant. Similar in method to commercial letters of credit and subject to UCP 500 but different in three significant aspects: (1) beneficiary's statement or claim of default suffices to draw (in contrast to a pile of detailed export documents under commercial L/C), (2) discrepancy rate is between low and zero, (3) expect banks to collateralize standby L/Cs somewhat differently from commercial L/Cs (i.e., 100 percent).

国家控制/控股贸易公司

state-controlled trading company   In a country with a state trading monopoly, a trading entity empowered by the country's government to conduct export business.

航运（运价）公会，轮船会议

steamship conference   A group of vessel operators joined together for the purpose of establishing freight rates. A shipper may receive reduced rates if the shipper enters into a contract to ship on vessels of conference members only.

担保提货，提货担保

steamship guarantee   A guarantee issued by a bank to a steamship line against financial loss arising from the release of a consignment without the appropriate transport document. Popular because goods frequently arrive at the port of discharge before documents are available to clear them.

存货分销商

stocking distibutor   A distributor that maintains an inventory of goods of a manufacturer.

记名提单，收货人抬头提单

straight bill of lading   A B/L consigned directly to a party who holds title to the goods. Straight B/Ls are discomforting to bankers if the consignee party is not the bank. A straight B/L cannot be endorsed to another party. See also *negotiable bill of lading*.

互惠信贷安排，互惠信贷协定

swap arrangements   A form of countertrade in which the seller sells on credit and then transfers the credit to a third party.

全球银行金融电讯协会

SWIFT   Society for Worldwide Interbank Financial Telecommunication. A cooperative owned by a consortium of banks designed to carry formatted messages between them in a secure environment. The messages all relate to financial transactions between banks and their customers.

互惠信贷协定

switch arrangements   A form of countertrade in which the seller sells on credit and then transfers the credit to a third party.

皮　重

tare weight   The weight of packing and containers without the goods to be shipped.

收费率表

tariff schedule   A schedule or system of duties imposed by a government on goods imported or exported; the rate of duty imposed in a tariff.

进　程

tenor   The time fixed or allowed for payment, as in "the tenor of a draft."

国际标准箱单位，以长度为 20 英尺的集装箱为国际计量单位

TEU   Twenty-foot equivalent unit. A measurement of cargo based on a standard ocean shipment container, which is 20 feet in length.

联运提单

through bill of lading   A single bill of lading covering both the domestic and international carriage of an export shipment. An air waybill, for instance, is essentially a through bill of lading used for air shipments. Ocean shipments, on the other hand, usually require two separate documents—an inland bill of lading for domestic carriage and an ocean bill of lading for international carriage. Through bills of lading, therefore, cannot be used for ocean carriage. See also *air waybill, inland bill of lading*, and *ocean bill of lading.*

远期汇票

time draft   A draft drawn so as to mature at a certain fixed time after presentation or acceptance.

贸易承兑

trade acceptance   A time draft in which the drawee signs the word "accepted" across the face and thus commits to pay the holder upon maturity. The instrument will be as valuable as the creditworthiness of the accepting party allows.

美国国务院贸易发展署

trade development program (TDP)   A program designed to promote economic development in the third world and the sale of U.S. goods and services to these developing countries. It operates as part of the International Development Cooperative Agency.

贸易代表团

trade mission   A mission to a foreign country organized to promote trade through the establishment of contracts and exposure to the commercial environment. Trade missions are frequently organized by federal, state, or local agencies.

不定期货船

tramp steamer   A ship not operating on regular routes or schedules.

运输单据

transport document   A bill of lading, an air waybill, a truck receipt, any other document acting as a receipt for goods and a contract of carriage. Of all these transport documents, only a bill of lading is a document of title.

转　运

transshipment   Shipment of merchandise to destination abroad on more than one vessel. Liability may pass from one carrier to the next, or it may be covered by a through bill of lading issued by the first carrier.

信托收据

trust receipt   Release of merchandise by a bank to a buyer in which the bank retains title to the merchandise. The buyer, who obtains the goods for manufacturing or sales purposes, is obligated to maintain the goods (or the proceeds from their sale) distinct from the remainder of his or her assets and to hold them ready for repossession by the bank.

交钥匙合同

turnkey   A method of construction whereby the contractor assumes total responsibility from design through completion.

国际商会《跟单信用证统一惯例》

UCP 500   Uniform Customs and Practice for Documentary Credits, Publication No. 500 of the International Chamber of Commerce. The indisputable authority on letters of credits recognized internationally, UCP 500 serves as the self-regulation of the L/C industry and renders L/Cs a more reliable form of payment. Importers and exporters are advised to be particularly careful of any L/C that does not clearly state (usually in the final paragraph) that it is subect to UCP 500.

不保兑信用证

unconfirmed letter of credit   A letter of credit that does not carry any confirmation by a second bank, usually located in the country of the beneficiary. Exporters intent on collecting payment under such L/Cs should hold a view as to risk of nonpayment for various reasons.

国际商会《托收统一规则》
URC 522   Uniform Rules for Collections, Publication No. 522 of the International Chamber of Commerce. An internationally recognized code for the handling of collections, clean or documentary.

远　期
usance   Banker's terminology, in use more commonly overseas than in the United States, indicating time allowed for payment of a bill of exchange (contrast with sight above).

远期汇票
usance draft   More often referred to in the United States as a time draft. See also *documents against acceptance.*

远期信用证
usance letter of credit   Sometimes referred to in the United States as a time L/C.

有效许可证
validated license   A government document authorizing the export of commodities within limitations set forth in the document.

垂直出口贸易公司
vertical ETC   An export trading company that integrates a range of functions taking products from suppliers to consumers.

签　证
visa   A signature of formal approval on an entree document. Obtained from a consulate.

水渍险
WA   With average. A marine insurance term meaning that a shipment is protected from partial damage whenever the damage exceeds a given percentage.

仓单，仓库收据
warehouse receipt   A receipt issued by a warehouse listing goods received for storage.

码头费
wharfage   Charge assessed by the carrier for the handling of incoming or outgoing ocean cargo.

毫无保留地
without reserve   A term indicating that a shipper's agent or representative is empowered to make definitive decisions and adjustments abroad without approval of the group individual represented. Compare *advisory capacity.*

网络术语

Don't be intimidated by Web jargon. Here, in simple English, are explanations of some basic terms you will encounter as you wander on the Web.

小应用程序
applet   A small program or application, usually written in java (see *java*) language. Applets run on your browser and power most of the fancier features, from animations to calculators.

带　宽
bandwidth   Measures the amount of information that can be transmitted over a connection. The lower the bandwidth, the slower the downloading of material, especially pictures. (Slang: A person with low bandwidth is slow on the uptake.) A very high bandwidth connection is known as a *broadband connection*.

博　客
blog   A Web log, which is usually shortened to *blog*, is a type of Web site where entries are made (such as in a journal or diary), displayed in a reverse chronological order. Blogs often provide commentary or news on a particular subject, such as food, politics, or local news; some function as more personal online diaries. A typical blog combines text, images, and links to other blogs, Web pages, and other media related to a topic. Most blogs are primarily textual although many focus on photo-graphs (photoblog), videos (vlog), or audio (podcasting).

网络书签
bookmark   A direct link to an often-visited site that you've saved on your browser for easy access.

［截短词］［俚语］机器人
bot   Short for *robot*. Performs a function on the Web automatically or electronically. A site that seeks out the cheapest prices for clothes is a shopping bot.

浏览器
browser   Program that allows you to interact with the World Wide Web. Examples include Netscape Navigator and Microsoft Explorer.

高速缓冲存储器（Cache Memory）
cache   High-speed memory that your computer sets aside to store frequently accessed data.

聊天室
chat room   A variation on the message board. A site for live, online conversation. Occasionally useful but usually rife with misinformation and inane chatter.

纯文本信息
cookie   The programming code from a Web site you visit that is stored on your computer. Visit the site later, and the cookie is sent back to the Web site to remind it of your preferences.

网络空间
cyberspace   A general term for the Internet and anything else online. Attach "cyber" to a business description, and you've got a hot stock.

域 名
domain name   Unique name that identifies a Web site (see *URL*).

下 载
download   To go online and bring a file from where you are into your own computer. The opposite of *upload*.

黑 客
hacker   The robbers of the Internet highway. Some are crooks, others just annoying pranksters. They use their computers to gain unauthor-ized access to networks and protected Web servers.

点 击
hits   How many visits a Web site gets, no matter how brief they are. Leading portal Yahoo! has 37 million hits a month.

主 页
home page   A Web site's main or central page, or, alternatively, the page that appears on your browser when you log on.

超文本标记语言
HTML   Stands for *hypertext markup language*, the programming language for most Web pages.

超链接
hyperlink   Or just plain *link* (to another site). Usually appears underlined and in a different color. Click on one, and you're transported to another Web page.

互联网服务提供商
ISP   Stands for *Internet service provider*. Organizations that charge monthly fees for providing Internet access. Examples include AOL and Earthlink.

Java编程语言（构建软件系统时使用）

java A programming language from Sun Microsystems that is used to create applets.

留言板

message board A place where people can post, read, and respond to messages written by other users.

插 件

plug-in Add-on program that enhances the capabilities of your Web browser, such as the ability to hear live audio feeds and see live video clips; for instance, RealPlayer and Shockwave.

代理服务器

server Computer that controls a network of computers or powers a Web site. Lots of Web traffic slows servers down, even for those that have a fast Internet connection.

［俚语］传统信邮方式

snail mail Mail delivered by the U.S. Postal Service.

垃圾邮件

spam Unwanted e-mail advertisements or solicitations. Too much electronic spam can clog your e-mail in-box and slow everything down to a crawl.

在数据网络上的音/视频数据流

streaming Audio or video that plays on your computer while being transmitted over the Web. Example: live tickers or radio broadcasts.

网上冲浪

surf Overused Web term that describes the action of moving from one Web site to another to another to another.

统一资源定位器

URL Stands for *universal resource locator*, the Internet address you enter into your browser window. Most begin with "http://www." and end with ".com" (commercial sites), ".gov" (government sites), and ".edu" (educational sites).

病毒程序

virus A program usually hidden in a file or e-mail that infects your computer by altering or deleting files.

INDEX